American Noir Film

American Noir Film

From *The Maltese Falcon* to *Gone Girl*

M. Keith Booker

ROWMAN & LITTLEFIELD
Lanham • Boulder • New York • London

Published by Rowman & Littlefield
An imprint of The Rowman & Littlefield Publishing Group, Inc.
4501 Forbes Boulevard, Suite 200, Lanham, Maryland 20706
www.rowman.com

86-90 Paul Street, London EC2A 4NE

British Library Cataloguing in Publication Information Available

Library of Congress Cataloging-in-Publication Data

Names: Booker, M. Keith, author.
Title: American noir film : from the Maltese Falcon to Gone Girl / M. Keith Booker.
Description: Lanham : Rowman & Littlefield Publishers, 2024. | Includes bibliographical references and index. | Summary: "American Noir Film explores how the popular genre and its tropes evolved from the early classics to neo-noir and beyond while maintaining the distinct features audiences love. Movies discussed range from Double Indemnity and Sunset Boulevard to Chinatown and Devil in a Blue Dress and recent films Under the Silver Lake and Promising Young Woman"— Provided by publisher.
Identifiers: LCCN 2024019711 (print) | LCCN 2024019712 (ebook) | ISBN 9781538194096 (cloth) | ISBN 9781538194102 (ebook)
Subjects: LCSH: Film noir—United States—History and criticism.
Classification: LCC PN1995.9.F54 B66 2024 (print) | LCC PN1995.9.F54 (ebook) | DDC 791.43/655—dc23/eng/20240521
LC record available at https://lccn.loc.gov/2024019711
LC ebook record available at https://lccn.loc.gov/2024019712

Contents

Introduction to Noir Film   1

Part I: The Noir Detective Film: Introduction to Noir Detective Films   19

Chapter 1: The Film Noir Detective: *The Maltese Falcon* (1941, Directed by John Huston)   27

Chapter 2: The Film Noir Detective: *Murder, My Sweet* (1944, Directed by Edward Dmytryk)   33

Chapter 3: The Neo-Noir Detective: *Chinatown* (1974, Directed by Roman Polanski)   39

Chapter 4: The Neo-Noir Detective: *Blue Velvet* (1986, Directed by David Lynch)   47

Chapter 5: The Revisionary Noir Detective: *Devil in a Blue Dress* (1995, Directed by Carl Franklin)   55

Chapter 6: The Revisionary Noir Detective: *Inherent Vice* (2014, Directed by Paul Thomas Anderson)   63

Chapter 7: The Revisionary Noir Detective: *Under the Silver Lake* (2018, Directed by David Robert Mitchell)   71

Part II: The Noir Film Lost Man: Introduction: The Noir Film Lost Man   77

Chapter 8: The Film Noir Lost Man: *Detour* (1945, Directed by Edgar G. Ulmer)   87

Chapter 9: The Film Noir Lost Man: *Out of the Past* (1947, Directed by Jacques Tourneur)   93

Chapter 10: The Neo-Noir Lost Man: *After Dark, My Sweet* (1990, Directed by James Foley)   101

Chapter 11: The Neo-Noir Lost Man: *The Man Who Wasn't There* (2001, Directed by Joel and Ethan Coen)   107

Chapter 12: The Revisionary Noir Lost Man: *The Killer Inside Me* (2010, Directed by Michael Winterbottom)   115

Chapter 13: The Revisionary Noir Lost Man: *You Were Never Really Here* (2017, Directed by Lynne Ramsay)   121

Chapter 14: The Revisionary Noir Lost Man: *Uncut Gems* (2019, Directed by Josh and Benny Safdie)   127

Part III: Women in Noir Film   **135**

Chapter 15: Women in Film Noir: *Double Indemnity* (1944, Directed by Billy Wilder)   143

Chapter 16: Women in Film Noir: *Sunset Boulevard* (1950, Directed by Billy Wilder)   151

Chapter 17: Women in Neo-Noir: *Body Heat* (1981, Directed by Lawrence Kasdan)   159

Chapter 18: Women in Neo-Noir: *The Last Seduction* (1994, Directed by James Foley)   165

Chapter 19: Women in Revisionary Noir: *Basic Instinct* (1992, Directed by Paul Verhoeven)   171

Chapter 20: Women in Revisionary Noir: *Gone Girl* (2014, Directed by David Fincher)   177

Chapter 21: Women in Revisionary Noir: *Promising Young Woman* (2020, Directed by Emerald Fennell)   185

Conclusion   193

Notes   195

Bibliography   207

Index   213

About the Author   217

Introduction to Noir Film

In one of the greatest feats of cultural expression ever performed, the makers of American film noir—working at a time when freedom of expression in American film was at an all-time low—managed to project onto American movie screens some of the darkest and most sharply critical visions of American life ever conceived. Throughout the run of the original cycle of noir films, Hollywood filmmakers were constrained by the limitations imposed by the Motion Picture Production Code that had gone into effect in 1934. Meanwhile, film noir itself arose at a time when the need to support the American effort in World War II made it difficult to criticize the American way of life without seeming unpatriotic. And most films of the original noir cycle were made during a time when the paranoid political atmosphere of the early Cold War years made it difficult to conduct such critiques without being suspected of communist sympathies. Yet noir filmmakers somehow managed to explore the dark side of the American dream with characters, plots, and visuals that pushed the limits of all these constraints, while nevertheless winning the hearts of American filmgoers.

Film noir was a key element of American film in the 1940s and 1950s. However, noir has shown a surprising staying power, and films building on the basic characteristics of film noir have continued to appear until this day. First, a wave of what has come to be called "neo-noir" films appeared in roughly the last three and a half decades of the twentieth century, driven largely by the collapse of the Motion Picture Production Code, which had greatly restricted how thoroughly the original noir films could explore the dark territory they consistently inhabited. Neo-noir films have continued to appear in the twenty-first century as well, but filmmakers of the new century have found innovative ways to explore noir territory. For one thing, noir has now become a genuinely international phenomenon (in addition to the contributions of European directors to American noir film throughout its history).

Noir-inflected films from Japan, South Korea, and Hong Kong have become a major element of twenty-first-century Asian cinema,[1] while the films and television miniseries associated with the Scandinavian cultural phenomenon sometimes referred to as "Nordic noir" have been one of the century's most successful modes of European cultural production.[2] The American film industry has also continued to produce new noir-inflected films (though often with international actors or directors), making noir one of the richest veins in twenty-first-century cinema as a whole.

This volume is partly intended to serve as a general introduction to noir film for those who are interested in the topic but have relatively little knowledge of it. But it also seeks, for both beginners and experienced viewers, to outline a new historical model for the historical evolution of noir film from its roots in the 1940s and 1950s to the production of a number of revisionary noir films in the twenty-first century (with the phenomenon of neo-noir falling roughly in between—in the period, say, from the 1960s through the 1990s). This introduction will seek to establish the basic characteristics that define "film noir," characteristics that neo-noir film uses and changes in only minor ways, but that revisionary noir film changes in more radical ways, potentially leading to a critical reevaluation of the original film noir cycle. For example, a neo-noir film such as *Chinatown* (1974) carefully draws upon film noir for its style and content, updating noir conventions primarily in ways that are related to the use of color and the collapse of the Code. In contrast, a revisionary noir film such as Robert Rodriguez and Frank Miller's graphic novel adaptation *Sin City* (2005) pushes the envelope of noir violence in exaggerated and even abject ways. *Sin City* thus calls attention to the sanitized and muted representation of violence in the original noir films, possibly suggesting that these films might have thus inadvertently made violence seem more palatable. *Sin City* is also technically innovative, producing digitized visuals that mimic the appearance of the comic series on which it is based, which is in itself essentially an exaggeration of the aesthetics of film noir. Presented mostly in extremely stark black-and-white visuals, this film also uses splashes of color for emphasis at key moments, such as red for blood, though it also effectively uses bright white and even yellow for blood in key scenes, a strategy that makes the black-and-white visuals seem even more striking. It also features a number of characters who might be described as noir lost men, though some go so far past the norm that they would make even the most extreme film noir characters seem tame. Thus, as Bould puts it, in both its visuals and its characters, this film reduces film noir "to its image(s) and the desire not to make a film noir but to somehow put the very idea, the megatext, of film noir on the screen" (114). This sort of representation clearly invites reevaluation of the characters, content, and aesthetics of noir, making *Sin City* an excellent example of revisionary noir.

WHAT IS NOIR FILM?

In this volume, I will use the term "noir film" as a blanket designation for all types of films that prominently employ noir motifs in any way. This term thus encompasses *all* the films discussed in this volume whatever their differences might otherwise be. (Though it will not be a primary focus in this volume, one might also use the term "proto-noir film" to indicate films that were made prior to the emergence of full-blown film noir but that had already begun to show many noir characteristics and that thus exerted an influence over the evolution of film noir.) I will use the term "film noir" in the same sense that it is typically used by both fans and scholars of the phenomenon—as a broad designation for the extensive cycle of films with noir characteristics that were produced roughly from John Huston's *The Maltese Falcon* in 1941 through Orson Welles's *Touch of Evil* in 1958. That is, "film noir" describes the prevailing paradigm in noir films from roughly 1941–1958. These are the films that establish what we think of as "noir." I will also sometimes refer to them as "original noir" films or "classic noir" films.

James Naremore, in a book first published in 1998, notes the significant amount of critical attention that has been paid to film noir, typically defined as a series of "thrillers or crime pictures of the 1940s and 1950s," characterized by their "cynical treatment of the American Dream, their complicated play with gender and sexuality, and their foregrounding of cinematic style." He then goes on to state that "film noir has become one of the dominant intellectual categories of the late twentieth century, operating across the entire cultural arena of art, popular memory, and criticism" (2). Naremore then does a great deal to characterize film noir, though noting that the concept has less to do with the films themselves than with a "discourse—a loose, evolving system of arguments and readings that helps to shape commercial strategies and aesthetic ideologies" (11).

The history of noir supports Naremore's claim, especially as the concept of "film noir" did not exist when the first wave of noir films was being made. Indeed, few observers in America realized, during World War II, that something genuinely new was happening in the relatively low budget, dimly lit crime dramas that were appearing with increasing frequency during the war years. Meanwhile, American films were largely banned in France during the Nazi occupation from 1940–1945, so that, once the war was over, French viewers suddenly gained access to a five-year backlog of American films all at once. Astute French critics, seeing these films together as a group, immediately recognized that much of what they were now seeing was distinctively different from the Hollywood films to which they had become accustomed before the war. Viewing films such as John Huston's *The Maltese Falcon* (1941), Billy Wilder's *Double Indemnity* (1944) and *The Lost Weekend* (1945), Otto Preminger's *Laura* (1944), and Edward Dmytryk's *Murder, My Sweet* (1944) for the first time, the French critics Nino Frank and Jean-Pierre Chartier declared these films to belong to a family of related works that represented a new breakthrough in American film realism—though many aspects of these films must have seemed familiar to French viewers in the sense that many French films of the 1930s anticipated film noir in a number of ways. Responding both to the thematic darkness of the films and to the literal darkness of the images they saw on the screen, Frank and Chartier dubbed this new kind of American film "film noir" (black, or dark film), a name apparently inspired by the *série noire* series of dark crime novels that had recently begun appearing in postwar France. It was thus that one of the most American of all film phenomena acquired its French name. Other French critics soon followed suit, remaining in the vanguard of critical appreciations of film noir for some time. For example, the first (and now classic) book-length study of the genre—only much later (2002) published in English—was *A Panorama of American Film Noir, 1941–1953*, by Raymond Borde and Etienne Chaumeton, published in France in 1955.

Basic Characteristics of Film Noir

Film noir is notoriously hard to categorize in a succinct way, largely because noir is defined more by mood and atmosphere than by specific settings or iconography. Still, the phenomenon of film noir is typically associated with a number of distinctive characteristics, even though no one film noir can possibly contain *all* of these characteristics. In fact, some of the best-known characteristics of film noir are actually absent from *most* noir films. For example, partly due to the association of the works of writers such as Dashiell Hammett and Raymond Chandler with the phenomenon, film noir is often thought of as typically featuring hardboiled private detectives. However, while detective films are certainly among the most important noir films, most noir films do not feature either private detectives or police detectives as their main characters. Similarly, because their depiction stood out in such stark contrast to the representation of women in most Hollywood films of the 1940s and 1950s, a focus on the figure of the femme fatale is often thought of as a key attribute of film noir. Again, however, most noir films do not contain a classic femme fatale, even though they do often contain a number of female characters who in one way or another stand apart from the Hollywood mainstream.

In their initial characterization of film noir, Borde and Chaumeton identified five basic characteristics of the series of films they were discussing. These films, they declared, were "oneiric, strange, erotic, ambivalent, and cruel," though different films focus on different elements in this list (Borde and Chaumeton 2). And, if this list of qualities seems a bit vague and general, many critics since that time have attempted to come up with a concise list of basic properties of film noir as a phenomenon. In a much-cited article (first published in 1972), director and screenwriter Paul Schrader has helpfully listed four basic "catalytic elements" from which he sees the original noir cycle as drawing its basic energies. These elements are: (1) war and postwar disillusionment; (2) a general turn to greater realism in postwar film as a whole; (3) the influence of German expatriates; and (4) the hardboiled tradition. He then discusses some basic stylistic and thematic tendencies in film noir, as influenced by these "elements."[3]

Deborah Thomas concentrates more directly on the properties of the films themselves. Taking an approach that is anchored in gender studies, she suggests the following list of basic characteristics of noir films:

1. These films tend to feature a "central male protagonist whose point of view is privileged through such devices as first-person narration . . . and subjective framing devices like flashbacks or dreams" (67).
2. They tend to undermine this point of view "through labyrinthine plots which seem to elude the protagonist's attempts to give them coherence through his narration" or through "breaks in the protagonist's consciousness" (68).
3. Film noir tends to feature protagonists with a divided or split consciousness, often figured in his simultaneous attraction to a "good" (i.e., domesticated) woman and a "bad" (i.e., strong and independent) femme fatale (68).
4. Such films tend to feature a "mood of pervasive anxiety" for their male protagonists, often resolved through the death of the femme fatale or a suggestion of normalcy and domesticity looming in the near future (68).

Any number of other lists might be (and have been) proposed. As a good starting point, I would suggest the following basic characteristics of film noir:

1. The noir "look." Almost always shot in black and white, the original noir films typically feature low-key lighting and striking shadow effects, often with odd camera angles or in a mode influenced by the style of German Expressionist cinema.
2. The noir protagonist, typically male, is an unconventional hero, even an antihero. Sometimes he is seriously flawed, even evil or psychotic. He might be unusually violent or misogynistic. Sometimes he is simply an ordinary person who is thrust into extraordinary circumstances with which he is ill-equipped to deal. Often, he is weak or ineffectual, confused and lost, particularly at the mercy of women. When he is strong and effective, he tends to be so on his own terms, often following his own moral code that differs substantially from the societal norm.
3. Women in film noir are often represented in stereotypical ways: the conniving bad girl and the virtuous good girl are the most common types, often placed in the same film in opposition to one another, perhaps competing for the affections of the same man. In many cases, though, noir women are actually far more complex than the classic Hollywood norm; they can be quite strong and capable (often more so than the male protagonist), but they sometimes have a tendency to use these characteristics to the detriment of the male protagonist, in which case they are usually given the label "femme fatale" ("fatal, or deadly, woman"). In a number of noir films, though, a woman character *is* the protagonist, and in this case, she tends to be more virtuous than the

typical femme fatale, though social pressures often force her into ruthless or unscrupulous actions.

4. Film noir tends to be informed by an air of moral crisis and uncertainty; characters are tempted by opportunities they know they should rightly decline or otherwise find themselves at a moral crossroads, knowing that the path they take will have crucial long-term consequences. Often the characters are morally ambiguous: they are neither fully good nor fully bad, nor are their actions. Borde and Chaumeton repeatedly emphasize the "ambiguity" of film noir and of the way in which noir films tend to break down easy distinctions, especially between good and evil, creating an effect of confusion that disorients viewers: "The moral ambivalence, criminal violence, and contradictory complexity of the situations and motives all combine to give the public a shared feeling of the anguish or insecurity, which is the identifying sign of film noir at this time." (13).

5. Film noir tends to be skeptical of high-minded pronouncements and pessimistic about the future. The films tend to suggest that life has no inherent meaning, though sometimes (in the mode of philosophical existentialism) characters are able to make their own meanings in life.

6. Film noir tends to be heavily stylized. The lighting, music, and camera placements are often intrusive, used to excess as a means of creating an atmosphere of tension, mystery, or uncertainty. Characters and plot events are not necessarily realistic in any conventional sense.

The Emergence of Film Noir

To understand film noir, it is helpful to understand the historical conditions under which it developed. One of these conditions was, of course, the Production Code, but broader historical conditions in the United States were crucial to the rise of film noir, as well. In fact, even conditions in Germany were important to the development of certain noir characteristics. In particular, the German defeat in World War I led to a period of intense crisis in Germany that eventually led to the tragic rise to power of Adolf Hitler and the Nazis. But the air of crisis in Germany after World War I proved a stimulus to some forms of artistic creativity, especially film, as the German film industry became for a time, arguably, the most sophisticated in the world. The most direct line of influence between the German postwar crisis and German film was in the rise of Expressionism, an artistic style that was perfectly suited to express a sense of crisis—and that ultimately exercised a strong influence on the visual texture of film noir. German silent film classics such as Robert Wiene's *The Cabinet of Dr. Caligari* (1919), F. W. Murnau's *Nosferatu* (1922), and Fritz Lang's *Metropolis* (1926) did a great deal to establish the Expressionist style. This style then continued to be a force in the German film industry into the sound era, and Expressionist sound films such as Lang's *M* (1931) and *The Testament of Dr. Mabuse* (1933) are both clear forerunners of film noir both visually and thematically.

Things were about to change in Germany, however, and Hitler's rise to the chancellorship in 1933 soon led to a tidal wave of oppressive policies that drove many top talents out of Germany. One of the first actions of the new regime, in fact, was to exert control over the German film industry, quickly leading to the banning of *The Testament of Dr. Mabuse* in Germany. Lang, a practicing Catholic whose mother had been born Jewish, fled to France before moving on to Hollywood to make his first American film, the proto-noir crime drama *Fury*, in 1936. He then worked in the Hollywood film industry for the next twenty years, becoming an important noir director and a key example of the influence of filmmakers who had formerly worked in the German film industry.

American filmmakers with roots in the German film industry (most of whom came to America in flight from the Nazis) included such noir masters as Wilder, Michael Curtiz, Otto Preminger, Robert Siodmak, and Edgar G. Ulmer. Their influence was no doubt one reason for the prominence of German Expressionist techniques in Hollywood by the 1940s. In the case of film noir, though, this prominence was greatly enhanced by the fact that the Expressionist style was so well suited to the thematic texture of film noir. This style, which emphasized low-key lighting and the inventive use of light and shadows to create atmospheric effects, was also well suited to low-budget filmmaking, another plus for noir film.

In short, the dark turn in German history between the world wars proved a boon to the American film industry, helping the period from the 1930s through the 1950s to become known as a sort of Golden Age in American film. During this time, an emergent Hollywood film industry developed a highly sophisticated system for making and distributing classic films that made Hollywood the world capital of cinema. Talent flowed into California from all over the country and even all over the world, enriching the Hollywood milieu even further and making the Los Angeles neighborhood a shining paradigm of America itself as a land of opportunity where anyone with the ability and willingness to work hard could have ample chance to succeed. Moguls such as Louis B. Mayer, Jack Warner, Carl Laemmle, Harry Cohn, and David O. Selznick became the kings of the industry. All these men were immigrants or the sons of immigrants; all were Jewish, and all came from working-class backgrounds. The building of this film industry was an impressive achievement, a highly visual demonstration of what American skill, ingenuity, and industriousness could accomplish. It was the American Dream in action. Meanwhile, Hollywood films became advertisements for America; distributed more and more widely across the globe, they became emblems of prestige, markers of quality that encouraged audiences around the globe to associate America with wealth, sophistication, and fine craftsmanship.

That, of course, is only one side of the story. The Hollywood film industry grew so impressively in the 1930s largely in order to provide a momentary diversion from the harsh realities of American poverty during the Great Depression. In the first half of the 1940s, Hollywood films provided brief moments of respite from the trauma and anxiety of World War II. Meanwhile, victory in that war brought anything but universal prosperity and contentment. Hollywood films continued to provide escapist entertainments in the late 1940s and through the 1950s, even as the industry itself became a central target of the anticommunist hysteria that swept across America like a plague. Thus, if the heyday of Expressionism occurred during a troubled period in German history, then the Golden Age of Hollywood corresponded closely with some of the darkest decades in American history, from the Great Depression in the 1930s, to war in the 1940s, to repressive anticommunist hysteria and terror of nuclear holocaust in the 1950s.

Hollywood film from the 1930s through the 1950s might have often provided escapist entertainment, but it also reflected the dark side of American history more directly. At the very beginning of the sound era, for example, films such as Universal's monster movies and Warner Bros.' gangster movies of the early 1930s grew out of the difficulties of their era. Such films were among the forerunners of film noir—and they were exactly the sort of films that the Production Code was designed to curb, leading to the rise of film noir to take their place. The connection between gangster films and noir films is fairly obvious, but it should also be clear that monsters such as King Kong and Frankenstein's creature are virtual prototypes of the noir protagonist: alienated, misunderstood, and basically innocent, but driven to crime and eventually destroyed by forces beyond their control.

Many films before the US entry into World War II anticipated film noir even more directly. In 1940, for example, *Stranger on the Third Floor* showed numerous characteristics that would later come to be associated with noir films. It also features performances by Elisha Cook Jr. (who would later become a key noir character actor) and Peter Lorre—who had starred in Lang's *M* (1931) back in Germany and who would play important roles in a number of American noir films, including *The Maltese Falcon*, which also features Cook. *Stranger on the Third Floor* includes a psychotic killer (played by Lorre), an innocent man (played by Cook) wrongly convicted of murder, and a protagonist (played by John McGuire) who is driven to near madness by the events of the film. The film ultimately deviates from most noir in its successful resolution, but it nevertheless has very much the look and feel of a noir film—especially in the strange dream sequence at the center of the film, which is an almost perfect example of German Expressionist visuals. The film also features the cinematography of Nicholas Musuraca, who would become a leading noir cinematographer.

The Motion Picture Production Code

No discussion of the basic characteristics of film noir would be complete without a consideration of the impact of the Motion Picture Production Code on these films, which in many ways were designed to do exactly what the Production Code was trying to prevent. The Production Code was a series of restrictions on the content of Hollywood film adopted by the film industry as a form of self-censorship, designed both to counter the public perception of film as a morally suspect form and to prevent the imposition of censorship from outside the industry. Adopted in 1930 and fully implemented in 1934, the Code was drafted by former US postmaster Will B. Hays, who resigned his cabinet post in 1922 to become the head of the Motion Picture Producers and Distributors of America (MPPDA), charged with creating a better public image of the film industry. The Code (often referred to as the Hays Code), established three general principles: First, no film should be produced that would tend to lower the moral standards of its audience. Second, films should present "correct standards of life." Finally, no film should ridicule the law (natural or human) or show sympathy with the violators of the law. It then spelled out a number of specific restrictions, most of which were oriented toward limiting the representation of sexuality, violence, or criminality on the screen. The Code had a major impact on Hollywood film from 1934 until the 1960s, when it began to appear more and more anachronistic. The Code was periodically updated to try to stay relevant but was abandoned in 1968. It was replaced by a film rating system, still in use today in modified form, instituted by the Motion Picture Association of America (MPAA), to which the MPPDA had changed its name in 1945.

Of course, virtually every film noir was in some way problematic according to this Code, and it is clear that many characteristics of film noir developed largely as an attempt to represent sexuality, violence, and criminality in ways that could pass Code review. Thus, noir filmmakers developed an elaborate language to suggest a variety of forbidden topics without actually showing or mentioning them directly, thus skirting the restrictions of the Code. Many film historians, in fact, feel that film noir was enriched by the limits placed on them by the Code, which forced the filmmakers to be cleverer and more creative than they might otherwise have been. Meanwhile, one reason for the emergence of neo-noir films at the end of the 1960s was that filmmakers wanted to revisit the possibilities of film noir in an era without Code restrictions. Indeed, the two major, obvious distinctions between noir and neo-noir films are the absence of Code restrictions on the latter and the tendency of the latter to be produced in color.

What Is Neo-Noir?

Though the original film noir cycle had seemingly run its course by the end of the 1950s, the changing nature of American society in the 1960s considerably disrupted the film industry—most obviously in the collapse of the Production Code, which opened the way for the resurrection of noir energies in the new and less restricted form that came to be known as "neo-noir." With the emergence of films such as John Boorman's *Point Blank* (1967), Roman Polanski's *Chinatown* (1973), Robert Altman's *The Long Goodbye* (1974), and Arthur Penn's *Night Moves* (1975), it soon became clear that the atmosphere, style, characters, and narratives of film noir were being self-consciously deployed in a new family of films, now unrestricted by the Production Code and mostly (but not always) made in color. By the 1980s, distinctive films such as Lawrence Kasdan's *Body Heat* (1981) and Joel and Ethan Coen's

Blood Simple (1984) helped to propel an explosion in the production of neo-noir films, an explosion that (predictably) included remakes of a number of noir classics. However, stretching the conventions of anything opens a much wider variety of possibilities than had following those conventions, so these films (the production of which continued apace in the 1990s) were much more diverse than the original noir cycle had been—as the example of Ridley Scott's science fiction noir classic *Blade Runner* (1982) amply illustrates. Even Tim Burton's original *Batman* (1989) clearly qualifies as a neo-noir film. Moreover, other influences (such as the French New Wave) also contributed to the greater diversity of neo-noir film.

It should also be noted that the rise of neo-noir was closely aligned with what has come to be known as the "New Hollywood," in which a new generation of young directors exercised unprecedented control over their films, thanks partly to the collapse of the studio system and partly to the fact that the rise of blockbuster films helped make directors a marketable "brand." Many of the key neo-noir films were also New Hollywood films, though it is also the case that some directors who were working within the bounds of what could rightly be considered neo-noir established such a distinctive brand that their films came to be associated more with their directors than with neo-noir. Thus, neo-noir directors from John Cassavetes (*A Woman Under the Influence* in 1974, *The Killing of a Chinese Bookie* in 1976, *Opening Night* in 1977) and Martin Scorsese (*Mean Streets* in 1973, *Taxi Driver* in 1976, *Raging Bull* in 1980), to David Lynch (*Blue Velvet* in 1986, *Wild at Heart* in 1990, *Lost Highway* in 1996) and Quentin Tarantino (*Reservoir Dogs* in 1992, *Pulp Fiction* in 1994, *Jackie Brown* in 1997), have more often been discussed as individual "auteurs" than within the genre context of neo-noir. Moreover, some of these directors— Lynch's *Mulholland Drive* (2001) is probably the best example, though all of his films contain strong revisionary energies—push the conventions of noir far enough that they might be considered revisionary noir directors.

The wide variety of neo-noir films—and the fact that some of the films are more clearly and self-consciously "noir" than others—makes neo-noir difficult to define. However, book-length studies, such as Richard Martin's *Mean Streets and Raging Bulls* (1997) and Foster Hirsch's *Detours and Lost Highways* (1999) have begun to map out a definition, while broader studies of noir, such as that by Bould, have paid significant attention to neo-noir as well. Meanwhile, if the beginnings of neo-noir are reasonably easy to locate in specific developments in the 1960s, there are no such developments to which one can tie the end of neo-noir. In fact, it is my argument in this volume that neo-noir films continue to be produced to this day, alongside revisionary noir films—and indeed that the distinction between neo-noir and revisionary noir is not an absolute one but a matter of degree, so that the revisionary noir films of the twenty-first century can be placed along a continuum from, say, the ultimate neo-noir of the Coens' *The Man Who Wasn't There* (2001), to the clearly revisionary noir of films such as Michael Winterbottom's *The Killer Inside Me* (2010) or Josh and Benny Safdie's *Uncut Gems* (2019). Meanwhile, other films of the twenty-first century remain mostly in the neo-noir camp, including such examples as otherwise different as Brian De Palma's *Femme Fatale* (2002) and *The Black Dahlia* (2006), Nicolas Winding Refn's *Drive* (2011), and Denis Villeneuve's *Blade Runner 2049* (2017).

What Is Revisionary Noir?

Neo-noir films self-consciously draw upon the conventions of film noir but in ways that do not encourage a reevaluation of those conventions or of the original noir films. Revisionary noir films use noir conventions but challenge them and go beyond them in ways that *do* encourage this sort of reevaluation. Again, though, the line between neo-noir and revisionary noir is not absolute: any given film that employs noir conventions might potentially inspire *someone* to rethink noir, just as any film that goes beyond noir conventions, no matter how radically, might find some viewers who are *not* inspire to rethink noir. I am speaking of matters of degree more than kind.

The historical line between neo-noir and revisionary noir is also particularly vague. Just as neo-noir films continue to be made today, so too were noir films with strong revisionary energies made well before the twentieth century. However, it should also be noted that the distinction between revisionary noir films and neo-noir films is not necessarily a value judgment: revisionary noir films are not necessarily "better" or more interesting films than neo-noir films. They simply push more firmly against the boundaries of what is conventionally regarded as "noir." *The Man Who Wasn't There* can be taken as a sort of limit case that pushes neo-noir as far as it can go without posing a critical challenge to our conventional understanding of "noir."[4] It thus opened the way for an increase in the prevalence of what I will call "revisionary noir," in reference to noir films that clearly and self-consciously draw upon noir tropes in both style and content but differ from the original film noir cycle in ways so substantial that they tend to encourage a reevaluation of those original films and of the meaning of "noir" as an umbrella concept. Such films do not merely use noir tropes but can lead to a substantial revision in those tropes. I will argue that this mode of noir film becomes particularly prominent after the first years of the new century and remains so today in 2024.

The Periodization of Noir Film

Cultural historians refers to the kind of historical model I am proposing here as a model of "periodization," in which history proceeds in stages, with a given "paradigm" being the dominant one in any given period. Some famous examples of this kind of periodization include the model of literary history proposed by the Russian formalists in the early twentieth century and the model of scientific history proposed by Thomas Kuhn in the middle of the twentieth century, but such models are commonly used in all sorts of situations, including the history of film. I should emphasize, though, that the periodization of noir film that I am proposing here (film noir, neo-noir, and revisionary noir) depends both upon developments within the films themselves and on external social and political forces that contribute to the shaping of film history. I should also emphasize that the transition from one period to the next is not sudden and absolute. For example, if I designate *Point Blank* as the "first" neo-noir film, that does not imply that this film represented a dramatic break in which noir history sharply veers off in a new direction. Indeed, one could just as easily suggest Jack Smight's *Harper* (1966) as the first neo-noir film without any meaningful change to the historical model. The boundaries between the three main periods I described above are fluid and porous. In addition, during each shift of paradigm, there will appear a number of transitional films that belong comfortably within neither the old nor the new paradigm. Thus, if one regards *Touch of Evil* as the "final" film noir, it might also be regarded as the first film in the transition to neo-noir. Similarly, if one regards *Point Blank* as the first neo-noir film, then it might also be considered the final film in the transition from noir to neo-noir. Moreover, in between *Touch of Evil* and *Point Blank*, there are a number of transitional noir films—such as *Harper* or Samuel Fuller's *Shock Corridor* (1963) and *The Naked Kiss* (1964)—that begin to push the boundaries of noir film beyond the original noir paradigm.

Of course, the emergence of neo-noir represents a sharper turn than the emergence of revisionary noir, largely because of forces that were external to the films themselves. The most obvious of these was the Production Code, which gradually collapsed over the course of the 1960s, due both to economic factors related to the rise of television and to changing cultural values amid the emergent countercultural movements of that decade. No such clearly defined external forces impacted the transition from neo-noir to revisionary noir, which is probably why that transition is less sharply defined (and is, in fact, being posited here for the first time).[5] Meanwhile, if neo-noir films have continued to be produced in the twenty-first century, it is also the case that, as the examples of films such as Paul Verhoeven's *Basic Instinct* (1992) and Carl Franklin's *Devil in a Blue Dress* (1995) show, films that clearly fit in the revisionary noir category were already being produced well before 2001.

It is helpful here to draw upon the work of the prominent British cultural theorist Raymond Williams to describe the transitions between periods. Williams argued (in much the same mode as the Russian Formalists, but with more awareness of external social factors), cultural production in any period is indeed largely shaped by a specific dominant paradigm. However, Williams notes, any period will also continue to see the "residual" influence of the preceding dominant paradigm, as well as to begin to see the "emergent" influence of what will become the dominant paradigm in the succeeding period (121–23). Thus, for example, the films of the neo-noir period not only draw upon the noir characteristics that were established in the original film noir cycle but also begin to anticipate the more radical deviations from those original characteristics that would emerge in the revisionary noir period.

Film Noir and Modernism

The specific vision of noir history put forth here is very closely related to larger models of cultural history during the same period—and especially to the theorization of postmodernism developed by the prominent cultural theorist Fredric Jameson through the 1980s and summarized in his 1991 book *Postmodernism, or, The Cultural Logic of Late Capitalism.* Before discussing the relevance of Jameson's work on postmodernism to noir history, however, it is first useful to note that both film noir and the related phenomenon of hardboiled detective fiction have been described as distinctively American forms of modernism.[6] Modernism is most commonly associated with the high-profile work of the early twentieth century, such as the fiction of James Joyce or Virginia Woolf, the poetry of T. S. Eliot or William Carlos Williams, or the paintings of Pablo Picasso. But modernism, though it never became a literary dominant (in the sense meant by the Russian Formalists), reflected a quite widespread sense that the radical changes underway in virtually every aspect of modern life had rendered older forms of art largely irrelevant. Modernist artists were thus willing to attempt radical experiments in an attempt to produce new forms of art that could respond to the new texture of life in the fast-paced modern world.

Film itself as an art form arose at about the same time as modernism—and was one of the many innovations that were changing Western societies at the beginning of the twentieth century. By the 1930s, though, a distinctive nonmodernist Hollywood style had become dominant in American film. This style was essentially realist in that it was designed not to call attention to itself, allowing audiences to concentrate on the story within the film, suspending their disbelief and treating the events on the screen as if they were really happening. There were few exceptions to this tendency in American film of the time, which is one reason why the most important exception—Welles's *Citizen Kane* (1941)—seemed so strikingly innovative. *Citizen Kane*, a major modernist work of art, was not a commercial success (for various reasons), and so it did not inspire a wave of direct imitators in Hollywood. It was, however, an important influence on the development of film noir, which was just beginning to appear when *Kane* was officially released in September of 1941, roughly a month before *The Maltese Falcon.* Often considered the greatest film ever made, *Citizen Kane* was certainly one of the most innovative, especially in its use of unusual camera angles and movements, play with lighting, unbalanced compositions, and flashback narrative structure. All these elements would subsequently become prominent in film noir, even though Kane is not typically thought of as a film noir, mostly because its central character is a larger-than-life figure, as opposed to the Everymen, outcasts, and losers who typically populate film noir. Of course, even the powerful Kane is driven by childhood trauma, has his life disrupted by a sexual obsession, and ends up a broken man, dying alone. Still, *Kane* is probably better considered a proto-noir film than a noir film proper, reminding us that *The Maltese Falcon* did not simply emerge from nowhere. Borde and Chaumeton mention *Kane* multiple times in their discussion of film noir, though they also regard *Kane* as an "unclassifiable" film that doesn't really fit in any category (2). It is also worth mentioning here that Welles himself would go on to become one of the greatest noir directors, directing such crucial noir films as *The Stranger* (1946) and *The Lady from Shanghai* (1947). And, if Welles's *Touch of Evil* (1958) is to be considered the end of the noir cycle, then that cycle can then be said to be bookended by *Citizen Kane* and *Touch of Evil*, making the films of Welles crucially important in the evolution of noir.

Noir Film and Postmodernism

Most cultural historians agree that, in the years after World War II, a new form of art that both drew upon and challenged the insights of the modernists began to emerge, becoming fully formed around the end of the 1960s. There has, as yet, been no complete consensus about the exact relationship of this new movement to modernism, but modernism seems so important as a predecessor in one way or another that this new movement has come almost universally to be known as "postmodernism." Original critical assessments of postmodernism (and especially of postmodern literature) were heavily influenced by the countercultural spirit of the 1960s, seeing postmodernism as an emancipatory movement that challenged the literary establishment via subversive carnivalesque strategies that refused to respect the authority of existing cultural norms. A number of critics in the 1960s and 1970s—Egyptian American literary scholar Ihab Hassan and French poststructuralist theorist Jean-François Lyotard were probably the most influential on American literary and cultural studies—saw postmodernism in this way, at the same time generally seeing modernism as an elitist movement that was largely aligned with the ruling forces in Western society.

Of course, these early theorists of postmodernism were working, not only in the midst of the 1960s/1970s counterculture, but also at a time when the modernist art and literature of the first decades of the twentieth century had been adopted as key parts of the official Western "canon," largely because the complex and sophisticated works of modernist artists were arguably aesthetically superior to the works of Soviet socialist realism, so that the canonization of modernism allowed it to be conscripted as a key element of Western Cold War rhetoric.[7] It was thus easy, after the 1950s, to envision modernism as supportive of official authority, even though the major modernist writers had mostly been marginalized outsiders when they were actually living and working. For example, Joyce's *Ulysses* (1922), perhaps the greatest single work of modernist literature, was powerfully critical of both the Catholic authorities in Ireland and the British colonial authorities that had by then ruled Ireland for centuries. Moreover, *Ulysses* was considered shocking and even pornographic by many. It was, for example, banned in the United States upon its initial publication, a ban that stayed in place until 1934.

Beginning his major work on postmodernism in the 1980s, Jameson was working at a time in which the 1960s and 1970s counterculture was largely a thing of the past—and had largely failed to achieve its supposedly radical goal of fundamentally changing the world. Jameson was thus able to see that the counterculture might not have been quite as radically transformative as it had been widely perceived to be at the time, primarily because it failed to imagine a genuine alternative to the capitalist system that was the most important factor determining the nature and organization of Western societies of the time. Accordingly, Jameson was immediately suspicious of claims of the emancipatory power of postmodernism, given that these claims were so clearly related to the energies of the counterculture. At the same time, he also sought to recover the initial subversive tendencies of modernism, which he saw as a (failed) last-ditch effort to resist the complete takeover of Western societies by capitalism.

In contrast, postmodernism, for Jameson, arose as a sign of the defeat of modernism by capitalism. Postmodernism, indeed, is for Jameson essentially the culture that arises when all of the major enemies of capitalism have been defeated, leaving the power of capitalism essentially unchallenged. Postmodernism, for Jameson, is the culture that arises when the process of capitalist modernization is virtually complete, leaving nothing that has not already been colonized by the capitalist system. Drawing upon the work of Ernest Mandel, Jameson refers to this new stage of capitalism as "late" capitalism, a global form of consumer-oriented capitalism when virtually everything (including culture) has been conscripted by the capitalist system and incorporated into the capitalist system of commodity production. Thoroughly aligned ideologically with late capitalism, postmodernism is thus the "cultural logic" of late capitalism.

As it so happens, Jameson uses neo-noir film as one of his key examples of postmodern art. In particular, he refers to neo-noir films such as *Chinatown* and *Body Heat* as "nostalgia films," arguing that the imaginations of postmodern filmmakers (and other postmodern artists) are typically held so firmly in the grip of late capitalist ideology that the artists are unable to develop distinctive styles of their own and must turn to the past for inspiration. On the other hand, for Jameson, this turn to the past is emotionally inert, bereft of the kind of genuine longing for something that has been lost that we typically associate with the emotion of nostalgia. This emotion, for Jameson, is unavailable to postmodern films because of a general postmodern loss of historical sense that makes filmmakers unable fully to understand the past as historically linked to the present. In particular, the nostalgia film thus becomes a special form of the "pastiche" that Jameson consistently regards as the crucial stylistic technique of postmodern art: unable to generate a genuinely personal style of their own, postmodern artists, for Jameson, simply borrow from the styles of the past, as if choosing them from a cafeteria menu.

For Jameson, such nostalgia films speak to the fact that we had (in the 1980s) become so estranged from our present, demonstrating the "enormity of a situation in which we seem increasingly incapable of fashioning representations of our own current experience" (21). Meanwhile, in the more than thirty years since *Postmodernism* was published, Jameson's book has remained the most influential theorization of postmodernism. Indeed, as the late capitalism he was describing developed into a new, more virulent neoliberal form, his analysis would seem to have become even more accurate. But if postmodernism is a cultural dominant, and if it is thoroughly aligned with late capitalism, how will anything ever change in the future? Jameson

doesn't know the answer to that, nor does anyone else. Yet, based on historical precedent, Jameson insists that the current prevailing system, no matter how total, will
change—and will change in ways that we cannot possibly anticipate:

> The postmodern may well in that sense be little more than a transitional period between
> two stages of capitalism, in which the earlier forms of the economic are in the process of
> being restructured on a global scale, including the older forms of labor and its traditional
> organizational institutions and concepts. That a new international proletariat (taking
> forms we cannot yet imagine) will reemerge from this convulsive upheaval it needs no
> prophet to predict: we ourselves are still in the trough, however, and no one can say how
> long we still stay there. (*Postmodernism* 417)

In addition, Jameson believes that postmodernism itself might evolve in ways that
ultimately give it the ability to contribute to future change. One reason why late
capitalism has such a grip on our imaginations, he argues, is that it is so complex
and widespread that it is impossible for us to understand how it works, where it
came from, or where we ourselves fit within the larger system. Late capitalism has, in
short, crippled our ability to perform what Jameson calls "cognitive mapping," after
the work of urban geographer Kevin Lynch on how individuals get their bearings
within the complex setting of modern cities. Jameson envisions a day, though, when
postmodern art can help us to regain the ability to perform this sort of cognitive
mapping. Thus, he concludes, "the political form of postmodernism, if there ever is
any, will have as its vocation the invention and projection of a global cognitive mapping, on a social as well as a spatial scale" (*Postmodernism* 54).

I would argue that, if neo-noir film is a quintessential example of postmodern
pastiche culture that fails to contribute to this project of cognitive mapping, the
emergence of revisionary noir films is possibly a sign that postmodern culture is
finally beginning to enter the political phase that Jameson speculated about when he
was writing over thirty years ago. Revisionary noir films acknowledge both film noir
and neo-noir as their predecessors but set themselves apart from these predecessors in
ways that help us to see those earlier periods as a past that is connected with the present through a process of historical change. By extension, if the past can change into
the present, then the present can change into a different future, possibly a better one.

ORGANIZATION OF THIS VOLUME

This volume will trace the historical evolution of noir film by looking at three important subsets of noir film, including those focusing on detectives, those centering
on the existential crisis of a "lost man," and those that are dominated by female
characters, including characters who belong to the classic noir category of the femme
fatale. There are, of course, other subsets of noir film (such as "heist" films or other
crime films that do not necessarily feature detectives or investigations), but these
three should be sufficient to characterize noir film in general. Each of the three

segments begin with an introductory historical overview of that subset of noir film. Each segment then proceeds with a detailed discussion of two films from the original noir cycle in order to clearly establish the characteristics of the films in that cycle. Each segment will then discuss two neo-noir films and three revisionary noir films from the requisite subset in order to explore the ways these categories differ from each other and from the original film noir cycle. The larger number of revisionary noir films is primarily included better to characterize this previously unidentified category, though it is also the case that these films differ so much from the original film noir cycle that they can cover a broader range of characteristics.

Part I

THE NOIR DETECTIVE FILM

Introduction to Noir Detective Films

Detective stories—especially stories involving hardboiled private detectives—are one of the principal narrative models for film noir. Of the five films initially identified with noir by Frank and Chartier, Otto Preminger's *Laura* (1944) is a detective story of sorts, while John Huston's *The Maltese Falcon* (1941) and Edward Dmytryk's *Murder, My Sweet* (1944) feature America's two best-known hardboiled private detectives. *Laura* is a much more idiosyncratic detective noir story, partly because it involves a police detective, the upright Mark McPherson (Dana Andrews), rather than a private detective. Otherwise, the on-screen clash between characters played by Clifton Webb and Vincent Price provides campy highlights to an otherwise straightforward whodunit that is nevertheless complicated by the fact that the eponymous Laura (Gene Tierney), supposedly a murder victim, turns up alive halfway through. There is a real murder victim, though, and McPherson manages to solve that case (along the way becoming obsessed with Laura), even if Webb steals the film with his performance. In any case, detective stories have come to be associated strongly with film noir in the popular consciousness, though such stories are probably actually more common in neo-noir films than in the films of the original noir cycle.

Still, many of the most important noir films have involved private detectives, and there are many reasons why detective films (as well as the larger and more general category of crime films) should be so central to such a crucial cultural phenomenon as film noir. For one thing, this focus on crime and detection generates compelling narratives that feature compelling characters. In particular, the private detective is the virtual embodiment of American individualism, a key element of the capitalist or "bourgeois" ideology that has long been crucial to the American national identity. The classic private detective, especially of the hardboiled type, is a lone individual living by his own code of ethics and trying to enact his own vision of justice, even though this vision might not match up with those of the police or of society as a whole. Moreover, as Ernest Mandel has argued, "The evolution of the crime story does indeed reflect, as if in a mirror, the evolution of bourgeois ideology, of social relations in a bourgeois society, perhaps even of the capitalist mode of production itself."[1]

Detective and crime stories present extensive opportunities for social critique. For example, they often feature characters who are driven to crime out of desperation because society does not provide appropriate support for the dire situations in which they find themselves. Or, as Mandel puts it, the history of the crime story is essentially the history of capitalist society, a society that "in and of itself breeds crime, originates in crime, and leads to crime."[2] It is thus perhaps no accident that the film conventionally considered to be the first film noir was a detective film. *The Maltese Falcon*, based on the 1930 novel of the same title by Dashiell Hammett, features Humphrey Bogart as the tough-talking (and genuinely tough) private eye Sam Spade. Perhaps the first fully noir detective film, it might also be the greatest noir detective film. Bogart, named the greatest American film legend of all time in a 1999 poll conducted by the American Film Institute, owes much of that status to his performances in film noir, and *The Maltese Falcon* is perhaps his most important noir film—though his own greatest noir performance is probably as a radically alienated screenwriter in *In a Lonely Place* (1950). In *The Maltese Falcon*, Spade (because of his strong, if rather eccentric, sense of right and wrong) stands out in a world full of corruption, as all the other characters—including femme fatale Brigid O'Shaughnessy (Mary Astor) scramble to achieve their own selfish goals, no matter who gets hurt—or killed. And yet there is a way in which Spade is very much at home in the world of the film, very much able to understand the motivations of the other characters.

This section includes a detailed discussion of *The Maltese Falcon* and *Murder, My Sweet*, the latter of which is based on Raymond Chandler's 1940 novel *Farewell, My Lovely*, featuring private detective Philip Marlowe (here played by Dick Powell). Chandler was especially important as a source of material for film noir. Ten films have been adapted directly from his writing, ranging from *The Falcon Takes Over* (1942), a loose adaptation of *Farewell, My Lovely*, to the 1998 neo-noir adaptation of *Poodle Springs*, the novel left unfinished on Chandler's death but finished by Robert B. Parker for publication in 1989.[3] Other especially important noir detective films include *The Big Sleep* (1946), another classic noir detective film based on a novel by Chandler (the 1939 novel of the same title). Here, Marlowe navigates a rather absurd Los Angeles landscape amid a famous for its complex, convoluted plot. *The Big Sleep* is clearly designed as a star vehicle for Bogart, who with this film became associated with the roles of both Spade and Marlowe. Bogart's Marlowe is a bit tougher than Powell's had been, but still lacks the rough-edged quality of Bogart's Spade from *The Maltese Falcon*. He also has a tender side here, including a subplot (significantly embellished from the novel) involving his relationship with Vivian Sternwood, played by Bogart's then-new wife, Lauren Bacall. Indeed, much of the marketing for this film attempted to capitalize on the public's fascination with the glamour couple, who had first been seen on screen together in the 1944 film *To Have and Have Not*. Possibly Chandler's raciest novel, this one required considerable modification to get past the Production Code, but director Howard Hawks, one of Hollywood's most successful mainstream directors, was a master craftsman who was up to the task. It probably didn't hurt that he had an all-star team of screenwriters, including the novelist William Faulkner, as well as Leigh Brackett and Jules Furthman (a Hollywood veteran who, among other things, had coscripted *To Have and Have Not*, along with Faulkner). And yet, the contrast between the source material of the original novel and the Hollywood craftsmanship of the finished film creates tensions and interesting effects that go beyond the craftsmanship itself.

In 1947, Marlowe returned to the screen in still another incarnation with Robert Montgomery's adaptation of Chandler's 1943 novel *The Lady in the Lake*. Though a generally undistinguished adaptation, this film is notable for being shot from the point of view of Marlowe (played by director Montgomery), thus mimicking Chandler's habitual first-person style of narration. Thus, except for an occasional insert in which he addresses the audience directly, Marlowe is never seen on screen, except when he is in front of a mirror and can thus see himself. This technique makes *Lady in the Lake* stand out, though in another way it is simply a specific example of a characteristic it shares with so many noir films—the tendency to put a great deal of emphasis on style.

Robert Aldrich's *Kiss Me Deadly* (1955), vaguely based on Mickey Spillane's 1952 detective novel *Kiss Me, Deadly*, updates the noir detective film to include Mike Hammer, the misogynistic, commie-hating protagonist who made Spillane a huge commercial success in the 1950s. Aldrich's film, however, adds a significant amount of Cold War anxiety to Spillane's novel, which had been about organized crime, by converting it into an espionage narrative centering on the threat of nuclear catastrophe. At the same time, the film presents Hammer (played by Ralph Meeker) in an extremely unflattering light that emphasizes his violence and brutality. Then the whole thing ends with a bang.

Finally, just to emphasize the versatility of noir detective stories, one might also take note of Fritz Lang's *While the City Sleeps* (1956). This film is rather late in the noir cycle, standing apart from high noir in the refinement of its visual style, which lacks the harshness and starkness of so many noirs, while still showing occasional signs of Lang's Expressionist roots. It is also an unusual noir in that it employs comedy extensively—and even has a comic ending. Otherwise, the film displays a number of crucial noir characteristics, including the dark nature of the troubled serial killer whose murderous attacks on women, motivated by his own gender insecurity, underlie the entire plot. However, the killer (dubbed the "Lipstick Killer" in the media and played by John Drew Barrymore) actually has relatively little screen time, most of which is taken up by said media. In particular, having just inherited his father's media empire but having no desire to run it, wastrel Walter Kyne (Vincent Price) decides to amuse himself by having the heads of his company's three major departments compete to see who can identify the killer before the police do, the winner to take over the leadership of the company. This contest initiates a competitive scramble in which all involved acquit themselves rather badly—making the key noir point that these respectable media executives are not that morally superior to the serial killer they are chasing. At least the killer has the excuse of being mentally ill, while the executives mostly seem to be just ruthless and ambitious.

Neo-Noir Detective Films

This section will include a detailed discussion of Roman Polanski's neo-noir film *Chinatown* (1974), which features Jack Nicholson as private detective Jake Gittes. *Chinatown* is a superb film with extremely high production values throughout, but it is perhaps most striking for the highly self-conscious way it plays with the tropes of noir detective films. Its success seemed to announce that neo-noir was a genuine phenomenon, though it was neither the first neo-noir film nor even the first neo-noir detective film. As early as 1966, Jack Smight's transitional film *Harper* (based on a novel by the Canadian Ross Macdonald, often compared with Chandler[4]) was moving close to neo-noir territory. *Chinatown* was also preceded in 1973 by Robert Altman's *The Long Goodbye*, based on Chandler's 1953 novel of the same title. *The Long Goodbye* mimics noir detective films rather playfully (but respectfully), updating the story to the 1970s, though Marlowe himself often seems to think he is still in the 1950s. Written by noir veteran Leigh Brackett, *The Long Goodbye* is another excellent example of the way neo-noir films often depart significantly from their noir predecessors, but in ways that do not ask us to revise our vision of those predecessors.

Arthur Penn's *Night Moves* (1975) quickly followed with another neo-noir detective film. Starring Gene Hackman, this unusually bleak film continues a neo-noir push into more erotic territory and might have been a bit ahead of its time. It was not a commercial or critical success at the time of its initial release, though its reputation has steadily grown over time. Released only a few years after *Chinatown*, *Night Moves* makes for an interesting comparison with that film, partly because it (like *The Long Goodbye*) modernizes its setting to the time of its making, while *Chinatown* places its action back in the 1930s. A number of other neo-noir detective films appeared in the 1970s, as well, including direct remakes of several classic noir detective films in the 1970s, including an undistinguished TV film remake of *Double Indemnity* in 1973. This remake was then followed by remakes of *Murder, My Sweet* and *The Big Sleep* in 1975 and 1978, both featuring aging noir star Robert Mitchum (in his sixties by the time of the release of the second of these) in the role of Marlowe. The first of these remakes was entitled *Farewell, My Lovely*, thus restoring the title of Chandler's original novel. It was, however, unable to recapture the magic of the original film. Meanwhile, the remake of *The Big Sleep* oddly shifts the action to London, thus losing the Los Angeles setting that was so crucial to Chandler's writing.[5]

Neo-noir detective films of the 1980s moved in a variety of new directions. For example, Brian DePalma, who made a string of neo-noir films during this period, made another standout in this category in *Blow Out* (1981), in which a sound effects man from the film industry plays detective—with shocking results. The year 1984 saw the release of *Blood Simple*, by Joel and Ethan Coen, featuring a highly quirky detective who isn't even the central character and announcing what would be an extensive career in noir film by the Coens. In terms of detective films, their most important contribution to neo-noir was *The Big Lebowski* (1998), which mimics the work of Chandler in a highly postmodern fashion that pushes the boundaries of noir about as much as possible yet shows a film-lover's respect for the original noir films.[6] Here, laid-back stoner Jeff Lebowski (Jeff Bridges), better known as "The Dude," fulfills the Marlowe role as he stumbles his way through an investigation that becomes increasingly more complicated—and that made him one of the most beloved film characters of recent decades.

David Lynch's *Blue Velvet* (1986) is also a neo-noir detective story in which an ill-suited nondetective plays the main detective role. Here, young Jeffrey Beaumont (Kyle MacLachlan) tries to solve the mystery of Dorothy Vallens (Isabella Rosselini), a decidedly unconventional femme fatale. Both *Chinatown* and *Blue Velvet* will be discussed in detail in this section as illustrations of neo-noir detective films.

In addition to *Blue Velvet*, many neo-noir films of the 1980s and 1990s featured nonprofessional detectives attempting to solve mysteries that lure them into decidedly noirish worlds. Meanwhile, many neo-noir detective films of the 1980s replaced private detectives with police detectives or other government operatives. For example, the main detective in William Friedkin's *To Live and Die in L.A.* (1985) is a Secret Service agent, in a film that brought new levels of action to noir. And Michael Mann's *Manhunter* (1986) features FBI agent Will Graham (William Petersen) but perhaps most memorably introduces film audiences to Hannibal Lecter (here played by Brian Cox). Some of the best neo-noir films of the 1990s were in this vein, as well. For example, the best-known version of the Lecter character made his first appearance in Jonathan Demme's *The Silence of the Lambs* (1991), which moved toward revisionary noir through its use of a female detective in FBI agent Clarice Starling (Jodie Foster). However, this film is so dominated by Anthony Hopkins's performance as Lecter that Foster's own impressive performance probably has less impact than it should have. Other neo-noir films of the 1990s—such as David Fincher's *Seven* (1995), the Coens' *Fargo* (1996), and Curtis Hanson's *L.A. Confidential* (1997)—also featured police detectives (and sometimes police villains). These films broke new ground in a number of ways, though they did not ask viewers to change the way they saw the original noir detective films. *Fargo*, by again featuring a female police detective, probably came the closest in this regard, but even something like Jake Kasdan's *Zero Effect* (1998), which spoofed the noir detective genre, did not do so in ways that would be likely to cause viewers to begin to look at the original noir films in new ways.

Revisionary Noir Detective Films

Neo-noir films of this period started to move beyond the original noir cycle in interesting ways, many by challenging viewers to play detective just to try to figure out what was going on in the film. Such films include Bryan Singer's *The Usual Suspects* (1995), Alex Proyas's *Dark City* (1998), Lynch's *Lost Highway* (1996) and *Mulholland Drive* (2001), Fincher's *Fight Club* (1999), and Christopher Nolan's *Memento* (2000). In addition, some noir detective films of the 1990s directly took on the original noir cycle in ways that might lead to a revision of our understanding of that cycle, thus anticipating the revisionary noir films of the twenty-first century. One of the most important of these is Carl Franklin's *Devil in a Blue Dress* (1995), which, in fact, can already be considered a revisionary noir film in its own right. Based on the 1990 novel by Walter Mosley, his first published book in what would become a distinguished literary career in a number of genres, this film introduced film audiences to African American detective Easy Rawlins (Denzel Washington), who would go on to be featured in fourteen novels and a number of short stories by Mosley. Rawlins owes some of his lineage to the classic noir detectives, but his Black cultural perspective places him in a distinctly different milieu that sets his world apart from the worlds of Spade or Marlowe, while also suggesting that the treatment of race (or lack thereof) in the original noir cycle needs to be reexamined. *Devil in a Blue Dress* is discussed in this section as an example of the revisionary noir detective film.

Going into the twenty-first century, revisionist noir films became more and more common, challenging the norms of the original cycle in new and reinvigorating ways. For example, in 2014 Paul Thomas Anderson's *Inherent Vice* (2014) became the first novel by the esteemed postmodern novelist Thomas Pynchon to be adapted to film. This film, clearly recalling the work of Chandler (perhaps as filtered through *The Big Lebowski*), is set in the hippie culture of 1970 Los Angeles, which already gives it a distinctly different feel from that of the original noir films, as does its largely comic tone. It will be discussed in detail in this section as an example of a revisionary noir detective film because of the way it potentially causes us to reassess the detective films of the original noir cycle. In somewhat of the same vein is David Robert Mitchell's *Under the Silver Lake* (2018), also discussed in this section. Here, an ordinary guy plays detective as he seeks a woman who mysteriously disappeared in some decidedly strange regions of contemporary Los Angeles society, taking him well outside the territory covered by predecessors such as Philip Marlowe.

Partly because neo-noir films had made noir motifs so familiar, such motifs appeared in any number of films of the early twenty-first century in modes that were somewhat decoupled from the original noir cycle, often allowing these motifs to be used in ways that might cause us to revise our assessment of their meaning in the original noir cycle. Other revisionary noir films that are either literally detective films (including police detectives) or function effectively like detective films include Jane Campion's *In the Cut* (2003), Rian Johnson's *Brick* (2005), Fincher's *Zodiac* (2007) and *The Girl with the Dragon Tattoo* (2011), the Coens's *No Country for Old Men* (2007), Debra Granik's *Winter's Bone* (2010), Denis Villeneuve's *Prisoners* (2013), and Edward Norton's *Motherless Brooklyn* (2019). Quentin Tarantino, all of whose work displays strong noir influences, deserves special mention in this group for *The Hateful Eight* (2015) because it is both a revisionary noir detective film and a revisionary Western.[7] All these films, though, illustrate the great versatility of noir motifs, which have demonstrated tremendous durability over time, partly because they can be used in so many different ways in so many different kinds of films.

Finally, one film worth mentioning partly because it illustrates the difficulty of making a sharp distinction between neo-noir and revisionary noir (or between detective noir and lost-man noir) is *Motherless Brooklyn* (2019). This film largely functions as a neo-noir detective film, as its central private detective figure uncovers a vast conspiracy involving some of the1950s most respected citizens of New York City, including one character based on notorious city planner Robert Moses. But the film, based on a 1999 novel by Jonathan Lethem (which was itself set in the 1990s), features an unusual detective in Lionel Essrog (nicknamed "Motherless Brooklyn" and played by Edward Norton, who also wrote and directed the film). What gives this film a revisionary twist is the unusual nature of this protagonist, an orphan whose struggles with Tourette Syndrome and obsessive-compulsive disorder have driven him into a life of radical loneliness and alienation. This condition also tends to push Essrog into lost-man territory, though he differs from the typical noir lost man in that he maintains his moral compass to the end (for him what might even be a happy one), an outcome that potentially causes us to reevaluate the way we see the moral downfalls of most noir lost men. In any case, this film well illustrates the range that can be covered by all types of noir film, which seems to promise a rich future for noir.

Chapter 1

The Film Noir Detective:
The Maltese Falcon

(1941, Directed by John Huston)

John Huston's *The Maltese Falcon* (1941) is the best known (and probably the best) of the various film adaptations of the novels of Dashiell Hammett. It is the third adaptation of the similarly titled 1930 novel on which it is directly based. Huston, who also wrote the screenplay, stays scrupulously close to the original novel, filming it virtually scene by scene (with only a couple of sexually suggestive scenes from the book deleted, probably to help get the book past the Code censors). The dark subject matter of the book is enhanced in the film by a dark look, complete with exaggerated atmospheric shadows. The film is thus often considered one of the first works of film noir—and it was indeed among the films discussed by the French critics who first gave film noir its name, though of course Huston was not consciously making a noir film at the time. The film was Huston's directorial debut; it also helped to establish Humphrey Bogart, via his portrayal of Hammett's tough-but-vulnerable detective, Sam Spade, as a major Hollywood star.

The Maltese Falcon begins by establishing its San Francisco setting via a shot of the Golden Gate Bridge. It then moves into the first scene, as a Miss Wonderly (played by Mary Astor) comes to Spade's office (through the window of which the bridge can be seen), ostensibly to hire him to help her find her missing sister, who has supposedly run off with a man by the name of Floyd Thursby. It's an iconic scene that would be repeated in innumerable detective films. The office is modest, slightly seedy—both because Spade's business is not that lucrative and because he is not one to be overly concerned with luxurious comforts. Meanwhile, Spade's secretary, Effie Perine (Lee Patrick), announces Miss Wonderly by flirtatiously assuring Spade that he will definitely want to see the potential client, because she is "a knockout."

It's 1941, of course, and such modes of assessing women were still common—this moment, in fact, was lifted virtually verbatim from the beginning of the novel, so the attitude goes back at least to 1930. Still, this scene tells us that Spade himself is accustomed to judging women according to their sexual attractiveness and that he is by no means oblivious to such things. We will learn, however, that he is no easy mark for a would-be seductress like Miss Wonderly.

Astor, incidentally, was a thirty-five-year-old actress with excellent screen credentials (she would win an Oscar for her performance in *The Great Lie* earlier in 1941), though she seems almost matronly compared with the character in Hammett's novel, who is only twenty-two and described as a striking red-haired beauty. Spade's caddish partner, Miles Archer (Jerome Cowan), meanwhile, seems an easier mark for Miss Wonderly's beauty than does Spade. Archer agrees to handle the case personally, after wolfishly ogling Miss Wonderly in a manner that makes the nature of his personal interest quite clear. That night, however, Archer is shot and killed while shadowing Thursby. Events move quickly in this film, and Thursby (who is never seen on screen) is shot and killed soon afterward. As Spade begins to investigate the killings (partly because the police seem to suspect *him*), it soon becomes clear that Miss Wonderly's original story was a ruse—and, as the film proceeds, it will become clear that she is one of film noir's first femme fatale figures.

Eventually, Miss Wonderly reveals that her real name is Brigid O'Shaughnessy and that she is in danger; however, she remains reluctant to explain the nature and source of this danger. Then, Joel Cairo (Peter Lorre) comes to Spade's office, and, after a complex encounter in which Cairo is at one point knocked unconscious by Spade, offers Spade $5,000 to help recover a lost statuette of a black bird: the Maltese Falcon.

Lorre is himself an interesting figure in film history. A Hungarian-born Jew who had starred in Fritz Lang's German Expressionist crime drama *M* (1931), a key forerunner of film noir, Lorre fled to America from the German Nazis, then continued his acting career in Hollywood. He portrays Cairo with an air of the exotic—his very name suggestive of the Middle Eastern and North African cultures that Edward Said[1] has seen as so central to Western stereotypical "Orientalist" depictions of non-Europeans, representations that were designed to demonstrate the superiority of the West to the East and to define the West through opposition to an inferior East.

For Said, one of the most common Orientalist stereotypes involves an air of mysterious and exotic sexuality, and it is probably no accident that Cairo seems vaguely homosexual—the Production Code made it impossible to make this characterization explicit, but it is quite clear in the novel. In any case, Cairo is clearly depicted as sneaky, conniving, and untrustworthy—all of which are standard stereotypes applied to Arabs in Orientalist discourse. Meanwhile, Cairo's depiction is only one of a number of aspects of *The Maltese Falcon* that seem to carry Orientalist resonances. For example, O'Shaughnessy reveals to Spade that she originally met Thursby "in the Orient" and that they had recently come to San Francisco from Hong Kong. Meanwhile, Kasper Gutman (Sydney Greenstreet), the portly art dealer who is the leading figure among a group of shady characters seeking the statuette, stays at the Alexandria Hotel while in San Francisco (and departs for Istanbul at the end of the film). The statuette itself is a rather exotic artifact with Orientalist intonations. It was originally made, we are told, by the Knights Templar (the on-screen text actually says "Knight Templars") in 1539. However, this attribution is problematic, given that the Knights Templar were officially active only from 1119 to 1312 AD. They were closely associated with the Crusades through which Europe attempted to seize control of the Holy Lands from Islam, an experience that was crucial to setting the terms for the development of Orientalist discourse. However, the Knights Templar were officially banned in 1312 by Pope Clement V for fear that they were gaining excessive power, though they subsequently became the stuff of legend and were widely rumored to still be operating in secret.

Spade soon concludes that Brigid is the only one who knows the location of this mysterious bird, though he himself seems more fascinated by Brigid herself than by the falcon or by the cash that the falcon might bring. However, his attempt to negotiate a deal between her and Cairo is soon complicated by the arrival on the scene of Gutman, accompanied by his noxious henchman, Wilmer Cook (Elisha Cook Jr.). Gutman tells Spade that the bird was made by the "Order of the Hospital of St. John of Jerusalem, later known as the Knights of Rhodes and other things." He goes on to explain (revising the opening on-screen text) that, in 1539, these Knights, also crusaders, persuaded Emperor Charles V to lease them the island of Malta, with the stipulation that they would subsequently pay a symbolic yearly tribute of one falcon to acknowledge that Malta was still officially ruled by Spain. To show their gratitude (and to display their wealth), they decided to pay a tribute for the first year, not of an actual live bird, but of a magnificent jewel-encrusted statuette of a falcon, which is the object indicated in the film's title. Then, the statuette was stolen by pirates in route to the emperor, subsequently disappearing and then periodically resurfacing in various places ever since, meanwhile picking up a coat of black enamel to disguise its true value. As Gutman explains of the knights in the film, indicating the probable value of the statuette, "For years they had taken from the East nobody knows what spoils of gems, precious metals, silks, ivory, sir. We all know the Holy Wars to them were largely a matter of loot." This story is reasonably believable in a historical sense. In 1530, Charles V (who was both the Holy Roman Emperor and the king of Spain) granted control of Malta to the Knights Hospitaller (aka the Order of St. John and the Knights of Malta), and they did indeed agree to pay an annual tribute of one live Maltese falcon to show their loyalty—though the motif of a fabulous bejeweled bird seems to have been invented entirely by Hammett and to have no basis in history. The knights then ruled Malta until it was captured by Napoleon in 1798, having successfully fended off an invasion from the Ottoman Empire in 1565.

After a series of twists and turns in which each character (except Spade) tries to out-betray all the others, the statuette finally emerges, but turns out to be a fake, apparently substituted for the real bird by the Russian general from whom it was stolen (just before the events of the film) by Thursby, O'Shaughnessy, and Cairo, acting as Gutman's agents. Meanwhile, it becomes clear that Cook killed Thursby, as well as Jacoby (Walter Huston, the Oscar-winning father of the director, in a brief, uncredited appearance), the captain of the ship that brought the statuette in from Hong Kong. Indeed, it is important to note the international background of the falcon statuette: it has moved about Europe and Asia for centuries and has only just arrived in America from the Far East, giving it an air of the exotic. Similarly, with the exception of Cook, Spade's antagonists in the film are all cosmopolitan figures who have just arrived in America. As Michael Walker notes, this film is made more politically conservative by the fact that the corruption of its noir world comes from abroad.[2] Spade, of course, is staunchly American, and to an extent the oppositions of the film can be seen as American virtue versus foreign corruption.

A staunch individualist, Spade is unswerving in his support of good versus evil, but he conceives that opposition in his own terms and refuses to have it defined for him by others, including official institutions. Thus, Spade is portrayed in the film as having an uneasy (one might even say antagonistic) relationship with the police, which helps to further his characterization as an independent thinker who plays by his own rules rather than submitting to the expectations of polite society. From this point of view, it is important to note that hard-boiled detectives such as Spade and Raymond Chandler's Philip Marlowe tend to be self-employed: too independent and individualistic to bow to the requirements of an employer, they are instead self-employed small businessmen, making them even more emblematic of the individualist American dream.

Eventually, though, Spade does cooperate with authority to an extent, as he puts the cops onto Gutman, Cook, and Cairo, who then arrest the lot of them. Spade then has a final confrontation with O'Shaughnessy, with whom he has developed an uneasy romantic relationship in the course of the investigation. The film adds much more of an element of romance than is present in the novel, among other things stipulating at several points that Spade is virtually irresistible to women: both O'Shaughnessy and Archer's widow practically throw themselves at him, while Effie clearly has an ongoing crush on him. Spade likes women, too, but not to the point that he would ever relinquish his cherished independence in order to be with one. He seems vaguely fond of Effie in a condescending way, but there is an element of outright hostility in most of his interactions with women in the film, something that was apparently, at the time, taken as an emblem of masculine strength. He deduces that it was O'Shaughnessy who killed Archer, hoping Thursby would be blamed and thus eliminated from the picture. She, in turn, pleads her love for Spade and asks him not to tell the police that she killed Archer. He admits that he might possibly be in love with her as well but explains that it is his duty not to let the killing of his partner go unpunished: "When a man's partner is killed, he's supposed to do something about it." In particular, he explains that, in the detective business, it is simply bad business to let someone in your organization get killed and then do nothing about it. He ultimately turns a deaf ear to her pleas and ultimately turns her over to the police as well, foregoing her considerable charms and once again demonstrating that his strength and rectitude cannot be compromised by a mere woman.

Of course, it helps here that O'Shaughnessy is a rather unscrupulous sort, and it is also the case that Spade's treatment of her is part of a pattern of antagonism toward almost everyone else in the film, to whom he seems to feel superior because they do not live up to his ethical standards. In fact, Spade is a bit of a bully. Not only does he run roughshod over the women he encounters in the film, but he seems to take pleasure in roughing up the small, effeminate Cairo and the small, ineffectual Cook. When Cairo complains about his continual rough treatment at the hands of Spade, the detective exerts his masculine dominance by declaring, "When you're slapped, you'll take it and like it." Then he slaps the smaller man a few more times. Minutes later, somewhat complicating the gender politics of the film, Cairo also gets knocked around by O'Shaughnessy, furthering his humiliation—which is then completed when he whines to the police about his mistreatment at the hands of both Spade and O'Shaughnessy. Spade then quickly talks himself out of trouble, but not before one of the police slaps *him*. In the novel, this blow is an actual punch to the chin, and one can speculate that it is downgraded to a slap to help placate the Code censors. In any case, the effect of all this slapping (more often than not figured as a feminine form of violence in American culture) is to complicate both the gender politics of the film and the characterization of Spade, who is humanized and made to seem less brutal once he himself becomes the recipient of a slap. He is not, however, made to appear weak: indeed, another cop has to intercede to prevent him from clocking the one who slapped him.

Later, when Cook confronts Spade and attempts to march him up to see Gutman, Spade easily disarms him and instead marches him up to see the boss, making a joke of the whole thing in order to humiliate Cook as much as possible. Meanwhile, comic musical cues accompany this sequence, emphasizing how ludicrous it had been for Cook to believe he could strongarm a man like Spade. For his part, Spade hands Cook's guns over to Gutman and sardonically claimed that a "crippled newsie" took them away from Cook, but Spade made the newsie give them back. Gutman seems amused at Cook's plight and impressed by Spade's bravado. "You're a chap worth knowing," he declares. "An amazing character!"

Cook, then, is clearly feminized in this scene, and it might be worth noting that Spade repeatedly refers to the small man as a "gunsel," a term that is used only once in the novel. A gunsel is, traditionally, a younger man kept as a subservient homosexual lover by an older, dominant male. Hammett reportedly used the term because he anticipated that his editors would merely think it referred to the fact that Cook was carrying a gun. That strategy carried over into the film, where the Code censors clearly missed its homosexual implications, allowing Spade to declare both Cook and Gutman to be gay and still get past the Code.

Of course, this film is clearly designed primarily for entertainment and does not seem particularly interested in delivering any sort of weighty message. For example, the exaggerated lighting effects work well with the equally exaggerated tough-guy dialogue to give the film a rather campy feel that never interferes with the suspense but merely adds to the fun. Spade's own behavior is highly theatrical, and he is often self-consciously playing roles. In one scene, for example, he displays a violent (and seemingly excessive) outburst of temper in the midst of a conversation with Gutman. He bursts angrily out of Gutman's suite and then is seen wearing a self-congratulatory grin as he walks down the hall—he had clearly staged his anger for Gutman's benefit. Naremore emphasizes the theatricality of the film, noting that *The Maltese Falcon* is "strikingly witty, especially at the level of performance."[3]

Nevertheless, *The Maltese Falcon* has considerable depth and numerous possible political implications. For one thing, the film's entire cast of characters is engaged in a furious and ruthless dog-eat-dog pursuit of wealth, as when Gutman at one point agrees to sacrifice Cook, who is "like a son" to him, to the police so the others can go free and share the bounty. Placed within the context of this suggestion that selfish concerns supersede personal relationships, Spade's rejection of O'Shaughnessy appears less laudable. In any case, the entire quest motif of the film has potential implications as an allegory of capitalist greed. On the other hand, though the characterization of Spade might sometimes read like a criticism of the ideology of individualism, it is also the case that the film seems to encourage an admiration for his strength in not letting his feelings (especially for a woman) cloud his judgment. Nor is Spade one who would ever be taken in by the lust for wealth that drives the others to the extreme of murder.

The tension between Spade's belief that virtually everyone is corrupt and his own refusal to be corrupted might be taken as an enactment of the basic mismatch between the dark vision of Hammett's hard-boiled fiction and the usual idealized products of Hollywood. This same tension, of course, is common in film noir as a whole, the cynicism of which conducts an ongoing subversive critique of the more saccharine products of the Hollywood dream factory. *The Maltese Falcon*, because it comes so early in the noir cycle, can be seen as a groundbreaking film in this respect. Thus, R. Barton Palmer argues that the film's refusal to smooth over the basic conflict between Hollywood and hard-boiled fiction is what makes *The Maltese Falcon* a landmark of American cinema. Palmer argues that the Huston film involves a "full accommodation of Hammett's pessimism and social critique," while earlier adaptations of this novel bowed to "the mainstream optimism of Hollywood film."[4] Granted, one might think that the stylishness of the film would interfere with its cynicism, but in fact this stylishness is itself cynical, providing a constant reminder of the artificiality of the film, which, like the counterfeit nature of the Maltese Falcon itself, potentially makes a statement about the mendacity and inauthenticity of American popular culture and American society as a whole.

Chapter 2

The Film Noir Detective:
Murder, My Sweet

(1944, Directed by Edward Dmytryk)

Murder, My Sweet (based on Raymond Chandler's 1940 novel *Farewell, My Lovely*) begins at the end and is then narrated in flashback—which would become a common noir plot structure. The out-of-kilter opening scene shows police interrogating private eye Philip Marlowe (Dick Powell) as part of a murder investigation in which he is apparently a suspect. For his part, Marlowe maintains his habitual wise-cracking cool, though he is a bit disadvantaged due to the fact that his eyes are covered in heavy bandages, making him a private eye without functioning eyes—which is, symbolically, a perfect beginning, given that Marlowe is essentially blind to what is going on through much of the film. By the time of this interrogation, though, Marlowe has unraveled the web of murder and deceit that will constitute the rest of the film, which essentially consists of the story Marlowe tells the police—though even he doesn't know the end of the story.

This device allows Marlowe to become the narrator of the film—just as he is the narrator of the original novel, from which many lines in his narration are taken directly, so that the film is able to capture much of Chandler's distinctive style. Indeed, Marlowe's highly stylized voiceover narration is identified by Andrew Dickos as one of the most "spectacular" examples of voiceover narration (along with that in *Double Indemnity*) in all of film noir.[1] This voiceover takes us into the flow of the story, which begins with a sort of missing-person case, in which the massive Moose Malloy (played by Mike Mazurki, a former professional wrestler who played many tough-guy roles) comes to Marlowe's office in the middle of the night to hire him to find his beloved Velma Valento, with whom he has gotten "out of touch" (thanks to his recent eight-year stretch in prison). Marlowe seems reluctant, but quickly changes his tune when the dim-witted Malloy throws two twenties at him—establishing the fact that Marlowe is in business to make money and that even a relatively small amount of money is significant to him. He does, however, have his standards, and we will soon learn that even a relatively large amount of money cannot persuade him to violate them.

Marlowe is probably a bit more virtuous in the film than he is in the novel, which is sanitized on the screen in other ways as well. The most important of these is the fact that Chandler's Los Angeles is altogether seedier and more corrupt than the one we see in Dmytryk's film. There is also significantly more social commentary in the novel, particularly in its representation of the racism and corruption of the Los Angeles police, an element that is entirely missing in the film. Thus, James Naremore argues that "law is where you buy it" is the central theme that runs through Chandler's novel but notes that the Production Code made it impossible for the film to follow suite.[2] It was probably also because of Code restrictions that the novel's commentary on racism is eliminated from the film, which makes Marlowe (himself somewhat racist in the film) into a more positive figure. Meanwhile, Velma (who emerges in the novel as an almost noble figure who just happens to have a checkered past) is portrayed in the film as a sinister femme fatale willing to lie, cheat, and kill to get what she wants.

In all versions of the story, Marlowe's search for Velma takes him in unexpected directions, partly because he soon takes on a second case that unexpectedly turns out to be related to his search for Velma. In the second case, the effete Lindsay Marriott—obviously portrayed as gay in the novel[3] and in the 1975 film, but not so obviously in the 1944 film, where he is simply described as a "pretty guy"—offers Marlowe $100 to facilitate a transaction in which he is supposedly buying back some jewels that were stolen from a friend. This job leads to Marriott's murder in a manner that seems designed to point to Marlowe as the killer, which motivates Marlowe to look further into the case, even though he is no longer employed to do so. Partly, of course, he just wants to clear himself of suspicion in the killing of Marriott, a man whom Marlowe clearly disliked from the moment he first saw him. But Marlowe also wants to solve Marriott's murder out of a sense of professional obligation, feeling that he should have been able to protect his client. This development points Marlowe in the direction of the wealthy Grayle family, whose aging patriarch (played by Miles Mander in the 1944 film) is married to a beautiful and much younger woman, Helen (Claire Trevor), the owner of the stolen jewels. Marlowe also meets Grayle's daughter Ann (Anne Shirley), who despises Helen, suspecting her stepmother of being a gold digger.

Helen does, in fact, seem to be a bit of a suspicious character, emerging fairly quickly as the film's femme fatale character. Meanwhile, Ann clearly emerges as the film's "good girl" character, forming with Helen one of the pairs of opposed female characters that are so common in film noir. It might be noted here that Ann Grayle replaces Anne Riordan (the daughter of a former cop) from the novel. This substitution places Ann in more direct opposition to Helen, thus enhancing the good woman versus bad woman structure. Among other things, the two women emerge in *Murder, My Sweet* as vague competitors for Marlowe's romantic attentions, though it quickly becomes clear that Helen is the manipulative sort and that any interest she has in Marlowe simply involves being able to make sure he doesn't uncover certain secrets—such as the fact that the jewelry theft was a hoax designed to pull Marlowe into the case so that he could be killed rather than continuing his search for Velma. Meanwhile, it is revealed that Helen did not want this search to go on because she herself is actually Velma, having now assumed a new identity that would make her more viable as the wife to a man such as Grayle.[4] Ann also gradually emerges through the film as a sort of love interest for Marlowe, seemingly impressed by his professional acumen and rectitude. For example, when he explains to her his interest in following up on Marriott's murder on the basis of the fact that "I'm just a small businessman in a very messy business, but I like to follow through on a sale," she seems to find this explanation admirable, rather than venal.

This follow-through will involve an investigation that centers on the stolen jewelry, a jade necklace that was supposedly stolen from Mrs. Grayle and that plays something of the same role in this film as the falcon statuette had in *The Maltese Falcon*. Like that statuette, the necklace, having come from China, introduces an element of the exotic into the text. This element, meanwhile, is further enhanced when Marlowe, in the course of his investigation, is taken by Helen to the Coconut Beach Club, where the entertainment is provided by a Chinese dancer undulating to Oriental-sounding music, providing exotic atmosphere.

As William Luhr notes, *Murder, My Sweet* "not only develops patterns of disorientation by means of strange camera angles, unexpected editing, and lighting strategies, but it also repeatedly places Marlowe in situations that are exotic or perverse."[5] These situations, meanwhile, span the range of Los Angeles society, from low to high. To this range of settings, one might add the hints of exoticism that are added to the text by the presence of the Chinese jade necklace and the Chinese dancer in the Coconut Beach Club. Such elements, as they frequently do in film noir (and as they memorably do in such neo-noir films as *Chinatown*), add atmosphere because (especially at the time *Murder, My Sweet* was made), audiences would have associated them with a panoply of Orientalist stereotypes. China, to Western audiences of the 1940s, was a mysterious and largely unknown realm. Its evocation in the text thus reinforces the ever-present notion of Marlowe's confusion and inability to decipher the strange events that are occurring around him. In addition, China was at the center of a number of associations in the popular Western mind between the "Orient" and a certain sexual exoticism. From this point of view, it is significant that the dancer in the club wears an exotic and (by the standards of 1940s Hollywood) skimpy costume.

Helen, as she had planned to do all along, ditches Marlowe at the club, knowing that Malloy will pick him up there and take him directly to see Jules Amthor (Otto Kruger), a "psychic consultant" the police have already warned Marlowe to stay away from and who is in league with Helen. Confronted with Amthor, Marlowe, confused as he often is in this film, is for once unable to come up with a snappy line. "I don't

Figure 2.1. A rumpled Philip Marlowe (Dick Powell) with Ann Grayle (Anne Shirley) in *Murder, My Sweet.* **RKO Radio Pictures/Photofest © RKO Radio Pictures.**

get it," he simply says. In this case it is Amthor who is ready with the smart retort. "You mean there are some things you do not understand," he says. "I've always credited the private detective with a high degree of omniscience. Or is that only true in rental fiction?" Minutes later, Marlowe is knocked unconscious for the second time in the text, his loss of consciousness visually signaled by a wavering pool of black that engulfs the screen. Indeed, *Murder, My Sweet* is marked by a number of inventive visuals, causing Andrew Spicer to note that this film was particularly striking for the way it built on the legacy of *Citizen Kane* in terms of "voice-over narration, expressionist lighting, distorting and disorienting reflections."[6] Indeed, made by the same studio that had made *Citizen Kane* three years earlier, *Murder, My Sweet* seems to have derived much of its visual style from Welles's film, without any conscious awareness that it was also contributing to the development of a "noir" style.

This style is perhaps most strikingly evident in the central part of *Murder, My Sweet*, which is taken up by a dreamlike sequence in which Marlowe awakens (sort of) to find himself held prisoner in an establishment where he has been interrogated under the influence of drugs administered to him by a Dr. Sonderborg (Ralf Harald), a sort of Nazi-esque mad scientist. Marlowe is, in fact, still under the influence of these drugs even as he partly regains consciousness. This sequence certainly verifies the claim by Borde and Chaumeton that film noir is "oneiric" (i.e., dreamlike) in ways that confuse and disorient audiences. Indeed, the sequence blends in quite nicely in a film in which Marlowe is so consistently confused and in which virtually no one can be counted on to be who they appear to be. Moreover, the surreal visuals in this middle sequence not only provide a pictorial representation of Marlowe's epistemological confusion throughout the film, they also represent one of the best examples in all of film noir of an attempt to use out-of-kilter visuals to represent an unbalanced state of consciousness.

Not overly tough or even especially masculine (in comparison, say, with Sam Spade, certainly not when compared with the powerful Moose Malloy), Marlowe is also seemingly always a step behind the events that surround him, especially in this central sequence at Dr. Sonderborg's, but he manages a stumbling escape from captivity even in his impaired condition. Then he again runs into Malloy again, who has now reassessed his relationship with Amthor and this time aids Marlowe in his getaway (and will soon afterward kill Amthor). Malloy's sudden shifts in allegiance are perfectly at home in this film, which is filled with sudden changes in direction, making the plot seem a bit incoherent, even though it has been simplified significantly in comparison with that of the novel. In fact, from this point forward, the plot of the film is made up of one abrupt shift after another, culminating in the final scene in which the ruthless Helen, having been revealed to be Velma, is about to shoot Marlowe but is instead herself shot and killed by Grayle, who subsequently shoots and kills Malloy in the midst of a struggle in which Grayle is killed as well. Marlowe is blinded by the flash of the gun as he tries to prevent the shooting of Malloy, thus looping us back to the beginning of the film (and at the same time completely changing the ending of the novel, which is more sympathetic to both Helen/Velma and to Grayle). The film then ends with its own coda that significantly expands the romantic conclusion for Marlowe and Ann, who seems remarkably unshaken by the recent death of her father.

If this ending seems slightly discordant, it might be because it deviates so much from the novel's, just as Ann Grayle in the film is a much more innocent and morally pure character than is Ann Riordan in the novel. Barton Palmer might also be correct that this ending was probably developed to provide a reward for Marlowe's own virtuous pursuits in the film, thus providing a sort of counterweight to the darkness of the world presented even in the film's sanitized version of the story. Indeed, Palmer goes on to argue that "the film as a whole still strongly makes Chandler's original and despairing point that American culture, from top to bottom, is sick with anomie, mindless pursuit of self-interest, and obsessive psychopathology."[7]

Palmer's "top to bottom" comment is worthy of exploration. One of the reasons why Chandler's fiction seems so cynical is that it contains so few genuinely positive figures. Marlowe himself stands apart from a world full of selfish, venal, manipulative operators, regardless of their class or gender. The film modifies this figuration in terms of gender by adding "good girl" Ann Grayle. But the film still avoids any sort of attribution of virtue on the basis of class. Moose Malloy is clearly a sort of proletarian figure; he avoids the sinister plotting associated with most of the upper-class characters, but that is largely because he is depicted as lacking the intelligence to conceive of any sort of connivance. And he, of course, is a killer who commits a number of other crimes in the course of the film as well. Velma, meanwhile, is also a working-class character, but she is depicted as an amoral woman who has conned her way into a posh life and is willing to do anything to keep it. The cops of the film are also essentially working-class figures, and they are relatively honest in comparison with the cops in the novel, but they are not particularly competent. Among the characters depicted as upper-class figures, Marriott and Amthor are depicted as effete (a code for gay) and morally bankrupt. Grayle, meanwhile, is essentially a pathetic figure, sexually inert and devoid of any assets except money. In the novel, he is depicted as a successful businessman, but in the film, he seems so hapless that it is difficult to imagine him acquiring his fortune in any way other than inheritance. And, of course, he turns out to be a killer as well. It is little wonder, then, that Marlowe seems to stand apart from the society around him in Chandler's fiction, though the film, in good Hollywood fashion, supplies him with a human connection in Ann Grayle.

This personal dimension is also indicative of the way in which almost all of the social critique in Chandler's *Farewell, My Lovely* has been transformed into personal and psychological drama in the film. As Jonathan Buchsbaum has pointed out, this transformation makes *Murder, My Sweet* an excellent example of the crucial role so often played in film noir by personal psychological forces, especially paranoia. Thus, in the novel, the plot revolves around the interactions among corrupt cops and an organized criminal mob that does not even appear in the film, where the plot revolves around the drama of the Grayle family and their circle of personal associates. In both cases, Marlowe must struggle to make his way through a dangerous world. In the novel, however, these threats come primarily from the organizational structures of the cops and the mob; in the film, the threats are centered on the sexually aggressive Velma/Helen, set in opposition to the innocent Ann, who provides a nonthreatening alternative that is nevertheless still contained within the Grayle family.

Like Buchsbaum, Luhr points to *Murder, My Sweet* as an exemplary noir text largely because of its ability to create certain psychological effects. For Luhr, the central strategy of the film is "disorientation," which is accomplished in virtually every element of the film: "This central perceptual problem works hand in hand with other strategies that are evident in the film's editing, cinematography, confusing timeline, character disorientation, and even in the questionable reliability of some of its images."[8] Thus, visually, thematically, and atmospherically, *Murder, My Sweet* is one of the iconic works of film noir and one of the films that helped to define noir as a mode. Powell's Marlowe, meanwhile, is one of the great noir characters, even though that character would soon come to be identified in the popular mind with his portrayal by Humphrey Bogart in *The Big Sleep* (1946). But Powell's portrayal of Marlowe is actually closer to Chandler's original than is Bogart's, which is much more inflected through mainstream Hollywood modes of characterization and through Bogart's own by then well-established screen persona. It is, in fact, an altogether more mainstream Hollywood film, though still well within the realm of the noir mode, which is versatile enough to encompass both films easily.

Chapter 3

The Neo-Noir Detective: *Chinatown*

(1974, Directed by Roman Polanski)

Chinatown has much in common with classic film noir, combining a complex detective story plot with a general air of corruption and a darkly claustrophobic look and atmosphere. The protagonist, J. J. Gittes (Jack Nicholson), is a paradigmatic film noir detective, willing to bend the rules but sincere in his quest for the truth. Similarly, the central female character, Evelyn Mulwray (Faye Dunaway), is at first glance a classic femme fatale. On the other hand, *Chinatown* is intensely self-conscious in its engagement with the legacy of its predecessors in the noir tradition, reminding us that it is a *neo*-noir film, not a film noir proper.

Despite its effective use of color, *Chinatown* is in some ways even darker than the typical film noir. Gittes succeeds in solving the film's central mystery, but it really does him no good, and he is no match for the mighty forces that are arrayed against him, powerless to prevent the realization of the complex, evil plot that his investigation uncovers. Ultimately, the film becomes a confrontation between Gittes (as a lone individual) and capitalist modernization, embodied in the central villain, Noah Cross (played by film noir pioneer John Huston), but also pictured as an inexorable historical force. This force is far too much for Gittes, whose final helplessness and even ridiculousness are emphasized in the way he goes through so much of the film with a huge, almost comical, bandage on his nose after a thug (played by Polanski) slits one of his nostrils open with a knife.

Chinatown is set in 1937 and employs exquisite period detail to create an old-fashioned feel, though it does so in an oddly indeterminate way that makes the film feel like it could have been set at any time from beginning of the 1930s through the end of the 1940s. In addition, it is based on actual Los Angeles water scandals dating back to the first decade of the twentieth century. Yet *Chinatown* is very much a film of the 1970s, both in its underlying ecological concerns and in its cynicism

Figure 3.1. Jake Gittes (Jack Nicholson) with bandaged nose in *Chinatown*. Paramount Pictures/Photofest © Paramount Pictures.

about the possibility of opposing the ruthless and greedy quest for profit that constitutes the context of the film. One of the most highly praised films of the 1970s, *Chinatown* garnered eleven Academy Award nominations but won only one Oscar, for Robert Towne's screenplay.

Gittes begins the main part of the film as an unwitting dupe, hired by a woman posing as Evelyn Mulwray to gather evidence of an extramarital affair on the part of Evelyn's husband, Hollis Mulwray (Darrell Zwerling), the chief engineer of the Los Angeles city water system. This apparent evidence is then leaked to the press in an attempt to discredit Mulwray, who is involved in a bitter political battle because of his opposition to the construction of a new dam near the city. Soon afterward, Mulwray is murdered, while the young woman with whom Gittes had spotted him, apparently in flagrante, disappears. Gittes is meanwhile hired by the real Evelyn Mulwray (Dunaway) to find out what happened to her husband, then is subsequently retained by Cross (Evelyn's father and Hollis Mulwray's former business partner) to find the missing woman, supposedly so that Cross can help her out of deference to Mulwray's affection for her.

Gittes' subsequent investigation reveals that Mulwray had been killed by Cross because Mulwray, Cross's former partner, had discovered, and opposed, an intricate scheme involving the city's water system. Indeed, Gittes, who becomes romantically involved with Evelyn, is able to ascertain the exact nature of the plot, which is part of a complex scheme to ensure that the proposed dam will be built. The perpetrators of this scheme, led by Cross, have meanwhile plotted to acquire large amounts of land in a valley north of the city. They then plan to divert the water made available by the new dam to the irrigation of this valley, vastly increasing the value of the land there and leading to huge profits for themselves at the expense of the taxpayers of Los Angeles. Gittes also discovers that the missing woman, Katherine, is both the daughter and the sister of Evelyn Mulwray, the product of an earlier incestuous liaison between Cross and the then-teenaged Evelyn.

Through most of the film, Chinatown itself functions simply as a (somewhat Orientalist) metaphor for mystery and corruption, in a way that is quite consistent with the Orientalism of classic film noir. Gittes's investigation then culminates in the only scene of the film that actually occurs in Chinatown, a final confrontation involving most of the final characters. In this scene, it becomes clear that Gittes's investigation will go for naught because the wealthy Cross "owns the police." Cross openly flaunts this fact in front of a helpless Gittes. Meanwhile, when Evelyn tries to escape with Katherine to keep her away from Cross, the police shoot and kill Evelyn. In the end, police lieutenant Lou Escobar (Perry Lopez), a former colleague of Gittes in the L.A. police department, sends Gittes home and advises him to forget the entire matter. Cross, with the power of his immense wealth behind him, is left to do as he will, with Katherine, the taxpayers' money, the L.A. water supply, and anything else he wants.

This ending probably goes beyond the cynicism that the Production Code would have allowed in the classic noir era. However, much American cinema of the 1970s, heavily influenced by the recent experience of Vietnam and Watergate, shows a very similar cynicism. In some ways, though, *Chinatown* shows a surprising amount of restraint and does not actually show very much that would not have passed the Code, even though it does stipulate some things, such as the incest between Cross and Evelyn, that the Code would have never allowed. One reason for this restraint is probably that *Chinatown* consistently and self-consciously seeks to be as reminiscent of classic film noir as possible, while still appealing to a 1970s audience. This intent, in fact, is foregrounded from the very beginning, as the opening credits role in a retro font that looks (despite the yellow letters) very much like something from a classic film noir, accompanied by Jerry Goldsmith's dreamy title music, which also has a noir feel—and which will run through the entire film as a recurrent theme in the soundtrack.

After these credits, the first actual visual of the film is a black-and-white still photograph of a man and woman apparently having sex, though in point of fact the sex is really just implied, with no graphic details shown. This photograph encapsulates one of the central strategies of this film, suggesting material that could not have been included in a classic noir, but *only* suggesting it. Meanwhile, we quickly learn that this photo has been taken by Gittes after being hired by one "Curly" (Burt Young) to shadow his wife (the woman in the photo), whom Curly suspects of having an affair. This photo is one of a series that confirms this suspicion, to which Curly responds with considerable agitation, nearly wrecking the new venetian blinds that Gittes has just had installed in his office. Curly's reaction thus calls attention to these blinds, which (knowledgeable viewers would know) are a key part of the iconography of the noir tradition. Indeed, venetian blinds will at several points in the film cast distinctive shadow patterns inside Gittes's offices, such patterns being perhaps the single most recognizable visual image in all of film noir.

This initial scene establishes Gittes as the type of low-rent private detective who takes on such tawdry assignments, helping to make clear his status as the kind of unheroic protagonist so often found in film noir. At the same time, Gittes seems to have a fairly successful practice, with a secretary and at least two "operatives" working in his employ. It is thus not entirely far-fetched that Curly is immediately succeeded by a much more upscale client in the apparent Evelyn Mulwray, who comes to hire Gittes for what is apparently a similar mission to the one for which Curly hired him: shadowing her "husband." In retrospect, though, it eventually becomes clear that this faux Evelyn has been sent to Gittes precisely because his somewhat shady reputation makes him an ideal candidate for the kind of scheme that is being set in motion here. Thus, when Gittes does indeed get and deliver what appear to be compromising photos of Mulwray with a young woman, Gittes is surprised to find that the photos are immediately published in the newspaper in an attempt to discredit Mulwray.

Gittes responds by deciding to investigate further, especially after Mulwray turns up dead soon afterward. Gittes subsequently stumbles upon Cross's complex intrigue, ultimately confronting Cross near the end of the film. Genuinely unable to grasp why the ultra-wealthy Cross would go to so much trouble to make even more money, Gittes asks him how much wealth he actually has, and Cross says he has no idea, but agrees that he certainly has much more than $10 million. Then Gittes gets right to the heart of the matter of capitalist greed. "Why are you doing it?" he asks. "How much better can you eat? What can you buy that you can't already afford?" "The future, Mr. Gittes," declares Cross. "The future!" This answer suggests that Cross wants to accumulate enough wealth that he will be prepared for whatever the future brings; it also suggests that he wants enough wealth to be able to have a say in shaping that future.

We can be sure, though, that Cross does not wish to shape the future for the common good, so Gittes's question still stands: In what way will controlling the future of Los Angeles make Cross's life any better than it already is? The answer, of course, is that Cross simply wants power for the sake of power, a drive that seems central to his psychology. Indeed, the drive to dominate and control others seems central to all of his major life decisions, including his decision to engage in incest with his teenage daughter, establishing a sexual relationship in which all the power is his. As far as we can tell from the film, he does not appear to be engaged in that sort of relationship with his other daughter (and granddaughter), Katherine, though it is clear that he will go to any extreme to maintain control over her. One could even argue that his killing of Mulwray was ultimately a reaction to Mulwray's refusal to be controlled as much as an attempt to prevent him from revealing Cross's water scheme. Indeed, Cross's lust for power and control is so extreme as to be clearly pathological, which would put him very much in the tradition of the pathological villains who inhabit much of film noir.

However, Cross is most decidedly not in the tradition of film noir psychos such as Richard Widmark's Tommy Udo in *Kiss of Death* (1947). He is calm, calculated, and coldly rational. He is thus more in the tradition of film noir psychos such as Horace Vendig in Edgar Ulmer's *Ruthless* (1948) or Smith Ohlrig in Max Ophüls's *Caught* (1949). In short, his pathological behavior is due less to mental illness than to a capitalist system for which he serves as a sort of allegorical standard-bearer. Viewed this way, Cross feels he must dominate and control, that he must *own*, anything and everything (and everyone) with which (or whom) he comes into contact because the capitalist system that produced him is driven by an uncompromising mania for accumulation that can never be satisfied.

Cross is an example of the extreme capitalist who has been produced by individualist ideology in its most vicious and ruthless form. It should be noted, however, that everyone else in the film is a product, in one way or another, of this same ideology. Gittes, the private detective, is a particularly interesting example, because private detectives in general have often been seen as paradigms of American individualism. Private detective characters in American culture, in their various ways, tend to be loners who believe in doing things their own way, often in opposition to the perceived norms of society. Gittes might be less tough and incorruptible than Sam Spade and he might be less contemplative than Philip Marlowe, viewing the world from less ironic distance. But he clearly belongs in the company of figures such as Spade and Marlowe in the way he approaches the world with a sense that he stands apart from everyone else in it.

In *Chinatown*, of course, there is an irony in this depiction due to the fact that Gittes is considerably less admirable (or formidable) than Marlowe or Spade. In the course of the film, for example, Gittes has several violent confrontations with various antagonists, almost all of whom get the better of him. About the only people he seems to get the better of in physical fights are a crippled farmer on crutches and a disoriented Evelyn, whom he slaps around in an attempt to get a straight story out of her concerning her complex relationship with her sister/daughter Katherine.

Meanwhile, though Gittes does eventually get to the heart of the film's central mystery, he does not seem to be a particularly brilliant detective. About the closest he comes to cleverness is the collection of cheap pocket watches that he carries in his car so that he can place them under the wheels of parked cars to be crushed (and thus stopped) when the cars drive off, thus revealing the times of their departure. But this device is clearly less remarkable than the James Bond-like gun dispenser that Marlowe has in his car in *The Big Sleep*—not to mention the fact that it is probably not very reliable and is certainly no substitute for actual surveillance. In addition, much of Gittes's work is also remarkably unexciting, bordering on the tedious and routine. In short, while the film consistently asks viewers to compare its representation of Gittes with those of the private detectives of the hard-boiled tradition, it also creates an ironic tension that makes Gittes a demythologized version of them.

Gittes begins his investigation of Mulwray by attending a public meeting at which a speaker drones on about the status of Los Angeles as a desert community that depends on outside water for its survival. This bit of exposition might be helpful to some viewers of the film in explaining why water seems so important in the film, but it certainly comes as news to no one in the audience, which is presumably composed of people who are already familiar with Los Angeles. Gittes himself yawns widely and starts to read an article in a racing newspaper about the famous racehorse Sea Biscuit as the speaker goes on and on with his presentation, urging the building of a new dam. Mulwray, though, does seem to get Gittes's attention when he then speaks against the project, arguing that the proposed dam would be unsafe and prone to collapse.

Gittes is additionally intrigued when a farmer drives his flock of sheep into the meeting hall to protest the theft of water from the valley where he raises these sheep, setting up a structural opposition between common people (like the farmer) and L.A.'s power elite that will run throughout the film. The opposition between common people and the wealthy elite is then furthered when Gittes discovers, while getting a shave in a barber shop, that the pictures have made their way into the newspaper. In response to these pictures, another, rather distinguished-looking, patron suggests that Gittes has "a hell of a way to make a living." Learning that the man is a mortgage banker, Gittes becomes angry at the man's sense of moral superiority. "Tell me," Gittes says, "did you foreclose on many families this week?" When the man suggests that Gittes had the photos published in the paper in order to garner publicity for himself, Gittes becomes particularly incensed, confronting the man and yelling that he actually tries to help people with his work: "I don't kick families out of their houses like you bums down at the bank do."

This encounter, among other things, provides a reminder of the Depression-era setting of the film, when mortgage foreclosures were particularly common and when banks had a particularly negative reputation for preying upon the poor. This setting, of course, makes Cross's schemes to accumulate more and more wealth all the more obscene, while this scene with the banker reminds us that what Cross is doing is not unique but quite typical of the way business is done in the capitalist world. Meanwhile, Gittes's angry confrontation with the banker helps to set him up as a sort of champion of the common people, a man whose heart is in the right place despite his own possibly problematic ethics in some cases. This scene also sets up the later opposition between Gittes and Cross, helping to make clear that the kind of predatory capitalism represented by Cross (and the banker) is precisely the sort of the thing that infuriates the struggling small businessman Gittes, whose ethics turn out to be far superior to those of Cross and the banker, despite the fact that they are respected leaders of a society in which Gittes is considered a somewhat shady character because of his occupation.

This same point is also made in Gittes's confrontation with the gangsterish thug played by Polanski, who accosts Gittes in the company of Claude Mulvihill (Roy Jensen), the chief of security for the Los Angeles Department of Water and Power.

That Mulvihill and Polanski's unnamed character seem to be working as a team makes it quite clear that, in the world of the film, there is little distinction between official power (as represented by Mulvihill) and gangsterism (as represented by Polanski's character). In any case, both Mulvihill and the gangster are really working for Cross, who essentially controls the Water and Power Department as part of what is little more than an organized crime syndicate, wrapped in the cloak of respectability afforded by Cross's extreme wealth.

Chinatown is a film with many ironies and much room for interpretation, but Constantine Verevis is surely correct when he calls the film a "damning critique of capitalism."[1] Whatever else it is, though, *Chinatown* is a quintessential example of neo-noir that seems to well illustrate Jameson's view of the film as a postmodern pastiche of a noir film, intensely aware that it is replicating a style and a mode of filmmaking from an earlier era. Indeed, *Chinatown* is one of Jameson's key examples of the "nostalgia film," which he sees as one of the most representative forms taken by postmodern culture. Jameson thus argues that all of the period detail in *Chinatown* represents an "aesthetic colonization" of the 1930s.[2] Moreover, for Jameson, *Chinatown* and other neo-noir films (he specifically mentions *Body Heat*) are key examples of what he calls the "nostalgia film," in which "our awareness of the preexistence of other versions . . . is now a constitutive and essential part of the film's structure."[3]

Chapter 4

The Neo-Noir Detective: *Blue Velvet*

(1986, Directed by David Lynch)

Blue Velvet (1986) is one of the central films discussed by Fredric Jameson, in his seminal book on postmodernism, as an exemplary cultural product of the postmodern era. Among other things, *Blue Velvet* is a particularly interesting example of the neo-noir detective film, though its principal detective is merely a curious amateur, rather than a professional. In fact, many aspects of the film reference film noir, the most important of which is its suggestion of a dark, corrupt underworld that exists just beneath the shiny surface of American society. At the same time, the dialogue between the film's present in the 1980s and its numerous echoes of the past period of the original noir cycle is quite complex and possibly contradictory.

The film begins with a full screen shot of a sort of crumpled blue velvet curtain, as Angelo Badalamenti's light classical theme (reminiscent of film noir) sounds in accompaniment. As this opening screen fades, we hear birds singing and the soundtrack shifts to Bobby Vinton's classic 1963 recording of the song that gives the film its title. The camera pans down to show a white picket fence with red roses blooming in front of it—an iconic image of American suburban domesticity (but one that here looks ostentatiously fake, providing an early warning of what it is to come in the film). We cut to a shot of a fire truck rolling down a suburban street, bearing a friendly fireman who waves to the locals as he passes by them, suggesting that we are in the sort of small town where everyone knows everyone else, and friendliness is the norm. A shot of more flowers in front of a picket fence is followed by one of innocent young school children being waved across a street by a kind and matronly crossing guard.

We then cut to the peaceful home of what we will learn is the Beaumont family, with the family patriarch out happily (and stereotypically) watering his lawn. A cut to the interior of the home shows Mrs. Beaumont sipping coffee and watching television, though what we see on the screen she is watching (a black-and-white clo-seup of a hand-held revolver, apparently moving in for the kill) is our first reminder that American culture and society might not be so peaceful after all. Subsequent images continue this dark turn, enhanced by sound effects. A closeup of Beaumont's hose, leaking badly where it is attached to the faucet, seems only a minor sign of trouble, which then becomes more serious when the hose becomes entangled in a bush, impeding Beaumont's progress across the lawn. He tugs at the hose, while the camera cuts back and forth between the leaky faucet and the entangled hose, which suggests more trouble. Suddenly, Beaumont grabs the back of his neck and collapses onto the ground with what will turn out to be a near-fatal stroke. An unidentified innocent toddler waddles toward the fallen man, while a small dog aggressively seeks to drink from the still-spewing hose, furthering the juxtaposition of idyllic, all-American images with a dark intimation of mortality. Then the camera slowly pans into the grass that was being watered, as ominous sound effects accompany the gradual revelation of a deadly battle among insects hidden in the grass. A quick cut to a billboard announcing "Welcome to Lumberton" then ends the opening sequence, accompanied by a hilarious ode to logs and wood on the soundtrack.

The stage has now been set for the entire course of the rest of the film, which will be concerned with the revelation of dark goings-on beneath the surface of this placid town, whose calm surface obscures a depraved underworld of sex, drugs, violence, and death. In some ways, the plot is a simple one that reads almost like a dark parody of old-time youth detective stories such as those featuring Nancy Drew or the Hardy Boys—except that it goes into noir territory that those stories would never explore. The plot is kicked off when young Jeffrey Beaumont (Kyle MacLachlan), home from college as his father recuperates in a hospital from his stroke, discovers a severed hu-man ear in a field. Such an abject discovery would certainly never occur in a Hardy Boys story, but the film shifts back to a relatively nostalgic mode as Jeffrey takes the ear to local police detective John Williams (George Dickerson), who of course knows the Beaumont family and agrees to check into the case of the severed ear.

However, impatient with the progress of the police investigation, Jeffrey decides to do some sleuthing of his own, aided by Williams's daughter, high school senior Sandy Williams (Laura Dern). This investigation immediately leads them to beauti-ful lounge singer Dorothy Vallens (Isabella Rossellini), who in turn leads the teenag-ers to discover a shocking world of crime and perversion lurking beneath the placid surface of Lumberton. Jeffrey, employing some rather problematic methods, learns that Dorothy is being terrorized by the deranged Frank Booth (Dennis Hopper), who forces her to submit to his weird, sadistic sexual proclivities by holding hostage her son and husband (the latter of whom was the owner of the ear found by Jeffrey earlier).

From this point, the double nature of the world of Lumberton is mirrored in Jeffrey's double love life. Wholesome, chaste young love blooms between Jeffrey and Sandy as they bond over their investigation, but a much more perverse sexual rela-tionship develops between Jeffrey and Dorothy, the latter of whom is so traumatized by her experience with Booth that she turns to Jeffrey for solace, exerting some power in that relationship in response to her complete lack of power in her dealings with Booth. But, of course, Jeffrey shows some doubleness of his own as he rather willingly responds to Dorothy's sexual invitations while at the same time pursuing his relationship with Sandy, the two women thus forming a "good girl-bad girl" pairing of the type that is so often found in film noir, a genre that provided important models for so many things in this film.

Meanwhile, Booth turns out to be involved in an elaborate drug ring (with the complicity of Williams's partner on the police force), but he is far too perverse to be a mere businesslike criminal. Instead, his criminal activity is merely part of what seems to be a general attempt to flout every possible aspect of acceptable bourgeois behavior. When Jeffrey falls into Booth's hands, he exposes the young man to some of his bizarre social circle before beating him senseless and leaving him unconscious. Ultimately, though, the police move in on Booth's operation, and Booth himself is shot and killed by Jeffrey, seemingly restoring order. Dorothy's husband is killed by Booth and his gang, but Dorothy's son is restored to her, and Jeffrey is restored to his family as well, including his recovered father. The romance between Jeffrey and Sandy seems set to proceed to a normal, socially acceptable conclusion. There are, though, hints that the dark side of Lumberton might be at least as authentic as the beautiful side, primarily in the way the film employs reminders of the tooth-and-claw nature of life in the animal kingdom. The film reminds us that the animal kingdom, like Lumberton, can be both beautiful and violent—as signaled by the film's final image of a robin that lands on a windowsill announcing the town's return to tranquility, but is at the same time eating an insect it has captured.

The whole Frank Booth/Dorothy Vallens storyline reinforces the film's central message, which is repeated several times in the film, almost like a mantra. This message ("It's a strange world") may go a long way toward explaining the tendency toward strangeness in Lynch's films, which thereby simply becomes mimetic. However, what Lynch's films represent is declaredly not reality but other representations of reality—which explains why they are sometimes so confusing to viewers who attempt to interpret them as being "about" the real world. Thus, the superficial tranquility of Lumberton—with its blooming flowers, singing birds, white picket fences, and friendly firemen—is quite transparently derived from nostalgic clichés of the American 1950s, with a look more reminiscent of a Disney World town than of any real town that ever existed in the 1950s or any other time. Meanwhile, the dark underside of Lumberton society seems equally stereotypical, deriving its material and look (cozy suburban homes suddenly replaced by stark urban red-brick buildings) from film noir—or what film noir might have been like without the Production Code, which placed strict limits on the kinds of images of sex and violence that could be included in Hollywood films between 1935 and the mid-1960s.

That *Blue Velvet* contains images that slide freely from the 1950s to the 1980s opens the way for a range of interpretations. For example, as opposed to the easily recognizable nods to nostalgic versions of the 1950s, the dark material related to

Figure 4.1. Jeffrey Beaumont (Kyle MacLachlan) and Dorothy Vallens (Isabella Rosselini) in *Blue Velvet*. De Laurentiis Entertainment Group/Photofest © De Laurentiis Entertainment Group.

Booth and his gang might be related to conditions prevailing in 1980s, Reagan-era America. Jameson, however, reads Booth as a marker of the 1960s counterculture, which presumably disrupted the seemingly placid texture of 1950s America (though that vision of the 1950s always obscured the reality of racism, sexism, and anticommunist paranoia that made the 1950s anything but placid for many Americans). For Jameson, though, the 1960s counterculture, represented by Booth, is represented in *Blue Velvet* as "more distasteful than it is fearful, more disgusting than threatening: here evil has finally become an image, and the simulated replay of the fifties has generalized itself into a whole simulacrum in its own right."[1]

This reading provides some interesting insights into the film, though one could also read the film in exact opposite way. Rather than see the depiction of Booth and his gang in *Blue Velvet* as a critique of the 1960s counterculture from the perspective of the Reaganite 1980s, I would argue that it is at least as possible to see the over-the-top representation of Booth as a mockery of the paranoid vision of the counterculture as drug-addled evil that was typical of Reagan and his followers. By this reading, the real object of critique in the film's representation of Booth is not the counterculture but the Reaganite 1980s and that decade's obscene caricature of the 1960s counterculture, while aligning Reagan's folksy, down-home declaration of his project of restoring the traditional values with a nostalgic vision of the 1950s that was always at odds with reality. As Coughlin puts it, *Blue Velvet* "is not pleading for a 'return to the fifties' or deferring to a 'nostalgia' of the past, he is actively criticizing the past to facilitate a greater understanding of the limitations of many of its representations."[2]

Many things about *Blue Velvet* are intentionally left unclear. For example, we don't really know where Lumberton is supposed to be or how big it is supposed to be. It is also at times hard to tell *when* it is supposed to be. As noted by Denzin, *Blue Velvet* includes a number of inconsistent historical markers, though its principal historical mix is between the mid-1980s, when the film was made, and the 1950s, from which many of the characters seem to emerge, returning us to the question of 1950s nostalgia, though this nostalgia is itself quite vaguely defined in the film.[3] In fact, the 1950s are never overtly identified as an object of nostalgia in the film, but fifties nostalgia was so well established by this time that Lynch could assume viewers would recognize the various cues that point in this direction. By the 2020s, of course, the 1950s nostalgia in *Blue Velvet* takes on an extra layer of irony because the film was made in the mid-1980s and is ostensibly (on the basis of automobiles and other items within the film) set there as well, while the 1980s had themselves become a common object of cultural nostalgia by the 2020s.

Blue Velvet, meanwhile, already calls into question the validity of 1950s nostalgia, supporting Jameson's argument that the turn toward a less authentic postmodern form of nostalgia was already well underway in the 1980s, even if it was not as mainstream as it is in the 2020s. Thus, while Lynch's film employs a panoply of retro images from the 1950s, it ultimately undermines any attempt to digest these images in a truly nostalgic way. The film's 1950s imagery is associated with youthful sexual innocence, with calm, crimeless streets, with safe, comfortable homes. But everything that happens in the film warns us that these images are superficial and unrealistic. Beneath the placid, idyllic surface of Lumberton lurks a dark world of sexual depravity and abject violence. Moreover, there is no sense of temporal sequence in which the film's images of tranquility and wholesomeness are associated with the 1950s, while the images of darkness and depravity are associated with the 1980s. Instead, all of these images are overlaid, existing simultaneously, with the ultimate implication that the stereotypical 1950s images represent what the citizens of Lumberton in the 1980s *wish* their world could be like with no implication that their world was ever that way, even in the actual 1950s.

As is typically the case with Lynch's films, music is crucial to the overall impact of *Blue Velvet* and to its evocation of particular time periods. For one thing, Angelo Badalamenti's score escapes association with any particular time period, though its refusal to point toward any other time makes it seem fairly contemporary to the 1980s. It also employs a range of styles (with a tilt toward jazz) to produce a vague sense of strangeness and threat, a sense that the placid surface of things in Lumberton might be disrupted at any moment—as, of course, it frequently is in this film. This score, though, is so thoroughly integrated into the texture of the film that it doesn't particularly leap out as a feature. What does leap out is the use of well-known popular songs that supplement Badalamenti's often-jazzy, noir-like original score in important ways. The fact that the film's very title is taken from a popular song signals to us the importance of music in *Blue Velvet*, which, among other things, serves as a key component of the film's complex cultural nostalgia.

Music is also used in *Blue Velvet* to evoke the dreamlike nature of film noir. For example, after Jeffrey and Dorothy fall into the clutches of Booth and a couple of his thugs, they are introduced to Booth's gang of drugged-out misfits, including the "suave fucker" Ben (Dean Stockwell), who, at Booth's request, performs a weirdly lit lip-synched rendition of Roy Orbison's "In Dreams." This 1963 hit fits perfectly with the oneiric character of so much of *Blue Velvet*, including this performance itself, which seems to move Booth almost to tears, until he interrupts it, grabs the cassette tape from which the song was playing, and leads his entourage to a remote sawmill, one of the few indications in the film that we are in a logging town. There, Booth starts to sexually abuse Dorothy. When Jeffrey tries to intervene, Booth responds by playing "In Dreams" on the cassette deck in the car while, seemingly energized to savagery by the song, he badly beats Jeffrey, leaving him lying unconscious on the ground.

The prominent use of the songs "In Dreams" and "Blue Velvet" might appear to support the notion that *Blue Velvet* is informed by a nostalgic vision of the 1950s, given that references to the music of the decade have long been crucial to 1950s nostalgia in general. However, the use of these songs in *Blue Velvet* actually *undermines* 1950s nostalgia. For one thing, both "In Dreams" and Vinton's version of "Blue Velvet" are from 1963, suggesting that our cultural memory of the 1950s might be a bit inaccurate, sometimes confusing the 1950s with the early 1960s. More importantly, Vinton's well-known rendition of "Blue Velvet" is undermined in the film by the tortured version performed by Dorothy, while "In Dreams" is subverted by Ben's bizarre pantomime of it.

All in all, it seems most advisable to read *Blue Velvet* as a critique of nostalgia more than as an example of it, even if the implications of that critique are not always simple or clear. For example, Lumberton is quite clearly depicted as anything but an ideal, peaceful small American town. Crescencia Chay concludes that "*Blue Velvet* masterfully paints an impressionistic and nightmarish dreamscape of small-town suburban America that highlights the problematic ideology of Americana in the postmodern condition. Through the deconstruction of this seemingly perfect American suburbia, the film highlights the ways in which postmodernism has engendered illusory feelings of nostalgia and wistfulness for a manufactured 'dream.'"[4]

That *Blue Velvet*'s intentions toward idyllic visions of small-town America (or 1950s America) are mostly subversive can also be seen in the film's ending, which at first glance might appear to endorse those idyllic visions. Normalcy seems entirely restored (though normalcy also includes a robin eating a bug.) More importantly, though, the normalcy that is restored is just a bit *too* "normal." As Berry puts it, this ending is "transparently ironic, a ridiculously happy ending to the small-town life of a nuclear family. The symbolic order of the 'normal' world has been shown by Lynch to be a mere sham and can never really be fully restored."[5] Given all that we have seen before about the kinds of things that really go on in Lumberton (and we have to wonder whether Booth's death will ensure that bad things don't continue to happen), the ending of the film seems quite contrived and inauthentic, somewhat like the inauthentic versions of American reality that were so consistently purveyed in American television sitcoms of the 1950s. Real American life in the 1980s was certainly not like what was shown in those 1950s sitcoms—and neither was real American life in the 1950s.

Chapter 5

The Revisionary Noir Detective: *Devil in a Blue Dress*

(1995, Directed by Carl Franklin)

Devil in a Blue Dress is an adaptation of a 1990 novel by Walter Mosley, the first in what would ultimately become a long series of novels featuring African American private detective Ezekiel "Easy" Rawlins (played in the film by Black megastar Denzel Washington). This series of novels is probably the most prominent body of detective fiction featuring a Black detective in all of American literature, though none of the other novels have been adapted to film as of this writing, possibly because this film was not a financial success.[1] In both the novel and the film, *Devil in a Blue Dress* is a sort of origin story that reveals how Rawlins became a private detective in the first place. Set in 1948 Los Angeles, the story takes place in the heart of noir territory in terms of both time and place. It also involves a classic noir narrative, as Rawlins is hired for the seemingly simple task of finding a missing woman, only to uncover a more serious web of treachery and crime that reaches into the realm of the rich and powerful—not to mention some thuggish racist cops. Indeed, where this film deviates from the films of the original noir cycle is in its emphasis on race—and in ways that would never have been allowed under the Production Code. This emphasis, in fact, is strong enough and integral enough to the texture and message of the film that it can be considered an early example of revisionary noir.

As *Devil in a Blue Dress* begins, Rawlins (recently back from serving in Europe in World War II) has just lost his job (in an incident apparently involving racial discrimination) as a machinist at Champion Aircraft. This situation thus immediately calls attention to the issue of racism, while also helping to contextualize the events of the film during a period when many African Americans were moving to Los Angeles in search of opportunities in the defense industries that had arisen there as part of the war effort.[2] Rawlins will then spend most of the first half of the film continuing to wear his Champion Aircraft jacket, emphasizing his working-class background, though the film also identifies him as an ambitious, upwardly mobile Black man. He is a proud homeowner whose well-tended suburban home is a far cry from the seedy offices that have served as the home bases for so many previous hardboiled detectives. In fact, by the end of the film, Rawlins is preparing both to invest in more real estate and to start his own detective agency. The film is thus quite hopeful in its presentation of the possibilities for advancement in American society for African Americans, though it is also open about the obstacles that Black Americans face at every turn.

The plot of *Devil in a Blue Dress* revolves around an upcoming L.A. mayoral election between two wealthy white men: Todd Carter (Terry Kinney) and Matthew Terell (Maury Chaykin). The woman Rawlins is hired to find is one Daphne Monet (Jennifer Beals), the former fiancée of Carter, who has disappeared. In the course of his investigation, Rawlins learns that the ostensibly white Monet is secretly a mixed-race woman,[3] that Terell has learned of this fact, and that he has used it to blackmail Carter into dropping out of the mayoral race, leading Carter's family to bribe Monet to disappear. In a further complication, however, Monet has acquired photographs revealing that Terell is a pedophile, which she hopes will eliminate Terell from contention and allow her to reunite with Carter. Rawlins, though, is unsurprised to learn that Carter still feels that he must break off his relationship with Monet due to her racial background. As Rawlins puts it in the voiceover narration that is one of the many nods to film noir tradition in this film, "Even though we had fought a war to keep the world free, the color line in America worked both ways, and even a rich white man like Todd Carter was afraid to cross it."

Monet's complex role in this film—in which she is both blackmailed and black-mailer—is typical of the nebulous ethical texture of noir film, making her both something of a femme fatale and something of a victim. Indeed, in some ways she occupies both ends of the "good girl-bad girl" pairing that is so often found on the films of the original noir cycle. In this case, though, the ambiguity in her status includes her ambiguous racial identity, introducing an element of uncertainty that goes beyond anything in the original noir cycle. For one thing, the extremity of the response to the revelation of Monet's racial identity is indicative of the deep level of racism that pervades the society of 1948 Los Angeles in the film.[4] But this indication may also point a finger at the original noir cycle itself, which Julian Murphet has seen as underwritten by a "racial unconscious" that was only beginning to be revealed, thanks to the work of filmmakers such as Franklin and writers such as Mosley.[5]

Devil in a Blue Dress employs a classic noir plot structure, but it moves into revisionary noir territory because of the role played by race in the film. We should not underestimate the importance of Monet in this sense, though this film is very much dominated by its protagonist, whose race and working-class background, combined with his aspirations to gain middle-class respectability, set him apart from the typical noir protagonist. Meanwhile, the effectiveness of *Devil in a Blue Dress* as a character study is also enhanced by the performance of the charismatic Washington, who makes it easy to root for Rawlins, even if he might be a bit too much into drinking and womanizing for his own good. However, if Washington alone helps to make Rawlins seem more likable, it is also the case that certain elements of the plot have been changed relative to the book to achieve the same effect. For example, the Rawlins of the novel has some of the same negative tendencies as the Rawlins of the film, only more so, including a greater willingness to break the rules to achieve his goals. What is also particularly effective about the film is that Rawlins so clearly evolves over the course of the action, beginning as a less formidable figure than he is in the novel but winding up having learned some valuable lessons that make him much better suited to perform as a private detective than in the beginning.

Rawlins is also made more likable through his contrast with the other characters in the film, most of which make him seem like a pillar of virtue by comparison. These characters include both of the film's wealthy white mayoral candidates, who together serve to provide a representation of corruption at the highest levels of Los Angeles society, though neither the miscegenation of Carter nor the perversion of Terell would have been allowed in the films of the original noir cycle due to Code restrictions. Another white character who serves as a counterpoint to Rawlins is DeWitt Albright (Tom Sizemore), a private detective who initially enlists Rawlins to search for Monet. Monet, Albright has heard, likes to hang out with Black people, which makes him of the "wrong persuasion" to be able to track her down—thus he turns to Rawlins. Albright is corrupt, vicious, and unscrupulous, generally coming off more like a gangster than a private eye. He thus provides a sort of reverse role model for Rawlins in his development as a detective. Meanwhile, many of the Black characters Rawlins encounters in the film are also pretty disreputable. The most important of these is "Mouse" (Don Cheadle), Rawlins's friend from Houston who comes to L.A. to help Rawlins work his way through the trouble he finds himself in. Depicted as so good with handguns that he is almost a superhero (or perhaps supervillain), Mouse is also completely willing to use his guns to commit cold-blooded murder if it can help him reach his objectives. He thus serves as a marker of the kind of life Rawlins must have been headed for had he not gone in another direction, perhaps thanks partly to his experience in the military and his ability, at least momentarily, to get a good job at a defense plant after the war. Mouse also poses something of a dilemma for Rawlins, both because he is extremely effective as backup and because their long-term friendship makes it difficult for Rawlins to turn his back on him. By the end of the film, however, Mouse has returned to Houston and Rawlins seems headed for a respectable middle-class life (though punctuated by the shadowy milieu in which he will no doubt occasionally find himself as a private detective).[6]

All in all, the treatment of race in *Devil in a Blue Dress* is particularly effective because it deftly acknowledges the racial inequality in American society but avoids the simple depiction of Rawlins as a Black outsider in a white world. It's 1948, and segregation is still a real thing, so the races do generally occupy separate spheres in the film. Thus, in one scene in which Rawlins stumbles into a conversation with a white girl on a pier, he finds himself quickly surrounded by hostile white boys ready

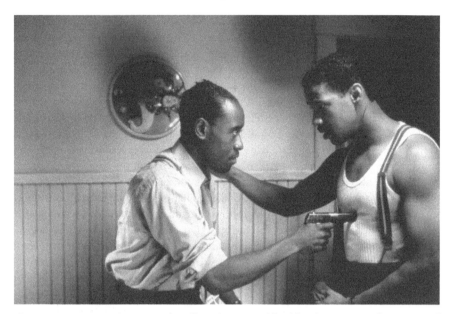

Figure 5.1. "Mouse" (Don Cheadle) threatens his friend Easy Rawlins (Denzel Washington) in *Devil in a Blue Dress*. Tristar/Photofest © Tristar.

to make an example of him (only to be rescued by Albright). However, the Black world in which Rawlins mostly travels is depicted as a fully functioning "normal" one. Granted, the nature of the narrative is that he meets up with some unsavory characters, but one of the key elements of the film (and the novel) is the middle-class suburban lifestyle to which Rawlins aspires—but on his own terms. Thus, one of the most important scenes in the film is the final one, unusually optimistic for noir film, in which Rawlins strolls through his all-Black neighborhood in a sort of utopian moment, nodding to his neighbors as they similarly go about their quest for the kind of safe, comfortable life promised them by the American dream, even as the society around them places so many obstacles in their path because of their skin color.

In his introduction to the thirtieth-anniversary edition of the novel, Mosley notes that he sees Rawlins very much in the tradition of the hardboiled private eye in that he operates according to his own personal code of ethics, regardless of what others might think. Then he nicely sums up his view of Rawlins and his neighbors:

> He and his friends face every morning having to scramble up the slippery slope that is America, that is business as usual, that is an unequal sense of innocence and guilt, that recognizes and prejudges race, gender, and class before wondering about the who, what, and why of the crime committed. Easy is an American hero. He does not expect recognition, acceptance, or any sense of equality in the land that defines his experience as something other. He knows that he will never be seen as equal to those that believe equality is weighted by color and class, gender and belief. But Easy doesn't care how he

is seen or perceived; as long as they know he is blessed with the willingness to fight back, then the rules begin to tip, ever so slightly, in his favor.[7]

Noting the many similarities between *Devil in a Blue Dress* and classic noir, James Naremore argues that "because the action is viewed from a different social, economic, and racial perspective, familiar motifs of urban noir are either intensified or neatly reversed."[8] In particular, Naremore notes that, though the Black clubs and pool halls in the film can be violent and dangerous places, they nevertheless seem more "accommodating" to Black characters than are the more up-scale locations in the white world. "Throughout," he concludes, "the white world is a dangerously alien territory at the margins of 'normal' life, and poor and semirural areas that were never represented by the classic studios are given an aura of peace and dignity."[9] One might compare here the Black jazz club that appears in *Out of the Past* (1947) as a sign of otherness and exoticism, in relation to the white "norm." In *Devil in a Blue Dress*, though, the terms are reversed, and the white settings seem much more like foreign territory than do the Black ones, which is a crucial part of the impact of this film.

But, of course, race was always there in film noir (as in American society), even when it was not acknowledged. For example, E. Ann Kaplan discusses the obliquely symbolic treatment of race (and gender) in such classic noir films as Jacques Tourneur's *Cat People* (1942) and Orson Welles's *The Lady from Shanghai* (1947), describing race as film noir's "repressed unconscious signifier."[10] Among other things, Kaplan notes how the famed visual style of film noir often led to an association of darkness or Blackness with the evil and the marginalized, using "tropes of Blackness as metaphors of White characters' falls from grace."[11] She goes on to note that Black directors have sometimes used the noir style as a way of commenting on the plight of African Americans within a racist American society, though her main example of this is actually a novel, rather than a film, Chester Himes's *A Rage in Harlem*. One might certainly see Franklin's work as an example, though Kaplan doesn't mention it, as an example of this phenomenon.

Perhaps getting more to the heart of the matter, Eric Lott argues that racial tensions and anxieties were a crucial part of the noir mood, even though it was seldom expressed directly in the films of the time:

> Noir responded to this problem not by presenting it outright but by taking the social energy associated with its social threat and subsuming it into the untoward aspects of white selves. The "dark" energy of many of these films is villainized precisely through the associations with race that generated some of that energy in the first place. Film noir is in this sense a sort of whiteface dream-work of social anxieties with explicitly racial sources, condensed on film into the criminal undertakings of abjected whites.[12]

From this point of view, the frank treatment of race (and the sympathetic treatment of blackness) in *Devil in a Blue Dress* seems particularly refreshing and important. Nevertheless, it is worth noting that *Devil in a Blue Dress* was not entirely without precedent in its exploration of race and racism via noir film, though in some ways it stands out even more when compared with other films that attempted to tackle such issues. For example, in one scene we can see from the marquee that the 1948 film *The Betrayal* is playing in an L.A. theater. This film, directed by pioneering Black filmmaker Oscar Micheaux, also features an ostensibly white woman who turns out to be Black, so the allusion is appropriate and clearly intentional, though *The Betrayal* is not really a film noir. There were, however, occasional critiques of racism even in the original noir cycle. The very first feature film performance of Sidney Poitier was in *No Way Out* (1950), a film noir that strongly condemns racism, though it clearly identifies its central racist (played with his usual aplomb by Richard Widmark) as a pathological figure, thus muting any critique of systemic racism. Similarly, Martin Ritt's *The Edge of the City* (1957) pits Poitier's character against a racist bully (played by Jack Warden) who is depicted as being outside the norm of American society. This film was, though, considered particularly daring because it depicted an interracial relationship between a Black woman (played by Ruby Dee) and a white man (John Cassavetes). Finally, Robert Wise's *Odds Against Tomorrow* (1959) features Harry Belafonte as a Black nightclub performer and Robert Ryan as a racist ex-cop, both of whom become involved in a bank heist with a tragic ending that makes its antiracist theme in a rather heavy-handed way: both characters are burned to death in an explosion, their corpses becoming unidentifiable by race.

The initial wave of neo-noir films was not strong in its treatment of race. However, the concurrent "blaxploitation" cycle of films, aimed primarily at Black audiences roughly throughout the 1970s, included a variety of genres including crime films that verged on neo-noir in their subject matter. Notable examples of the latter include Melvin Van Peebles's *Sweet Sweetback's Baadasssss Song* (1971), Gordon Parks's *Shaft* (1971), and Jack Hill's *Foxy Brown* (1974). However, the look and feel of these films—enhanced by their typically funk and soul soundtracks—is very different from what is normally considered to be noir, and film historians have generally considered them to be a separate phenomenon than the neo-noir films that were also emerging at this time.

It was thus not until the 1990s that genuinely noir films began to treat race seriously as a systemic social problem. Franklin's own *One False Move* (1992) is a neo-noir film in which race is an important issue, though it is not foregrounded as much as it is in *Devil in a Blue Dress*. Indeed, the lead character in this film is one Dale "Hurricane" Dixon (Bill Paxton), the white police chief of the small Arkansas town of Star City. Meanwhile, the plot revolves around a three-person gang that eventually flees to Star City after committing a series of grisly murders in Los Angeles and Houston. The gang consists of a Black woman ("Fantasia," played by Cynda Williams), a Black man ("Pluto," played by Michael Beach), and a white man (Ray Malcolm, played by Billy Bob Thornton). Meanwhile, of the two LAPD detectives who track the gang to Star City, one is Black and one is white. Malcolm and Fantasia are involved as an interracial couple. Meanwhile, it turns out that Dixon had been involved with Fantasia (then called "Lila") years earlier when she was living in Star

City—and that he unknowingly fathered her now-five-year-old son at that time. There is little commentary on these interracial relationships, however, and little direct commentary on race in general, other than the subtle suggestion that Dixon is an unconscious racist, despite his lack of open hostility toward the Black characters in the film.

The lack of open commentary on race keeps *One False Move* within the realm of neo-noir. Thus, probably the closest predecessor to *Devil in a Blue Dress* is Bill Duke's *Deep Cover* (1992), in which Laurence Fishburne is an undercover cop dedicated to taking down a Latin American drug cartel—fueled by his memory of the death of his junkie father, shot down in front of the boy's eyes while trying to rob a liquor store. Race becomes an issue at several points in this film, though it is never *the* issue, and this film remains toward the neo-noir end of the spectrum, though it is unusually cynical even in a genre noted for its cynicism.

If *Devil in a Blue Dress* was clearly a major step forward in the production of noir films that openly address the question of systemic racism in American society, it is also the case that filmmakers of the ensuing three decades (including Franklin himself) have not really gone beyond what Franklin accomplished in this film. Recent events such as a rise in white supremacist political activity suggest that this lack of development is not because the US has entered a "postracial" era. Instead, it would seem to be largely attributable to the fact that the most interesting critiques of racism in American film have been conducted in other generic contexts, with the horror films of Jordan Peele providing the most obvious examples. Nevertheless, *Devil in a Blue Dress* suggests that noir can be an excellent mode for the exploration of such issues given the right script and the right combination of cinematography, character, plot, and setting.

Chapter 6

The Revisionary Noir Detective: *Inherent Vice*

(2014, Directed by Paul Thomas Anderson)

Paul Thomas Anderson's *Inherent Vice* is, to date, the only film to have been adapted from the novels of Thomas Pynchon, arguably the greatest American novelist of his generation and possibly the most important of all postmodern novelists. Indeed, Pynchon is such an important figure that it is almost impossible to talk about this adaptation without also addressing the original novel. At the same time, Pynchon is such a complex novelist that his work has typically been regarded as virtually impossible to adapt to film; the fact that *Inherent Vice* was adapted so successfully can be attributed, at least in part, to the fact that this particular novel is unusually cinematic due to the extent to which it draws directly upon film noir. One of the distinctive features of Pynchon's fiction is his ability to incorporate, through both style and content, the energies of any number of different genres from both high and low culture, including film and television as well as various forms of literature. *Inherent Vice* draws upon a narrower range of genres than do Pynchon's longer and weightier works—such as *Gravity's Rainbow* (1973) and *Against the Day* (2006)—given that it draws the vast majority of its material from hard-boiled detective fiction and film noir (while also including material from genres such as horror and science fiction, as well as the typical Pynchon allusions to things such as *Star Trek*, *Gilligan's Island*, and *Godzilla*). Importantly, though, the genres imported into *Inherent Vice* represent more than the "blank parody" described by Jameson. They interact to produce an entirely new, potentially subversive, message. Or, as Casey Shoop puts it, "Through combining noir with other familiar genres, *Inherent Vice* challenges both the mediums and the messages of American ideology."[1]

Multiple critics have noted how extensively Pynchon draws upon film noir in *Inherent Vice*, while also noting that he challenges many of the conventions of the genre. John Miller writes of the novel's "assimilation and parody of noir conventions," suggesting that it draws in particularly important ways on the convention of Los Angeles, the ultimate noir city, as a place of both promise and corruption.[2] Eleanor Gold, meanwhile, describes the novel as an "adjustment" to film noir that combines film noir with other genres to challenge "both the mediums and the messages of American ideology."[3] And Sean Carswell, drawing upon Christian Moraru's concept of "rewriting," argues that Pynchon's novel actively rewrites Chandler's novels, especially *The Long Goodbye* (1953).[4] It is certainly the case that the cultural context of *Inherent Vice* (in both the novel and the film) is so radically different from that of film noir and Chandler's fiction that audiences are given an opportunity to reevaluate those predecessors from an estranged, renewed, and refreshed perspective.

This estrangement is accomplished partly by simple temporal displacement of so many identifiable film noir tropes into the world of the counterculture in 1970, which seems so different from the noir world of the 1940s and 1950s (though it still contains much of the same corruption and vice). The black-and-white cinematography of the original noir films is replaced by the full-color world of hippie tie-dyes (though the film still contains a number of scenes that occur in fog or darkness). The edgy, jazz-inflected scores of the original noir films are replaced by a collection of mostly familiar hits from period artists such as Neil Young and slightly earlier artists such as Sam Cooke, though it also includes tracks from edgier artists, such as the German experimental rock group Can. The tough-guy private detective is now a hippie; the femme fatale has been replaced by an ex-girlfriend of the detective, while sex is now so freely available that she has largely lost the mysterious aura of forbidden access, her mystery replaced by a mutual sense of longing and loss for the failed relationship between the detective and the femme fatale (which rhymes with the sense of loss due to the failure of the counterculture to realize its utopian dreams).

"DOC" SPORTELLO, P.I.

Inherent Vice begins with a voiceover narration by one Sortilège (Joanna Newsome), who is a minor character in both the novel and the film but assumes a more prominent role as narrator of the film. This use of voiceover is a common film noir technique, though it is unusual in classic noir to have a woman narrator. What is even more unusual is that Sortilège is a sort of hippie earth mother, whose point of view is much different than the typically cynical point of view of the film noir narrator. Then the action begins with a classic noir scene when a seductive woman client (as close as anyone in this film comes to being a femme fatale) comes to a private investigator to seek his help. In this case, though, the woman is former hippie chick Shasta Fay.

6.1. Hippie detective "Doc" Sportello (Joaquin Phoenix) on the beach with ex-girlfriend Shasta Fay Hepworth (Katherine Waterston) in *Inherent Vice*. Warner Bros./Photofest © Warner Bros.

Hepworth (Katherine Waterston) and the detective is her former lover (still a hippie) Larry "Doc" Sportello (Joaquin Phoenix). Shasta wants Sportello to help extricate her from a difficult situation in which she has become the girlfriend of wealthy real-estate developer Michael "Mickey" Wolfmann (Eric Roberts), whose wife (along with the wife's lover) has attempted to enlist her in a scheme to have Wolfmann committed to a mental asylum so they can make off with his money before he (having undergone a recent "conversion") can give it all away to counter-cultural causes. Sportello's subsequent investigation then takes him into a dark and dangerous world of corruption and violence in both high and low places. In short, it takes him into the typical world of film noir—with the twist that Sportello's "native" environment is the counterculture of the 1960s and early 1970s, which adds a distinctively new element to the noir lifeworld.

Sportello is strongly anchored at the center of the film as its point-of-view character, which sometimes makes things a bit hazy for viewers, given his drug-addled consciousness. Still, given the clear Chandler-esque qualities of *Inherent Vice*, it seems natural to compare Sportello directly with Chandler's Philip Marlowe, especially as he is represented in the prominent classic noir films *Murder, My Sweet* (1944) and *The Big Sleep* (1946). To understand the relationship between *Inherent Vice* and the entire history of film noir, though, it is also useful to compare Sportello with the

Marlowe of Robert Altman's *The Long Goodbye* (1973), a key neo-noir film based on Chandler's fiction—and one that bears a special relationship to *Inherent Vice* because it has been modernized to be set in the early 1970s and thus is essentially contemporaneous with *Inherent Vice*.

Because of his appearances in so many works by Chandler (and in so many film adaptations of those works), Marlowe is probably one of the better-known characters in modern American literature. At the same time, he is a somewhat nebulous figure, and Chandler's descriptions of him can be somewhat inconsistent. As a result, he has been interpreted in widely varying ways in film adaptations. Dick Powell's Marlowe in *Murder, My Sweet*, Humphrey Bogart's Marlowe in *The Big Sleep* (1946), and Elliott Gould's Marlowe in *The Long Goodbye* are so different that they hardly seem the same character, except for sharing a name and profession. One thing they also share is a consistent and honorable adherence to a basic personal code of morality, even as they find themselves surrounded by corruption, violence, and even depravity. The code followed by the Marlowe of Chandler's fiction allows him to be a relatively heavy drinker and to engage in a reasonable amount of sexual activity, even though he tends to choose his partners carefully and not to be taken in by the machinations of the femmes fatales he frequently encounters. Both of these characteristics are necessarily tamped down in the film adaptations that were made during the Code period, though they do provide a point of contact with the pot-smoking, free-loving Sportello. It should be said, though, that Sportello still maintains an updated code of his own (commensurate with the vast historical changes that have occurred between the time of the original noir films and the 1970s). Indeed, the gap in ethics between Sportello and the corrupt society around him remains as large as that gap had ever been in Chandler or in the original noir films, suggesting that, in some ways, Marlowe was as much a countercultural figure as Sportello, but without such an established subculture with which to identify.

Indeed, while Sportello's bad memory and a sometimes-poor connection with reality set him apart from the keenly observant and analytical Marlowe, in some ways the difference between Sportello and Marlowe is more a matter of style than substance. Visually, Chandler's, Powell's and Bogart's Chandler are all clean-cut and well-groomed, generally dressed in a coat and tie. Gould's Chandler is a bit more rumpled, in keeping with the more relaxed styles in his 1970s, but he still operates primarily in coat and tie. Sportello is scruffy and slovenly even by the standards of the 1970s, especially for a "professional," in many ways more directly related to the Coen brothers' Jeff Lebowski than to Marlowe.[5] Whereas Marlowe runs his professional practice out of a somewhat seedy office (thus maintaining a certain professionalism), Sportello has an office of sorts (which he shares with a quack doctor) but seems to operate mostly out of his own rather shabby surfside crash pad. Indeed, Sportello often seems more like an amateur than a professional, solving crimes and finding missing people almost more out of a wish to do the right thing than of a desire to make a profit, suggesting the contempt for materialism in his countercultural ethic.

However scruffy he might be, Sportello shares with the various versions of Marlowe a seemingly easy access to virtually all levels of Los Angeles society. One of his former clients is the ultra-wealthy Crocker Fenway (Martin Donovan), whose runaway daughter Japonica (Sasha Pieterse) he once recovered (and whom he encounters again in *Inherent Vice*). And if the relationship between Shasta and Wolfmann seems surprising, it should also be noted that Sportello's current girlfriend is the uptight, highly respectable deputy district attorney Penny Kimball (Reese Witherspoon). Meanwhile, Sportello has extensive connections within the highly corrupt Los Angeles Police Department—especially including Detective Christian "Bigfoot" Bjornsen (Josh Brolin)—though his relationship with them is even more antagonistic than Marlowe's had been. In addition, Sportello (like Marlowe) makes many connections among the lowest rungs of L.A. society as well, encountering a variety of prostitutes, drug dealers, gangsters, and hit men. Marlowe, however, is endowed with a certain moral superiority to the lowlifes he encounters, while Sportello moves among these figures with a certain democratic ease.

THE POLITICS OF *INHERENT VICE*

At first glance, *Inherent Vice* might seem to be simply another example of the "nostalgia film" that Jameson associates directly with both postmodernism and neo-noir. Meanwhile, the 1970 setting would also seem to invite nostalgia, both for film noir and for the 1960s counterculture. It is certainly the case that both versions of *Inherent Vice* display an antiauthoritarian political perspective that is strongly informed by the 1960s counterculture. Of course, the strong influence of the counterculture on Pynchon has long been recognized[6] and can be seen by the fact that two of his earlier novels—*The Crying of Lot 49* (1966) and *Vineland* (1990)—bookend the history of that counterculture, the first detailing the early years of its gestation and the second detailing the aftermath of its defeat by the forces of regression from the years of Richard Nixon to the years of Ronald Reagan, both of whom lurk in the margins of *Inherent Vice*, providing important political atmosphere.[7]

Inherent Vice, though, is the only Pynchon novel actually set *during* a fully formed counterculture, but it is already informed by a sense of the *defeat* of the counterculture. For one thing, Sportello is somewhat of an aging hippie (Phoenix was forty in 2014, when the film was released). Meanwhile, 1970 is already late enough that the counterculture is in decline, having peaked, for many observers, in the "Summer of Love" in 1967, after which 1968 saw a series of calamities, including the assassination of Dr. Martin Luther King Jr. in April, the assassination of Robert Kennedy in June, and the police riots at the Chicago Democratic Convention in August. In July and August 1969, the Manson murders (which lurk in the background of *Inherent Vice* throughout[8]) further darkened the utopian dreams of the counterculture, especially when they were quickly followed by the violence at the Altamont Free concert in December 1969.

In 1970, the Vietnam War was still raging, something that is reflected in *Inherent Vice* in a number of ways, perhaps most importantly in the mysterious Golden Fang, various manifestations of which haunt *Inherent Vice*. Of course, this motif echoes the hints of Orientalism that run through much of film noir. However, in this case, the motif of an Asian drug cartel evading American authorities can be taken as a more specific reference to Vietnam, or to what Doug Haynes sees as a "representation of the resistance of a non-Western people to American superpower."[9] Thus, as opposed to the Orientalist motifs that are typically used in film noir simply to create an exotic (and perhaps decadent atmosphere), *Inherent Vice* gives a more active role to Asian culture, while also reminding us of the irony of the long-time motif of the "yellow peril," when it was, in fact, the US that was invading Asia at this time, rather than the other way around.

Haynes (writing about the novel) sees *Inherent Vice*'s historical setting as particularly important because it marks a crucial moment of transition in American history (the end of the counterculture) and in the history of capitalism, with a transition from Fordism to the beginnings of today's neoliberalism, a period that would be marked by "the acceleration and refinement of the culture industry, the privatization of pleasure, and the conspicuous consumption of the Apple generation."[10] This notion of 1970 as a turning point is also hinted at in the film, though the emphasis there is mostly on the fading of the counterculture, rather than the coming of a new, more consumerist culture.

Inherent Vice stands strongly apart from the postmodern nostalgia films discussed by Jameson, partly because there is no attempt to mimic the actual style of film noir, while any nostalgia for the lost days of 1970 is disrupted by the specter of Vietnam that hovers in the margins throughout and by the hints of the impending collapse of the counterculture (partly at the hands of conspiratorial capitalist forces) that are woven into both film and novel. Indeed, in both the novel and the film, any nostalgia is not *for* nostalgia but is located in a 1970 that is itself already nostalgic for the time a few years earlier when the hopes of the counterculture were still high and when Doc and Sasha were still together.

The ending of the film particularly tops off this note of displaced nostalgia. In this ending, a stoned Doc, hearing Sasha's voice in his head as she describes one of their best earlier moments together, starts to lay that head down on a table, possibly to sleep. Then, the scene dissolves into another, in which Doc is driving along a freeway with Sasha at his side. This setup clearly invites us to interpret the entire final scene of the film as a dream sequence, especially as the Sasha in the car seamlessly continues the speech that Doc had been hearing in his head in the previous scene. Meanwhile, they are surrounded by fog, which enhances the dreamlike atmosphere, as does the odd tenor of the entire scene, including the mysterious light that keeps showing up in the rearview mirror, which reflects the light onto Doc's face. Perhaps it is just Bjornsen tracking them down, but it seems more likely that this is the lost light of a brighter past. As if to emphasize that this past cannot be restored, Doc's final line in the film (a callback to an earlier moment in the film) is, "This don't mean we're back together," to which Sasha agrees. We'll never know for sure what this final moment means, which is a very noir way to end the film.[11]

Chapter 7

The Revisionary Noir Detective: *Under the Silver Lake*

(2018, Directed by David Robert Mitchell)

A basic plot outline of *Under the Silver Lake* might make it sound like a typical neo-noir film: alluring young woman mysteriously disappears; young man acting as detective investigates her disappearance; in the process, he uncovers a surprising web of secrets and conspiracies. However, numerous aspects of this film take it outside the norm for noir film—or for any film, thus pushing it into revisionary noir territory. Indeed, the most defining characteristic of this film might be its sheer strangeness—and its overt refusal to abide by the normal conventions of Hollywood film. For example, the film frequently introduces characters or plot elements that appear to be significant but then never make any real contribution to the development of the main plot. In terms of noir conventions, though, the film does not so much violate them as push them to absurd extremes, so that it often spills into different genres, such as horror or off-beat comedy. Ultimately, the film takes the atmosphere of confusion and uncertainty that so often reigns in noir films to such an extreme that it is virtually impossible to form any concrete conclusions about just what is going on in this film. At the same time, it presents us with a noir detective so problematic that we are forced to question the implications of detective fiction as a whole.

Under the Silver Lake is a complex and clever film—possibly a bit too clever for its own good, leading to a number of negative or at least ambivalent reviews. Peter Bradshaw, in a one-star review for *The Guardian*, called it a "catastrophically boring, callow and indulgent LA mystery noir."[1] In another negative *Guardian* review, Simran Hans saw the film as a "spoof of pop culture-obsessed man-boys" but felt that it was too self-indulgent to be effective.[2] On the other hand, Brian Tallerico applauded Mitchell for the ambitiousness of *Under the Silver Lake*, even though he didn't feel that the film was entirely successful.³ In the most detailed review of the film, Ethan Warren mostly likes the film, but he is particularly hard on the protagonist and point of view character, identified in the film only as "Sam (Andrew Garfield)." Noting the film's connection to earlier L.A. noirs, Warren argues, "Nobody could deny that Mitchell intentionally utilizes and revises noir tropes. . . . Sam does function as a sort of dirtbag riff on the classic noir gumshoe. . . . Sam serves as a funhouse reflection of the existential state of the noir protagonist, a figure often characterized as a bleak and sardonic womanizing functional alcoholic. Sam is the noir detective made realistically toxic."⁴

Sam is a completely directionless (and unemployed) young man whose personal fascination with conspiracy theories and the possible presence of secret messages in works of popular culture is so extreme that it clearly distorts his perception of reality. He's also a pretty creepy voyeur. In addition to his basic paranoid personality, he is often drunk or stoned, sometimes to the point of losing consciousness, so that his perceptions become even less trustworthy. Meanwhile, the events of the film are conveyed to us so strongly from his point of view that our perception is distorted as well; it is ultimately impossible to determine from independent evidence in the film whether many of the ultrastrange experiences that he encounters in the course of the film are actually happening to him or are simply figments of his paranoid imagination.

At first, we have no reason to question the reality of the strange things that Sam seems to experience so often, until we look back on them with knowledge of the even stranger things that will happen later. Thus, it is not at first hard to imagine that he might be as attractive to women as he seems to be. After all, Andrew Garfield is a good-looking guy, even if Sam is a bit unkempt. However, he is so poorly groomed that virtually every woman he meets in the course of the film comments on his bad odor (which serves something of the same function as the bandage on the nose of Jake Gittes in *Chinatown*), something that he attributes to all the skunks in his neighborhood, though the skunks oddly don't seem to have had an impact on anyone else. By the end of the film, however, we have to wonder whether his success with women is largely a matter of his own fantasies.

The first truly shocking event that occurs in *Under the Silver Lake* is Sam's encounter with two young boys who are vandalizing cars in his neighborhood, including Sam's own car. He is understandably upset at the vandalism (and is feeling frustrated over an interrupted potential sexual encounter with his sexy new neighbor Sarah [Riley Keough]), but it certainly comes as a surprise when he attacks the boys and literally beats them up. His namesake Sam Spade might occasionally be something of a bully in *The Maltese Falcon*, but it is extremely difficult to imagine Spade, or Philip Marlowe, or any of the other protagonists in noir film punching out children. Still, this encounter is not entirely impossible to believe at the time. However, we have to reassess how we see it in the light of some of the later events of the film, which make us think that either Sam is a dangerous attacker of children, or he might have just been fantasizing about beating up the young vandals.

We see Sam resort to even more extreme violence when he kills an old man ("The Songwriter," played by Jeremy Bobb) by bashing his face into pulp with Kurt Cobain's guitar. (We know from a poster over the head of Sam's bed that he is a big Cobain fan.) This particularly graphic moment is the culmination of what is perhaps the film's strangest scene—and one that verifies Sam's paranoid theories about popular culture so exactly that it seems as if it must almost certainly be occurring only in Sam's mind. In this scene, the aging songwriter claims to have been the author of virtually all the popular hit songs that have appeared from Beethoven's Ninth Symphony forward (a span of roughly two hundred years), while further claiming to have cobbled together these supposedly brilliant compositions simply as a means of making money while manipulating Sam and the other young people who might have seen their own experiences and emotions reflected in the songs, encouraging them to think they are being rebellious when in fact they are doing exactly what the powers that be want them to do. As The Songwriter puts it, "Oh look at you! Everything that you've hoped for, that you've dreamed about being a part of, is a fabrication. Your art, your writing, your culture is the shell of other men's ambitions—ambitions beyond what you will ever understand."

Of course, Sam lives in L.A., so there is no shortage of colorful characters who might share his view of the world. Much of the film clearly can be interpreted as a satire of certain elements of L.A. culture—as in its presentation of the musical group Jesus and the Brides of Dracula or in its presentation of an escort service that is staffed by aspiring Hollywood actresses. The film takes its title from a local zine built on various L.A. conspiracy theories—and whose creator Sam is eventually able to track down. Identified in the credits as "Comic Fan" (played by Patrick Fischler), this man turns out to be possibly even more paranoid and devoted to conspiracy theories than is Sam. (Comic Fan's collection of "life masks" is also one of the strangest images in a film filled with strange images.) When Sam shows the man a mysterious symbol he found left behind at Sarah's apartment after her disappearance, Comic Fan immediately identifies it as a known symbol from 1930s "hobo code": "It means stay quiet," he tells Sam. "Our world is filled with codes, subliminal messages. From Silverlake to the Hollywood Hills."

One clear thing from the film is that the encounter with Comic Fan only feeds Sam's paranoid fantasies, especially after the man turns up dead soon afterward. The police call it a suicide—though Sam seemingly finds suspicious surveillance footage of a naked masked woman (apparently a character known as the "Owl's Kiss," from the zine) whom he clearly thinks might have been involved in Comic Fan's death. Later, Sam seemingly spots the same woman in his own apartment, though she disappears after he turns a gun on her, calling the sighting into question.

Meanwhile, Sam does occasionally run into more sensible characters, as in the case of the unnamed character (listed as "Bar Buddy" in the credits, played by Topher Grace), who at various points suggests reasons why people might be paranoid these days, including video games and the internet. In perhaps his best explanation for why people such as Sam might find conspiracy theories attractive, he argues, "Used to be, a hundred years ago, y'know, any moron could kinda wander into the woods and look behind a rock or some shit and discover some cool new thing, y'know? Not anymore. Where's the mystery that makes everything worthwhile? We crave mystery, 'cause there's none left." This sensible explanation is essentially identical to the answer that Fredric Jameson finds for the ongoing popularity of "magical narratives" in a modern capitalist world that has been, as initially described by the pioneering German sociologist Max Weber, thoroughly rationalized, routinized, and stripped of magic. It is, argues Jameson, exactly because that process of rationalization has led to the "radical impoverishment and constriction of modern life" that magical narratives remain attractive, due to their ability to restore, at least in an imaginary way, some of the magic and mystery that has been lost in the process of capitalist modernization.[5]

If "Bar Buddy's" explanation for the popularity of conspiracy theories thus makes perfect sense, it also makes Sam's attraction to these theories seem all the more divorced from reality. However, at least part of Sam's paranoid view of popular culture does seem to be accurate, in the sense that the popular culture he has encountered through his life seems to have had a large impact on the way he processes reality. It is thus no surprise that he is so accepting of the dark secret conspiracies touted in the *Under the Silver Lake* zine. But more official kinds of popular culture seen to have influenced Sam, as well. Thus, at one point, we see him watching the famous scene near the end of *Invasion of the Body Snatchers* (1956) in which Kevin McCarthy runs screaming into traffic, sounding insane as he tries to convince the drivers that they are in danger from sinister alien invaders.

That Sam's encounters with culture might influence his fantasies is also suggested in a scene in which he meets Millicent Sevence (Callie Hernandez), the daughter of billionaire Jefferson Sevence (a man who has at this point apparently been murdered, along with Sarah). Millicent is surprisingly friendly to Sam, whom she quickly invites to the Silver Lake Reservoir to go skinny dipping. Then someone starts shooting at them, and she is apparently hit and killed, leaving her floating upside down in the water, suspiciously replicating the shot on the cover of a vintage *Playboy* magazine that Sam still keeps by his bedside and that he has identified as a picture of the first woman he ever masturbated to, suggesting that this whole encounter has been a fantasy, though Sam himself often seems unable to distinguish fantasy from reality.

Perhaps the most interesting intrusion of pop culture into Sam's mind occurs when, soon after he and Sarah meet, the two of them get stoned while watching Marilyn Monroe in the 1953 film *How to Marry a Millionaire*, of which Sarah is apparently a huge fan, given that her bedroom is decorated with memorabilia related to the film. Watching this film with Sarah seems to have had a major impact on Sam, who begins to associate Sarah with Monroe in his mind, though that will not become clear until later. Sam and Sarah seem to be getting along swimmingly, though their tryst is interrupted by the return of her roommate (along with some strange characters, including a guy dressed as a pirate who keeps appearing throughout the film). Meanwhile, the next time Sam "sees" Sarah, he is walking along and finds her small dog horribly killed and partly disemboweled, then spots Sarah apparently gorging on the entrails of a dead man. But when "she" turns toward him, we see that she now has a man's face and starts barking at him like a dog, whereupon he wakes from a nightmare. This scene is one of the clearest suggestions in the film that what we see on the screen might not always be happening.

The next time Sam seemingly sees Sarah, she has already disappeared, yet he suddenly seems to hear her swimming in the pool at their apartment complex. When he looks out, he finds that she is naked, seductively beckoning him to join her. Then she, too, begins barking like a dog, after which she seems to disappear. Then the camera cuts to Sam, again awakening, suggesting that he has once again been dreaming. In addition, the content of this dream is quite telling. For one thing, Sarah's actions in the pool replicate almost exactly those of Marilyn Monroe in a notorious scene that was filmed by director George Cukor in 1962 for the film *Something's Got to Give*, which was abandoned after Monroe's death, following several delays due to Monroe's health and personal problems.[6] That Sam might be familiar with this footage is no surprise: the numerous film posters that decorate his apartment make it clear that he is a film buff. Further, we learn in the film that he doesn't simply enjoy popular culture—he studies it meticulously as part of his search for hidden codes and messages. That this footage might invade his dreams is also not surprising, given his association of Sarah with Monroe, something that is clear from the fact that, in this particular scene, Sarah has suddenly acquired a facial mole like the one for which Monroe was famous.

That Sam might dream about Sarah is not extraordinary. But that both of his dreams about Sarah would involve her, or an avatar of her, barking like a dog is certainly odd, especially given the motif of dog killings that circulates through the entire film. That so many of Sam's dreams and fantasies involve either dogs or graphic violence (or both) is especially disturbing in light of the fact that someone apparently really *is* killing dogs in his neighborhood, while we also learn that Sam was apparently traumatized by a dog attack in his childhood. This combination of ingredients raises the question of whether Sam himself might actually be the dog killer. This question is not answered in the film, but the very fact that it is worth contemplating indicates the way the air of paranoia that pervades this film tends to make even viewers paranoid, attempting (like Sam) to interpret codes, especially as there are so many moments in the film that are difficult to understand or interpret.

Once we accept the possibility that Sam might be the dog killer, several other moments in the film take on new meaning. In the very first shot of the film, we see an employee of a coffee shop attempting (unsuccessfully) to remove graffiti that reads "BEWARE THE DOG KILLER" from the shop window. The camera then pans directly from that warning to our first view of Sam, as if applying the warning to him. Later in the film, Sam approaches a group of young women who are gathering for a rather sketchy-looking movie audition. As he approaches them, we see that they are standing around that same dog-killer warning, this time written on the pavement—as if to alert the women that Sam might be dangerous (instead of just smelly, which is the first thing they notice).

In short, while this film overtly casts Sam in the role of detective, it also asks the audience consciously to act as detectives—and in a sort of metafictional way that raises all kinds of questions about Sam but also about detective stories in general. For example, does the popularity of detective fiction suggest a tendency toward paranoia in American culture that has led to the current prevalence of conspiracy theories and other forms of disinformation?[7] This film also raises questions about films in general. Sam might not ultimately come off as a voice of wisdom, but his insistence that media might have multiple messages and perform multiple functions simultaneously does seem to be supported by the overall structure of this film, which contains elements of so many different genres and operates in so many different modes. It does raise serious questions about the prevalence of conspiracy theories in contemporary American society. It also contains moments of abject horror that go beyond anything normally found in a noir film, as well as moments of comic silliness that would again be out of place in most noir films.

For example, when Sam awakens from his first horrifying dream about Sarah, he grabs a Spider-Man comic book that is lying on a table next to him. His hand gets stuck to the comic, and he frantically tries to shake it loose in a moment of slapstick comedy that is made funnier by the fact that Andrew Garfield first became widely known to American audiences when he starred as Spider-Man in two films (in 2012 and 2014). But even this amusing moment leaves questions. After he shakes the comic loose, we see that his hand is covered by something that looks like pizza sauce. (The table is littered with dishes and beer containers,[8] after all.) Could it be blood? Could he have blacked out and killed a dog before returning to his couch?

After noting the evidence in the film that points to Sam as the dog killer, Warren concludes that the identity of the dog killer cannot ultimately be decided from evidence in the film. Meanwhile, though admitting that Sam seems to be suffering from "manic psychosis," Warren argues that the strange events of *Under the Silver Lake* are perhaps best explained as evidence that the film itself is "suffering a nervous breakdown"—in the sense that "the camera's eye," reflecting Sam's mental state, "seems to function as an active and independent agent in the film, one that's often in tangible, even dissociative, distress." Warren does not quite take the step of overtly concluding that most of the film's strangest events are probably figments of Sam's distressed mental state, preferring to see the film as more metafictional and arguing that Sam exerts "lunatic power over the very material reality of his environment" to the point where he "finds his natural world reassembling itself to suit his needs."

However one chooses to phrase it, *Under the Silver Lake* makes it very clear that the things we see in this film should not necessarily be taken at face value. It's a film, a fictional construction of writer/director Mitchell and his cast and crew. And, like all such films, anything can happen that Mitchell wants to happen. It is our task to decide whether to see any lack of verisimilitude as being there simply for our entertainment or whether we want to draw more serious lessons from it, including reassessing how we think about noir films, especially noir detective films.

Part II

THE NOIR FILM LOST MAN

Introduction: The Noir Film Lost Man

While it is often noted for its strong (and sometimes deadly) female characters, film noir remains a male-dominated genre. The vast majority of film noir protagonists are male, though these protagonists are often a different sort of male than the typical film protagonist. Many of them are more villain than hero; some are downright psychotic. They are often weak, confused, unsteady; they are anything but the strong, capable protagonists that are typical of mainstream classic Hollywood films. They are typically alienated from the society around them, often to the point of suffering extreme psychic damage. Sometimes, they are led to their doom by conniving women—or by perfectly innocent women who just happen inadvertently to bring out the worst in these men. More often, however, the lost men of film noir are led to their doom by the circumstances in which they live, so that their failures can be taken as a criticism of the capitalist system and of the whole concept of the American Dream.

That such characters would arise in a genre rooted in the anxieties of the Depression and World War II should come as no surprise. But, of course, a whole generation of American men in the years after the war were suffering from considerable (often undiagnosed) psychic damage as a result of their traumatic wartime experiences. Meanwhile, the postwar years were filled with a number of anxieties of their own, as American men had to adapt to changing gender roles in the domestic space as well as changing roles in the increasingly corporate public world of the workplace. Any number of American films beyond film noir expressed these anxieties. For example, the embattled state of American manhood in the late 1950s is perhaps best captured in Jack Arnold's memorable *The Incredible Shrinking Man* (1957), scripted by Richard Matheson based on Matheson's 1956 novel, *The Shrinking Man*. In the film, protagonist Robert Scott Carey (Grant Williams) is accidentally exposed first to a strange, floating, radioactive cloud, then to pesticides, causing him to start to shrink. The film thus reflects contemporary concerns about both radioactive and chemical contamination, but the real focus is on the psychic impact of the shrinkage on Carey, who grows increasingly bitter and withdrawn (even toward his loyal and faithful wife, Louise, played by Randy Stuart) as his decreasing size makes him feel more and more like a freak, unlike anyone else in the world.[1]

If Carey thus becomes a marker of the general alienation felt by so many in the 1950s, his predicament also dramatizes a typical 1950s fear of being overwhelmed by forces larger than oneself. The fact that he remains entrapped in his own home gives those forces a particularly domestic twist, especially in the way Carey experiences his decreasing size as a loss of virility. Size does matter, apparently, and much of his resentment toward Louise comes from his realization that, as he gets smaller and smaller, he is increasingly unable to fulfill his conjugal obligations, coming to feel more and more emasculated.

The Incredible Shrinking Man actually has a great deal in common with film noir, anticipating later films—such as *Blade Runner* (1982)—that would more famously combine science fiction with noir. All boundaries tend to be porous where noir is concerned, and virtually any kind of noir film might potentially contain a lost-man character. I am concerned here, though, with films in which a classic lost man is the principal (typically the point of view) character. Of the films originally associated with film noir by Frank and Chartier, two might be considered lost-man films of this type, both directed by Billy Wilder. In *Double Indemnity* (1944), insurance salesman Walter Neff (Fred MacMurray) leads a soulless existence—then thinks he has spotted a chance to achieve wealth, romance, and adventure thanks to meeting Phyllis Dietrichson (Barbara Stanwyck). The resulting web of seduction, murder, and deceit makes this film a classic noir films, while making Dietrichson the prototypical femme fatale character and Stanwyck the ultimate femme fatale actress. Cowritten by Wilder and hardboiled legend Raymond Chandler epitomizes film noir as much as any other single film. However, because the character of Dietrichson has played such a crucial role in noir history, *Double Indemnity* will be considered among the female-oriented noir films in the third section of this volume.[2]

The other Wilder film identified as an original noir film was *The Lost Weekend* (1945), one that is these days often considered not to be noir at all because its plot differs so substantially from those of most noir films. *The Lost Weekend* also seems a bit outside the noir tradition in that it was accepted so enthusiastically into the

Hollywood mainstream, winning the Academy Award for Best Picture, an Oscar for Best Director for Wilder, and an Oscar for Best Actor for Ray Milland. (It won a fourth Oscar for Best Adapted Screenplay for Wilder and the female science fiction writer Leigh Brackett.) Here Milland stars as Don Birnam, an alcoholic writer who gradually unravels as a result of his malady. In this sense, it is very much a lost-man noir film, except for the fact that, in the end, Birnam (with the help of a good woman) triumphs over his demons, gives up drinking, and resolves to write a novel about the evils of alcohol. Even this ending, though, cannot obscure the essential darkness of the remainder of the film.

Fritz Lang, the other great master of the lost-man film noir, was (like Wilder) an import from the German film industry. In Lang's *The Woman in the Window* (1944), mild-mannered psychology professor Richard Wanley (Edward G. Robinson) bemoans the fact that middle age finds him living a stodgy, routine, and increasingly uninteresting life. Then he spots a portrait of a woman in a store window that sends him drifting into fantasy, only later (apparently) to meet the woman who is the subject of the painting. Predictably, especially with his matronly wife and their kids out of town for the summer, Wanley's meeting with femme fatale Alice Reed (Joan Bennett) leads only to trouble. But the trouble becomes surprisingly intense when Reed's paramour, millionaire Claude Mazard (Arthur Loft), bursts into her apartment and attacks Wanley, who then kills Mazard in self-defense. Things go from bad to worse, until Wanley finally decides to commit suicide, in an ending made more tragic by the fact that, in an apparent deus ex machina twist, Heidt is shot down by police, seemingly letting Wanley and Reed off the hook, but too late. Never fear, though, Wanley then awakes to find that the whole misadventure was a dream—an ending that was necessitated by the Hollywood Production Code, which sometimes forced film noir to become more complex and cleverer, but in this case simply imposed a fairly lame ending on what is otherwise a genuinely interesting film noir. In particular, *The Woman in the Window* indicates the ways in which bourgeois comfort and respectability can lead to a numbing routinization, but can also be taken away in a heartbeat, especially if one breaks even the tiniest rule of bourgeois propriety. The depiction of the professor as out of his element in this world of seductive women and violent men is also a variation on a key noir theme (the ordinary man unable to cope with extraordinary circumstances and thus driven to his doom), though the fact that he seems to act so stupidly when faced with the real world, rather than the theoretical one of his books, is a bit problematic and potentially anti-intellectual.

Similar themes would be revisited in Lang's *Scarlet Street* the very next year, with much the same cast. This time Robinson stars as Chris Cross, a henpecked middle-aged husband and lowly cashier who dreams of being an artist. Bennett returns as Kitty March, a femme fatale who becomes the focus of Cross's fantasies of escape from the boring routine of his life. Duryea returns as Johnny, her boyfriend, who helps her con Cross into stealing money to rent an apartment for her, with predictably disastrous results. This one ends with another would-be suicide—which couldn't succeed, due to the Production Code—though what follows is perhaps even darker.

Robinson's two films with Lang show the way in which the American Dream can fail, even for respectable, seemingly ordinary American men. Edgar G. Ulmer's *Detour* (1945), on the other hand, focuses on a much more marginal figure. Here, Al Roberts (Tom Neal) is one of life's outcast losers, excluded from the American Dream altogether. *Detour* is a much more marginal film as well, shot quickly and on a shoestring budget. The result, though, is a noir masterpiece that illustrates much of what has made film noir such an important part of American cinematic history. Though he attempts to achieve his dreams, Roberts is a pessimist who finds it hard to believe that life can bring him anything but misery. As discussed in detail in this section, events of the film tend to suggest that he is right, though they also suggest that capitalism, rather than fate, is the real culprit.

The year 1947 was good for lost-man noir, seeing the release of two key examples from the genre. The lost man of Jacques Tourneur's *Out of the Past* is a former private detective (played by Robert Mitchum, one of noir's biggest stars), so it combines lost-man noir with detective noir. It also features another key example of a femme fatale in Jane Greer's Kathie Moffatt, who leads the protagonist astray. It thus joins *Double Indemnity* as an excellent example of a film noir that spans multiple categories. *Out of the Past* will be discussed in detail in this section. Edmund Goulding's *Nightmare Alley*, based on the 1946 novel by William Lindsay Gresham, had to considerably tone down both the politics and the lost man of the novel (played here by A-list star Tyrone Power), but it is still a solid film noir.

André de Toth's *Pitfall* (1948) is something like *Double Indemnity* lite. Here, ethically lost insurance man John Forbes (Dick Powell) is ultimately led to kill by his illicit love for a woman, but the killing isn't really murder (since it is partly a form of self-defense) and the woman involved, Mona Stevens (Lizabeth Scott) is just a lonely girl trying to get ahead and not quite manipulative enough to be a true femme fatale. In fact, the real villain of the piece is a private detective named MacDonald (Raymond Burr), whose (barely encouraged) lust for Stevens and unscrupulous methods in pursuing that lust are the real source of all the film's trouble. Even MacDonald, though, doesn't rise to the level of psychopathic evil that is often found in film noir, remaining at the level of mere smarminess. Silver and Ward call *Pitfall* "the key film noir detailing the fall of the errant husband from bourgeois respectability."[3] This aspect of the film, of course, is a bit clichéd, but the film's exploration of the emptiness of the American Dream is, in fact, quite cogent.

D.O.A. (1950), directed by the talented noir cinematographer Rudolph Maté, features another bored American male who gets into trouble while in search of adventure—though in this case the trouble actually emanates from his routine work and not from his attempt to escape that work. This film also, as much as any other noir film, illustrates the tendency of many noir protagonists to be doomed, no matter what they do in the present day of the film, possibly for something they did much earlier. The film begins with a frame narrative in which Frank Bigelow (Edmond

O'Brien), an accountant in the small California town of Banning, staggers into a Los Angeles police station to announce that he has been murdered. Most of the film is a flashback, detailing the story he then tells the police.

Among the many other "lost-man" noir films, special mention should be reserved for *In a Lonely Place* (1950), directed by Nicholas Ray, whose *Rebel Without a Cause* (1955) would become one of the great cinematic exploration of 1950s male alienation. Among other things, *In a Lonely Place* features Humphrey Bogart in what is perhaps his greatest noir performance. Though set within the Hollywood film industry, this genuinely dark postwar film actually contains little overt criticism of the film industry, leaving it for audiences to draw their own conclusions in that regard. Instead, the darkness of this film itself derives almost exclusively from the personal demons of protagonist Dixon Steele (Humphrey Bogart), a bitter and violent screenwriter. Steele's radical alienation may arise in part from his experiences with the film industry (and with capitalism as a whole), but that possibility is never overtly explored in the film. Instead, we are left to speculate on the causes of his angst, with hints that it might be rooted in his experiences in World War II.

THE NEO-NOIR LOST MAN

Lost men continued to populate noir films in the neo-noir era, especially given the fact that the collapse of the Production Code allowed neo-noir film to feature more extreme characters. Perhaps the clearest example of this phenomenon concerns neo-noir adaptations of the novels of Jim Thompson, who had been the mad genius of lost-man fiction during the time of the original noir cycle. However, his men were so radically estranged (and deranged) that his works simply couldn't be adapted to film under the terms of the Production Code. The collapse of the Code made it more thinkable to adapt the works of Thompson, though the first neo-noir adaptations of Thompson's work—Sam Peckinpah's 1972 adaptation of Thompson's 1958 novel *The Getaway* and Burt Kennedy's 1976 adaptation of Thompson's 1952 novel *The Killer Inside Me*—were both considerably bowdlerized in relation to the original novels. There was then some movement toward more faithful adherence to the spirit (if not the details) of Thompson originals in two slightly later French films: *Série noire* (1979), Alain Courneau's adaptation of *A Hell of a Woman* (1954), and *Coup de Torchon* (1981), Bernard Tavernier's adaptation of *Pop. 1280* (1963). Thompson himself was also the subject of a literary revival in the 1980s and 1990s; a revival partly spurred by the crucial role given Thompson in Geoffrey O'Brien's excellent survey of pulp crime fiction, *Hardboiled America: Lurid Paperbacks and the Masters of Noir* (first published in 1981). This revival saw the majority of Thompson's novels come back into print and led to the publication of two book-length biographies: Michael McCauley's *Jim Thompson: Sleep with the Devil* (1991) and Robert Polito's award-winning *Savage Art: A Biography of Jim Thompson* (1995). Amid this revival, Hollywood again turned to Thompson with a flurry of film adaptations of his work, beginning with *The Kill-Off* in 1989 and then two films from 1990: James Foley's *After Dark, My Sweet* and Stephen Frears's *The Grifters* (based on Thompson's 1963 novel). These two films were then followed by a second adaptation of *The Getaway* (1994) and by *Hit Me*, a 1996 adaptation of Thompson's 1954 novel *A Swell-Looking Babe*.[4] Of all these neo-noir adaptations of Thompson, *The Grifters* was probably the most successful as a film, though *After Dark, My Sweet* was probably the most faithful to Thompson's original vision. It also features a protagonist who is a classic noir lost man, even if lacks the murderous insanity of the typical Thompson protagonist.

Other neo-noir lost men appeared in remakes of classic noir lost-man films, including such examples from the 1980s as *Against All Odds* (a 1984 remake of *Out of the Past*) and an updated *D.O.A.* (1988). Among original lost-man neo-noir films of that decade, Ivan Passer's *Cutter's Way* (1981) stands out as a competent thriller whose lost men are essentially emblems of the lost potential of the failed counterculture of the 1960s and 1970s. Meanwhile, Rutger Hauer's title character in Robert Harmon's *The Hitcher* (1986) is one of the most chillingly deranged villains in all neo-noir film.

Moving into the 1990s, the three central criminals of Carl Franklin's *One False Move* (1992) represent the key noir trope of soulless criminals on the run, wreaking havoc while the cops close in. Paul Schrader's *Affliction* (1997) is neo-noir at its most bleak. It nominally features a police investigation, but the real focus is on the character (and the existential angst) of the film's central cop, Nick Nolte's Wade Whitehouse, whose descent from a position of respect to the role of unhinged killer is the real topic of the film—and the real aspect of the film that takes it into noir territory. And, of course, Bryan Singer's 1995 neo-noir hit *The Usual Suspects* is a particularly interesting case of a noir lost man because it revolves around one "Keyser Söze," who might not even exist. Then again, "Söze" might just be an alias for Kevin Spacey's Verbal Kint, whose overtly unreliable narration provides most of the plot of the film—which thus might not have ever happened, throwing pretty much everything about this film into doubt.

The neo-noir period of lost-man film was then topped off by the Coen brothers' *The Man Who Wasn't There* (2001), perhaps the most extensive attempt to make a neo-noir film that looks and feels exactly like an original noir film, yet still adds additional updating touches. Heavily influenced by *Double Indemnity*, this film features Billy Bob Thornton as protagonist Ed Crane, a barber whose profession is typical of the pointlessness of his life: he keeps cutting hair, but the hair keeps growing back, and he ultimately gets nowhere. Indeed, as the very title of the film makes clear, Crane is a classic lost-man character, emotionally dead and completely alienated from the world around him, feeling that his life is pointless and empty.

While *The Man Who Wasn't There* might well be the quintessential neo-noir lost-man film, such films continued to be made well into the twenty-first century. One example that is worthy of note is David Cronenberg's *A History of Violence* (2005), in which a former gangster (played by Viggo Mortensen) has settled down into a peaceful small-town life, only to have his violent past come back to haunt him, somewhat in the mode of *Out of the Past*. Based on a 1997 graphic novel written by John Wagner and drawn by Vince Locke, Cronenberg's film eschews the gritty, noirish black-and-white art of the original, opting for a more straightforward realistic style. It also tones down the horrifying violence of the graphic novel, which keeps it in neo-noir territory, while a more faithful adaptation would have probably pushed it into the realm of the neo-noir.

Having noted that *A History of Violence* qualifies as neo-noir, it should probably also be recalled that I noted in the introduction to the volume that another graphic novel adaptation from 2005, Robert Rodriguez and Frank Miller's *Sin City* (2005) is clearly a revisionary noir. In this sense, one might also mention Sam Mendes's 2002 graphic novel adaptation *Road to Perdition*, which opts for a realistic visual style and tones down the violence of the original comic, thus keeping the film within the realm of neo-noir. Other comic adaptations that might be considered neo-noir lost-man films include *From Hell* (2001) and *V for Vendetta* (2006).

THE REVISIONARY NOIR LOST MAN

A number of key revisionary noir films featuring lost men have been remakes of earlier noir or neo-noir novel adaptations that went beyond the original film and captured more of the spirit of the novel in portraying the travails of lost men. Examples of such remakes include Michael Winterbottom's *The Killer Inside Me* (2010), which goes well beyond the 1976 neo-noir adaptation to capture more of the dark spirit of Jim Thompson's 1952 novel. Meanwhile, Guillermo del Toro's 2021 remake of *Nightmare Alley*, the original 1947 film noir adaptation of that novel, captured considerably more of the texture of the original novel. The remade *The Killer Inside Me* will be discussed in detail in this section.

Noir film in the early twenty-first century has been marked by considerable variety, as noir motifs have been used to enrich any number of films, including some that go well beyond the narrative models that were typical of the original noir cycle. For example, Dan Gilroy's *Nightcrawler* (2014) features Jake Gyllenhaal as Lou Bloom, a petty criminal with big ambitions, just looking for the proper gimmick that will help him strike it rich. He finds something that works when he hits on the idea of shooting video of crime and accident scenes, then selling the video to the news department of a local TV station. Predictably, the unscrupulous Bloom pushes things too far, leading to the death of his assistant in a shutout between police and drug dealers that has been set up by Bloom himself. The truly lost Bloom feels absolutely no remorse, however, and ends the film expanding his highly successful operation with new employees. Meanwhile, his unethical, sensational approach seems to infect the TV news department as well, suggesting that his attitude is typical of a media environment that is willing to trade ethics for spectacle (and thus higher ratings). The original noir cycle occasionally veered into media critique—as in Billy Wilder's

Ace in the Hole (1951), about an unscrupulous newspaper reporter—but never to the extent seen in this film (though the cinematography of nighttime Los Angeles in this film is often classic noir).

Particularly notable among recent examples of revisionary lost-man noir is Lynne Ramsay's *You Were Never Really Here* (2017), which could have easily been called *The Man Who Wasn't There* had that title not already been taken. But Ramsay's film is a far more radical exploration of the theme than the Coens' film had been, moving into revisionary noir territory in the depth of its exploration of its central character. Here, Joaquin Phoenix delivers an outstanding noir performance as "Joe," a man so damaged by a lifetime of trauma that he hardly has any selfhood left. "I'm just a hired gun," as he says at one point, and he is indeed essentially reduced to his function in that capacity (though he tends to prefer the brutality of a ball peen hammer as a killing weapon). Joe does have some personal connection to his aging (and also damaged) mother, perhaps because of their shared trauma at the hands of Joe's abusive father in Joe's childhood. Joe now specializes in rescuing young girls who have been the victims of sex trafficking, but his attempt to rescue the daughter of a New York state senator leads him into a powerful political conspiracy that drives the plot of the film. He rescues the girl, but almost everyone he knows (including his mother) is killed in the process, leaving us to wonder exactly where Joe (and the girl, whose only remaining parent is also killed) will go from there. (One might compare here Fincher's 2023 Netflix film *The Killer*, which also features a professional killer, but one who is motivated primarily by money and who is explored in far less interesting ways, keeping the film in the realm of neo-noir.)

Among other standout examples of revisionary noir films about lost men are two films that, at first, seem to belong to other genres. Andrew Dominik's 2012 *Killing Them Softly* is, on the surface, a gangster film involving two Mafia hit men. But both Brad Pitt's Jackie Cogan and James Gandolfini's Mickey also qualify as lost men. The once-formidable Mickey has broken down into almost complete dysfunctionality by the time the action of the film begins, while Jackie, though still a competent hit man, has descended into total cynicism. In fact, almost everyone in this film is cynical or broken, or both, though placing the action in the midst of the 2008 financial crisis suggests that there might be systemic reasons why the characters would be in this condition. As Cogan puts it, in a classic noir expression of cynicism about the American dream, "I'm living in America, and in America you're on your own. America's not a country. It's just a business." In a somewhat similar multigeneric vein, S. Craig Zahler's brutal *Dragged Across Concrete* (2018) is a combination heist film and cop buddy film, but its central character, Mel Gibson's Detective Brett Ridgeman, clearly qualifies as a lost man. Ridgeman has not advanced in his career (largely due to his own questionable behavior), but he clearly blames the system for his loss of advancement and for his inability to provide for his wife and daughter in the way he feels he should. As a result, he resorts to a life of robbing criminals, rather than arresting them, with deadly results for himself (while one of his criminal targets ends up living in luxury, proving that crime can pay, after all).

Finally, the third film to be discussed in detail among the revisionary noir films in this section is *Uncut Gems* (2019), directed by Josh and Benny Safdie. Here, protagonist Howard Ratner (Adam Sandler) is a New York jeweler who travels in some decidedly questionable company, mostly because of his gambling addiction. He conceives a plan to make a big score in the gem business that will solve his ever-pressing money problems, but (being a noir lost man) all of his best-laid plans of course go astray—with tragic results. Ratner is a particularly interesting lost man, while this film's inside look at the New York jewelry business gives us an especially vivid milieu. However, what really pushes this film into the realm of revisionary noir is the overt Jewishness of the cultural world in which Ratner lives, something that is unprecedented in noir film, a fact that in itself calls attention to the substantial contributions made to noir film by Jewish filmmakers and performers, contributions that have hitherto been significantly underappreciated.

Chapter 8

The Film Noir Lost Man: *Detour*

(1945, Directed by Edgar G. Ulmer)

The Austro-Hungarian immigrant Edgar G. Ulmer built an almost legendary reputation as a low-budget auteur, famed for being able to produce artfully made genre films quickly and on a minuscule budget. His daring 1934 horror masterpiece *The Black Cat* (starring both Boris Karloff and Bela Lugosi) and his film noir masterpiece *Detour* (1945) are especially impressive achievements. Shot in a few days on a shoestring budget, *Detour*, in particular, has become a noir classic. Its vision of a down-and-out protagonist whose difficulties mirror larger problems in American society as a whole, captures the absolute essence of the noir spirit, while its visual texture very nicely matches its thematic content.

Detour begins as protagonist Al Roberts (Tom Neal) hitchhikes the back roads of America, stopping off at a roadside diner in Nevada. There, he hears a love song ("I Can't Believe That You're in Love with Me," a popular standard that dates back to 1926) playing on the jukebox, which triggers a chain of memories that explains how he got to this point and that provides the actual narrative of the film. This diner setting and this flashback structure are both quintessential noir motifs, just as Roberts will turn out to be a paradigmatic noir lost man, done in by a seemingly malicious fate, not to mention by a venal, malicious woman and an economic system built on exploitation and inequality. But this scene also tips us off that there might be some special artistry in this film. As Roberts begins to sink into memories, the camera focuses in on the coffee cup on the counter in front of him, which suddenly seems absurdly huge, giving the moment a surreal touch. The camera then moves from the round rim of the coffee cup to zoom in on the round record spinning in the jukebox. A cut then takes us to a closeup of the round bass drum of a drum kit, huge and white like the coffee cup, filling the screen with what at first looks like a full moon. These circular images thus provide a transition to Roberts's past in New York, while also providing a kind of visual key to the narrative structure of the film, which is, itself, circular. In addition, all of these circles can be taken to suggest the way in which Roberts is trapped in his life, continually moving in circles.

The early moments set in New York provide crucial background to the main narrative of Roberts's cross-country journey to Los Angeles, establishing that he was already bitter, broken, and cynical, even before his journey began. The drum belongs to the band playing at the somewhat seedy Break O' Dawn Club back in New York, where Roberts works as a piano player. He is, the film makes clear, a gifted pianist, adept at a number of different musical styles, including classical. However, due to events that are not explained in the film, his career has never really gotten off the ground, relegating him to playing in this dingy club.

Roberts is thus established as a man with considerable talent who has never gotten the opportunity to use it and has thus never gotten the recognition he deserves. In this sense (and in the film's later treatment of the Hollywood film industry), it is difficult not to see this film as being heavily influenced by Ulmer's own sense of having never gotten the appreciation he deserved for his talents as a director. Viewed in this way, the various artistic flourishes that punctuate *Detour* take on an additional significance. If the film's artistry seems a bit out of place in such a rough-hewn, low-budget film, this disjunction might be interpreted as a suggestion of the mismatch between the high-art films that Ulmer might have made if given the chance, and the B-grade films he was actually allowed to make. As Roberts himself says in the film, "Those guys out in Hollywood don't know the real thing when it's right in front of them."

Roberts's fiancée, Sue Harvey (Claudia Drake), works in the Break O' Dawn Club as a singer but dreams of bigger and better things. One of the songs that she performs most frequently is "I Can't Believe That You're in Love with Me," explaining its special significance for Roberts. She attempts to be supportive of Roberts, as when she suggests, on hearing him play, that he will "make Carnegie Hall." "Yeah," he says bitterly, "as a janitor. I'll make my debut in the basement." Meanwhile, convinced that she will never be able to fulfill her own dreams in New York, Sue decides to go to Hollywood to try to become a star, even though she and Al are apparently on the verge of marriage. However, both Sue and Al seem oddly uncommitted to pursuing a life together, so Roberts, skeptical of the whole Hollywood idea, decides to stay behind. His dreams having already been crushed in New York, he can't imagine Sue's dreams faring much better in Hollywood. Meanwhile, in Hollywood, Sue finds that stardom is not so easy to come by and ends up working as a waitress. Learning of this in a long-distance phone call that is presented in the film as a sort of technological miracle, Roberts decides to travel across the country to marry her, after all.

Sue's dream of making it big in Hollywood can be taken as commentary on the function of Hollywood in the American popular imagination, suggesting that the film industry serves as a sort of stand-in for the whole American culture of upward mobility.[1] At the same time, her subsequent failure to achieve her dreams suggests just how misleading this culture—with its suggestion that anyone can be a success if they simply work hard enough—can be. Hollywood, of course, is the perfect illustration of this point, given that so many young people (especially young women) have in fact gone there with hopes of becoming stars, only to have those hopes dashed on the rocks of reality. At the same time, it is also tempting to see this use of Hollywood as another somewhat bitter commentary on Ulmer's own career.[2]

In any case, Hollywood quickly fades into the background as *Detour* shifts into a focus on Roberts's attempts to get across the country to join Sue in California, placing the film within the great American genre of the road narrative. However, he has no cash for the trip, triggering Roberts's speech about the evils of money—or at least of the lack of it—that forms a crucial gloss on the film as a whole:

> Money: you know what that is. It's the stuff you never have enough of. Little green things with George Washington's picture that men slave for, commit crimes for, die for. It's the stuff that has caused more trouble in the world than anything else we ever invented, simply because there's too little of it. At least I had too little of it.

This declaration, at first glance, seems to resemble the traditional Christian notion that the love of money is the root of all evil. Roberts, though, sees the *lack* of money as the real problem and would presumably see having money as a good thing, indeed. Roberts's statement about money, then, is not a rejection of wealth, but a rejection of economic inequality of the kind that reigns in capitalist America, when guys like himself remain mired in poverty, while the more fortunate (though no more deserving) might be rolling in wealth. Roberts, though, is no socialist, and one gets the impression that he has no objection to wealth in general—he just feels that there must be something fundamentally wrong with a system in which he has none.[3]

Lacking the cash to travel any other way, Roberts decides to hitchhike to California. Things look up when he is picked up by the seemingly prosperous Charles Haskell (Edmund MacDonald), who is driving to Los Angeles and offers Roberts a ride the rest of the way. Roberts cheers up momentarily, envisioning a future "which couldn't have been brighter if I had embroidered it in neon lights." In this upbeat mood, he imagines Sue as a star in Hollywood, performing a glitzy version of "I Can't Believe That You're in Love with Me." However, his vision is shown on the screen at a skewed angle, giving it a dreamlike quality and perhaps suggesting that it is unrealistic.

Reality immediately intrudes into Roberts's fantasies, however, as a sudden outburst of rain begins to drench the open car—almost as if the gods can't stand the idea of Roberts being happy, even for a moment. Haskell, who has been popping pills the entire trip, is asleep (or unconscious, or dead) in the passenger seat, and Roberts, driving, is unable to awaken him. He stops the car to put the top up and opens the passenger-side door to try to get to Haskell to wake him up. Instead, Haskell falls from the car, hits his head on a rock—at this point definitely dead. In this film, Roberts's luck is almost comically bad, and Roberts himself suggests in his voiceover that people would probably laugh in disbelief when he explained how Haskell died; in fact, the very unbelievability of the story causes Roberts to panic and to assume that he will be accused of killing Haskell.[4] He decides to hide the body and continue on in the car. Realizing that he cannot get far without money, he reluctantly takes Haskell's wallet, which contains $768 and identification that will allow Roberts to pose as Haskell.

Roberts manages to reach California, where he picks up an attractive, but embittered and bedraggled, woman hitchhiker, who tells him to call her Vera (played by Ann Savage). Vera soon becomes Roberts's worst nightmare, attempting to exploit him in her own effort to achieve the American Dream. In another unlikely turn, she had earlier hitched a ride with Haskell. She accuses Roberts of murdering Haskell, then threatens to tell the police if Roberts does not do as she says. He then becomes her virtual prisoner as they make their way to Los Angeles. For her part, Vera is one of the meanest, nastiest, and most poorly groomed femmes fatales in all of film noir. As Dickos puts it, she is "one of the most unrelenting and frightening females in noir cinema."[5] Filled with hate, Vera not only exploits Roberts mercilessly but seems to take great pleasure in inflicting suffering on him, as if seeking revenge on all the men (including Haskell) who have previously wronged *her*. She is almost like a force from another world, so malignant as to seem more at home in a horror film than in a noir film. Unlike the typical femme fatale, meanwhile, she makes no effort to use her sexual charms to maneuver Roberts into doing what she wants; instead, she employs a combination of bullying and threats, while Roberts accepts her domination rather meekly. At the same time, Vera seems sexually experienced (she clearly has the aura of a prostitute around her), even predatory; she seems willing to use Roberts for her own sexual pleasure more than she is inclined to offer him favors as a way of inducing his cooperation. In any case, without giving any details, the film portrays Vera in such a way that one suspects that some very bad things have happened to her, making her at least a partly sympathetic figure.

Knowing that Haskell had been estranged from his family for more than fifteen years, Vera concocts a plan for Roberts to go on pretending to be Haskell (hoping they won't notice the switch) so that he can claim the inheritance when Haskell's ailing father dies. When Roberts finally balks and refuses to cooperate, a drunken Vera decides to call the police. Roberts then accidentally strangles her with the phone cord (through a closed and locked door) in the subsequent altercation—in a scene even more improbable than the one in which Haskell has been killed. This moment seems ridiculous, but Coursen notes that "it is the very implausibility of the action, juxtaposed with the ordinariness of the milieu—a nightclub, an apartment, a used car lot, and, of course, the road—that gives the film much of its force," emphasizing that sense that Roberts is doomed by forces beyond his power to resist, or even understand, forces that are "irrational, relentless, malevolent."[6] Roberts, of course, is once again convinced that he will be blamed for the killing (this time with a bit more justification), but it is also clear that Vera's death is almost a relief, seeming at the time almost a divine intervention, allowing Roberts to escape her domination.

This death also triggers one of the film's most famous moments, as the camera moves about the room, going in and out of focus, suggesting Roberts's confusion and panic and again giving the scene a dreamlike quality. The oneiric quality that appears so often in film noir is, in fact, on full display in *Detour*, which features a number of such scenes, many of them in actual dreams. There are also other genuinely strange moments in the film that seem designed to reflect Roberts's psychological state. On two different occasions, for example, he complains about the saxophone music that is driving him crazy. Saxophone music can indeed be heard on the soundtrack at both these moments; however, it does not appear to be coming from the world of the film but is instead part of the soundtrack. One possibility, of course, is that the film's low budget simply did not allow for the kind of sound editing that could make this music appear to be literally coming from outside Roberts's hotel and that the filmmakers just had to make do with the resources at their command. Another interpretation might be that Roberts, becoming increasingly divorced from reality, is merely imagining the music.

In any case, the actual effect of these saxophone references is to introduce a moment of strangeness into the film that is similar to the effect that occurs during an earlier scene in which Roberts is hitchhiking and the negatives seem to have been flipped, so that cars are suddenly shown driving on the left side of the road. There are, in fact, a number of minor continuity errors in the film, most of which were no doubt a result of the hurried, low-budget production schedule. There are, however, enough intentional artistic flourishes introduced into the film to make it clear that it would not have been inconsistent with the overall texture of the film for these "errors" to have been introduced intentionally, so that seeing them as enhancing the texture of the film, however inadvertently, is not inappropriate.

Vera's death forces Roberts to give up his dream of marrying Sue and to go on the lam, hitchhiking back eastward across America. For a moment, things seem to be looking up, as Roberts informs us that Haskell's body has been mistaken for Roberts's and that Vera has been assumed to have been killed by Haskell. But Roberts then imagines a future moment when he will nevertheless be stopped by police, then arrested and loaded into their cop car, the implication clearly being that he is headed for a conviction for murder. Meanwhile, he presents this expectation as an illustration of the fact that, at any moment, "fate, or some mysterious force, can put the finger on you or me for no good reason at all." This mysterious force has, after all, already put its finger on Roberts multiple times—little wonder that he expects the future to be no different.

Isenberg speculates that this last scene was probably added because the Code censors were adamant that Roberts could not be seen to be escaping from the consequence of his deeds in any sense.[7] At the same time, this sudden swerve in the narrative is perfectly consistent with the cobbled-together nature of the whole film, and Roberts's imagined demise at the end seems very much in keeping with the pessimism of the rest of the film. Roberts seems to regard himself as the victim of blind fate and pure bad luck, but it is also clear that his main misfortune is simply a lack of cash, thus suggesting that the American Dream, which so thoroughly fails to materialize in this film, is only available to those who can make the payments. The emphasis on luck and fate, in turn, suggests that those who can make these payments can do so more by chance than because of their own hard work or ability, except perhaps their ability to exploit others.

This message is a subversive one for an American film in 1945, and Ulmer was probably able to get away with it largely because his low-budget films were considered so insignificant that the powers that be simply took no notice of them. Meanwhile, for Naremore, *Detour* "provides justification for the idea that down-market thrillers are more authentic, less compromised by bourgeois-liberal sentiment or totalitarian spectacle, than the usual Hollywood product."[8] In any case, *Detour* is one of the oddest and shabbiest masterpieces in all of world culture. But it is a masterpiece, nevertheless.

Chapter 9

The Film Noir Lost Man: *Out of the Past*

(1947, Directed by Jacques Tourneur)

Jacques Tourneur's *Out of the Past* is one of the most representative of all noir films. It contains some of film noir's most famous cinematography (courtesy of Nicholas Musuraca), stars one of its most important actors (Robert Mitchum), and features one of its most seductive and dangerous femmes fatales (played by Jane Greer). Its narrative structure, which involves a series of intrusions of the past into the present, is a classic device of noir storytelling. And its central theme, as the title indicates, involves a classic noir message: the difficulty of escaping the mistakes of the past—though in this case there is an extra wrinkle involving a larger historical vision.

In *Out of the Past*, protagonist Jeff Markham (Mitchum) is a private detective, though he ultimately functions in this film as more of a noir lost man, careening from one personal crisis to another and doing very little actual detective work. He is hired by gambler/gangster Whit Sterling (Kirk Douglas) to find his runaway girlfriend, Kathie Moffat (Greer). Markham finds Greer hiding out in Mexico, but then falls in love with her himself and decides to try to have a life with her without Sterling's knowledge, literally trying to become "lost." This decision initiates a web of deceit with disastrous consequences for almost everyone involved. The plot, however, is quite complex. For example, in keeping with the frequent nonlinear narrative style of film noir, *Out of the Past* begins late in the story, as Markham (now calling himself Jeff Bailey and having parted ways with Moffat) is attempting to live a quiet life running his own gas station in the California mountain town of Bridgeport, enjoying the peaceful, natural surroundings and having at last apparently found a good woman to love. This woman, Ann Miller (Virginia Huston), thus serves as a symbolic counterpart to Moffat's femme fatale, though the two never come into direct contact. The opposition between Moffat and Miller is thus a relatively small part of the film, serving as only one of many stark contrasts in the film. For example, the idyllic setting in Bridgeport stands in sharp opposition to big-city corruption of the kind that prevails in New York, Sterling's home base at the beginning of the film. In addition, Bailey's deaf-mute employee—generally referred to simply as "The Kid," though played by twenty-two-year-old Dickie Moore—is presented as a paragon of innocence and virtue, standing in sharp contrast to the fallen condition of most of the older characters. Such contrasts help to highlight the central theme, suggesting that, once one enters the corrupt world of modern civilization, it is impossible to escape back into the purity of nature.

Bailey's plan to settle down is immediately disrupted when Whit's lieutenant Joe Stefanos (Paul Valentine) happens into town and discovers Markham, who subsequently realizes that he has not escaped his past, after all. Stefanos informs Markham that Sterling wants to see him at the gangster's new home in Lake Tahoe, only a short drive away. Under the circumstances, Jeff decides he had better tell Miller about his past. The majority of the first half of the film is then an extended flashback that dramatizes the story he tells her, showing how (roughly three years earlier) he tracked Moffat to Acapulco, where he immediately realized that he wants her for himself. The two struck up a relationship, living in a sort of dream world that allows them to avoid dealing with the difficult situation in which they find themselves. In this sense, Mexico serves, as it often does in film noir (and in Golden Age Hollywood film in general) as a sort of alternative to modern American civilization, a pastoral land where life is slow and easy, free of the bothers of the competitive world of modern capitalism.

Kathie herself is figured as such an escape for Jeff. When he sees her coming toward him on the beach in Acapulco, it gives him a feeling "like school was out," making clear the sense in which she provides for him an escape from the chores and responsibilities of everyday life and into a world of adventure and romance. He will, in fact, show a tendency to imagine women as solutions to his particular problems throughout *Out of the Past*. In this case, bored with the routine of the workaday world, he sees Kathie as a key to a more exciting life. Later, having discovered that this exciting life brings only disaster, he sees Ann Miller as a respite from adventure and as the key to a more stable and secure domestic existence.

Jeff and Kathie escape to San Francisco, where he supports the two of them by running his own shabby, "bottom-of-the-barrel" detective agency, which he is willing to do in order to be with Kathie. In this film, however, the past is inescapable. Jeff's smarmy former partner from New York, Jack Fisher (Steve Brodie), shows up in San Francisco and spots them, forcing the couple to split up: Jeff heads for Los Angeles, making sure that it is easy for Fisher to follow him, thus throwing him off the trail of Kathie. The characters of this film are constantly on the move from one location to another, and one of the film's key contrasts is between the constant movement of characters in the modern world and the relative stasis of life in Bridgeport.

Figure 9.1. Jeff Bailey/Jeff Marham (Robert Mitchum) and Kathie Moffat (Jane Greer) in
***Out of the Past*. RKO Radio Pictures/Photofest © RKO Radio Pictures**

This contrast, though, is complicated by the fact that Bailey's gas station is something of an emblem of modern mobility. Indeed, Bailey, despite his attempts to fit in, is viewed with suspicion by many of the locals as an intruder from a more modern (and less stable) outside world. As Stefanos arrives at the station and begins to ask The Kid about Bailey, we see an old-fashioned wooden church building in the background, emphasizing the function of Bridgeport as a bastion of old-fashioned values, as does a subsequent shot of their conversation from a different angle, showing an American flag flying in the background. Learning that Baily is not in, Stefanos then walks across the street to Marny's Café, another rather old-fashioned establishment, one that clearly caters to regulars rather than to travelers like Stefanos. Thus, though it might at first glance seem to be in the same family as the diner and roadhouses so prevalent in film noir, those establishments are places of mobility and impermanence, stopping off points for weary travelers such as Al Roberts in *Detour*. The cafe, run by the loquacious Marny, is a sort of home away from home, featuring countrified items of decor such as deer's heads on the wall and offering services to local fishermen such as freezing their fish for them.

The film then cuts immediately from Marny's to an idyllic mountain lake, where The Kid has just arrived in a convertible, while Jeff and Ann (accompanied by romantic musical cues) are doing some fishing but are clearly more interested in each other than in the fish. The small-town girl that she is, Ann hasn't been a lot of places and she sometimes dreams of what other places might be like. "You've been a lot of places, haven't you?" she asks Jeff. "One too many," says Jeff, cryptically. He then assures her that Bridgeport is his favorite place and that he would like nothing better than to marry her and settle down there forever. Jeff has lived a life of flux and uncertainty; he now wants nothing more than to ease into the comforts of home. Ann knows nothing but those comforts; she is perfectly willing to marry Jeff and stay in Bridgeport, but exploring the wider world also seems appealing to her.

When Stefanos's visit spurs Jeff to take the drive to Lake Tahoe, the trip marks a major shift in the narrative (marked by Jeff's return to his private detective uniform of trench coat and fedora), which will remain in the present tense from the end of this car trip forward. Meanwhile, it is significant that the main narration of the flashback portion of the film takes place in a car on the road, reinforcing this film's emphasis on movement and travel. The action itself becomes even more frantic from this point forward, with one plot twist after another driving the narrative.

The flashback portion of the film begins in Sterling's apartment in New York, shifting us suddenly from small-town Bridgeport to the ultimate big American city. Sterling's apartment itself is a gaudy exercise in ostentatious opulence, decorated at considerable expense but with little taste, bursting at the seams with artwork, lamps, candelabras, and furnishings. Sterling explains that Kathie shot him and made off with $40,000 of his money, but that he badly wants her back. When he promises not to hurt her, Markham, accompanied by Fisher, agrees to take the case, though Markham insists on handling it personally.

The search first takes Markham to a Black jazz club, a classic noir setting that adds an extra element of otherness, such Black clubs feature in a number of noir films as a source of exoticism that supposedly have more life and energy than the routinized locales of white, domestic spaces but that are also vaguely outside the realm of the entirely respectable in white, bourgeois terms. It's an upscale club, filled with well-dressed, middle-class African Americans, but they are African American nevertheless. It is also a setting with a different sense of time, Black culture typically being imagined by white filmmakers during this period as being almost outside of time, a slow-paced world of celebration and leisure, providing a respite from the pressures of the workaday world.

This notion of a slow-paced, *precapitalist* milieu is developed further as Markham flies to Mexico City, then takes a bus further south. In this modern world of rapid transportation, everyone moves about so easily that it is difficult for anyone anywhere to truly get away, as Markham will soon learn to his detriment. Acapulco, then, is still easily within reach of Sterling, even though it is depicted in the film as a sleepy oceanside hamlet, with most of its inhabitants seemingly spending most of their time drinking beer and drowsing. The Mexican cantina where Markham first spots Kathie thus serves somewhat the same function as the African American club he had visited in New York, only more so.

Even in sleepy Acapulco, it is impossible to escape the onslaught of modernity completely. As Markham sits in a quiet cantina drinking beer and drifting off, he is continually "jarred awake" by the music from a movie house next door. The town also includes a Western Union telegraph office that he nearly uses to inform Sterling that he has found Kathie, but then he thinks better of it. And, despite the seemingly slow pace of life in Acapulco, the inhabitants are constantly hustling, constantly trying to sell anything they can to "tourists" like Kathie and Markham. Those tourists, meanwhile, have their own spaces in which they are catered to, as when Kathie takes Markham to a casino where an immaculately dressed French-speaking croupier spins a roulette wheel for an upscale, Western clientele.

For a brief time, Acapulco functions for the two new lovers as a sort of tropical paradise, their emerging passion sealing them off from the outside world and the passing of time. Shots of lush, tropical vegetation emphasize this function of the setting, but even the lovers know it can't last. Given that Sterling knows Markham is in Acapulco, they decide to catch a boat for an unspecified destination so that they can stay a step ahead of the gangster. Unfortunately, Sterling and Stefanos show up in Acapulco before Jeff and Kathie can depart.

Jeff and Kathie manage to flee by steamship to San Francisco, where they struggle to maintain their two-lovers-apart-from-the-world life, despite the modern urban surroundings. And, for a while, they manage, keeping to themselves and visiting out-of-the-way parts of the city they would never, as Jeff explains to Ann in his narration, have seen on their own. Then they get overconfident and go to a racetrack, where Fisher spots them. They separate, and Jeff makes sure that Fisher follows him to L.A. Eventually, he concludes that he has lost Fisher and so can arrange to meet Kathie at a remote cabin.

Unfortunately, Fisher follows Kathie to the cabin, arriving just after the two lovers. After he and Jeff fight, Kathie (always quick on the trigger) shoots and kills him, then drives away while Jeff is examining the body, which he subsequently buries. Jeff ends his story to Ann at this point, as they arrive at Sterling's estate in Tahoe. Ann and Jeff agree that they still want to make a life together, but first he has to square things with Sterling. She drops him off at the gate and drives away. Sterling's Tahoe estate contains an even more impressive display of wealth than had his New York apartment. In contrast, Markham notes his own modest situation: "I sell gasoline; I make a small profit. With that I buy groceries: the grocer makes a profit. We call it earning a living. You may have heard of it somewhere."

In addition to this class figuration, the opposition between Bailey and Sterling is a temporal one: Bailey represents the traditional values of small-time America and is thus associated with the past. Sterling, on the other hand, is associated with modern, big-city corruption and is thus associated with the present of modernity. (Markham, incidentally, is also associated with modernity, so that Markham and Bailey, though the same person, play two different allegorical roles in the film in this sense.) This same opposition between tradition and modernity also inheres in the collection of locations found in the film. New York, Los Angeles, and San Francisco (the three most important film noir cities) all figure in the text as modern, urban settings where violence and corruption reign. On the other hand, places such as Acapulco and its beaches or Bridgeport and its placid surroundings serve as quiet, pastoral settings. It is important, however, to recognize that this opposition is not complete or absolute. In the modern, postwar world there are already no places that have not been impacted to some extent by modernity, thus the telegraph office and the Western-style casino in Acapulco and the cars and gas station of Bridgeport.

Critics have typically seen *Out of the Past* as a film in which Jeff's attempt to build a new life in the present is disrupted by the emergence of forces from his past, in a sort of return of the repressed. Thus, Barton Palmer concludes that the lesson of *Out of the Past* is that the past "cannot be escaped," while "the present is . . . subject to a sudden, often thoroughgoing disruption that is connected somehow to what has been left behind but is not, as the story begins, in any sense 'over.'"[1] It is true that Markham and, to an extent, Moffat do try and fail to escape their past lives. Palmer also seeks to broaden his reading into the social realm of history, but still sees the film in the same way, arguing that the postwar world of the film was still struggling to escape the traumas associated with the experience of the war. And he is surely correct here in terms of the short-term individual memory of recent events. I would argue, however, that the sociohistorical dimension of *Out of the Past* derives more from the long view of history as the hundreds-of-years-long process of capitalist modernization in which it is the precapitalist *past* that is viewed as the locus of stability and tranquility, while the present is viewed as a time of contingency, precarity, and change. Viewed in this way, what really occurs in *Out of the Past* is not that Jeff attempts to escape *from* the past *into* the present, but that he attempts to escape *to* the past *from* the present. Put differently, Jeff attempts to build an idyllic life in a world of the past, a project that fails because of the emergence of forces representing the present world of modern capitalism. The film, in short, functions in a nostalgic mode that idealizes the past and identifies the present as destructive, which is essentially the opposite of what most critics have felt that it was doing.

The script for the film is shot through with suggestions of anxieties about the destruction of traditional ways of American life by the forces of modernization. One might say the same thing about *Out of the Past*, which would seem to make the film's ending a happy one. The outside forces that have been threatening the peacefulness of Bridgeport have all been removed (Sterling, Stefanos, Markham, and Moffat are, in fact, all dead), and life in the quiet mountain town seems set to return to normal, with Ann now apparently willing to settle for marriage to childhood sweetheart Jim (Richard Webb), having been convinced by The Kid that Jeff had betrayed her and was running away with Kathie.

There are, however, a number of problems with this seemingly recuperative ending, leaving openings for readings that undermine the film's apparent intentions. For one thing, Jim—though a native of Bridgeport—now works for the State of California Department of Highways and travels freely about the state. He is himself thus, to some extent, an agent of modernity, suggesting the difficulty of maintaining a completely traditional existence in the modern age. Indeed, as the film ends, he and Ann drive away together in his state car, headed out of town, though their departure is presumably only temporary. In any case, Ann seems to regard Jim as more of a friend than anything and is willing to marry him only because Jeff is out of the picture (and only because The Kid—presumably trying to protect her feelings—has lied to her about Jeff's intentions). In addition, the marriage is something of a defeat for her (built on murder and lies) that safely transcribes her within the patriarchal structures that are such a prominent component of the traditional ways of life that the film seems to want to romanticize. After all, it's 1947 in small-town America, and she has to marry *somebody*.

Out of the Past is a complex film that can be read in a number of ways. And these complexities go far beyond the complex twists and turns of the plot to include the film's complex engagement with history. The specifics of its story reflect the disruptions in American life of the past few years, disruptions from which Americans were still trying to recover in the postwar years. But the film also shows the impact of the larger historical narrative of capitalist modernity, which brings about a world informed by constant, vertiginous change and transformation, in a process that sweeps away traditional modes of life like dust in the wind. This world brings with it progress and opportunity (especially of the economic variety), but it is unsettling and disorienting in a way that destabilizes institutions, social practices, and personal relationships. In this world, as Marx and Engels so aptly put it, "All that is solid melts into air."

Chapter 10

The Neo-Noir Lost Man: *After Dark, My Sweet*

(1990, Directed by James Foley)

If film noir suggested a dark side to the American dream, it was significantly limited in how dark it could go, thanks to the Hollywood Production Code. Meanwhile, American culture as a whole was limited in the extent to which it could directly critique American society during the years of the original noir cycle, first out of a need to show solidarity with the American cause during World War II and then because of the repressive McCarthyite atmosphere of the postwar years. Nevertheless, certain pulp novels of that period were able to go beyond what the Code allowed in film in terms of social critique. And while some of these novels—such as William Lindsay Gresham's left-leaning novel *Nightmare Alley* (1946) or Mickey Spillane's brutal right-wing novel *Kiss Me Deadly* (1952)—were adapted to film noir, the process required a considerable amount of bowdlerization. Thus, novel adaptations in the original noir cycle typically drew upon earlier novels, such as those by the hard-boiled trio of Hammett, Chandler, and Cain. Meanwhile, the novels of Jim Thompson, in some ways the most "noir" of all 1950s novelists, were simply too extreme for the original noir cycle.[1]

It should then perhaps be no surprise that, after the collapse of the Code opened the way for neo-noir, filmmakers immediately began to draw upon the rich trove of noir material represented by Thompson's novels. However, even neo-noir adaptations typically had to water down the original material considerably, at the loss of much of the distinctive texture of Thompson's work. Of the neo-noir adaptations of Thompson's novels, *After Dark, My Sweet* is probably the one adaptation that is actually closest in spirit to the (1955) novel on which it was based.[2] This unusual faithfulness to a Thompson original, meanwhile, was enabled partly by fact that the original is relatively mild in content by Thompson's standards and partly by the fact that the novel version of *After Dark* might simply be unusually cinematic to begin with. Polito notes that the novel "exchanges the verbal or structural pyrotechnics of its predecessors for bold, cinematic imagery. Thompson, in fact, projected *After Dark, My Sweet* as a movie right from conception."[3]

After Dark, My Sweet is in many ways a classic example of lost-man noir, the kind of noir in which Thompson specialized, creating some of the most thoroughly lost men in all of American literature, typically expressing their sense of exclusion from the American dream through their own first-person narration. *After Dark* is narrated by a character whose sanity is questionable at best, creating a great deal of interpretive instability due to the unreliability of the information supplied to us by that narrator. The novel is narrated by one William "Kid" Collins, whose first name has been changed to "Kevin" in the film, presumably to avoid the potential corniness of his being called "Billy the Kid" (though he is almost never addressed by his first name, anyway). Collins is a former professional boxer and escaped mental patient, whose psychological downward spiral was apparently hastened when he lost his temper and killed an opponent in his last prize fight.

Collins's former profession aligns him with an important subset of noir films that focus on boxers, typically using the competitive ethos of boxing as an oblique commentary on capitalism, with boxers standing in for exploited workers (and played by leading noir actors such as John Garfield and Humphrey Bogart). Key noir boxing films include *Body and Soul* (1947), *The Set-Up* (1949), *Champion* (1949), and *The Harder They Fall* (1956). Meanwhile, there are also a number of characters in film noir who are clearly mentally ill. For example, Richard Widmark originally made his mark as an American actor playing deranged characters in noir films, with his turn as Tommy Udo in Henry Hathaway's *Kiss of Death* (1947) standing as an iconic noir performance. Where Thompson's work stands apart from the original noir cycle is that deranged characters in film noir are typically villains or otherwise marginal characters. In Thompson's novels, the deranged characters are centered, typically serving as protagonists and narrators. They may commit villainous, even heinous acts, but there is a certain amount of sympathy for them due to their marginalized social status and their potential lack of rational control over their actions due to mental illness.

In the film version of *After Dark*, Kid Collins is played by Jason Patric, who also serves as a typical noir voiceover narrator. Patric is an actor who is known for his good looks, but here he is ill-shaven and ill-groomed, with a wild-eyed look that well conveys his troubled condition. Voice over narrators in film (whose narration is supplemented by so much action on the screen) dominate their texts less thoroughly than do the narrators of novels (who are typically our only source of information). Moreover, voiceover narration is used sparingly in this film. Still, Collins is also strongly positioned as the film's point-of-view character, so we really see almost everything from his perspective. Unfortunately, that perspective is a bit shaky due to Collins's precarious mental condition. The instability of Collins's perspective is reflected effectively in the film, sometimes through strictly visual effects. In some scenes, for example, we see him moving about like the ex-athlete he is, leaping and running about quite gracefully. In other scenes, he shuffles along, dragging his feet as if he has trouble walking. Such changes are not explained in the film. Does Collins's physical ability vary with his psychological mood? Might he even have multiple personalities? Or does he at times simply feign disability in order to appear less threatening and more sympathetic?

As the action begins, Collins arrives (on foot) at a small desert town in the vicinity of Palm Springs (which, in the 1950s, was fast developing a reputation as a resort spot for the rich and famous). Collins, against his own best judgment, immediately stops in at a bar, where he quickly runs afoul of the bartender (and the bar's owner), whom he punches out, indicating his quick temper (though the barman is also unaccountably rude to him). In the bar, Collins also meets the film's femme fatale in the person of widow Fay Anderson, played by Rachel Ward, who had played such characters in the noir spoof *Dead Men Don't Wear Plaid* (1982) and *Against All Odds* (1984), a neo-noir remake of the noir classic *Out of the Past* (1947). Fay, however, is a somewhat unconventional femme fatale in that she greets Collins in with a combination of seductiveness and outright hostility, as when she decides to call him "Collie" because he looks like a dog. Collins accepts this appellation willingly, though some of her insults cause Collins (clearly sensitive about the matter) to insist to her that he isn't stupid, despite what people seem to think. Whether or not he is actually stupid is never entirely clear, though it is certainly clear that he is not in full possession of his faculties, presumably due to the impact of having taken so many punches during his boxing career. The lonely Fay, meanwhile, seems to suspect that he is stupid but also finds him attractive.

At times, Fay slinks about seductively like a classic femme fatale, but at other times she seems much more vulnerable than the typical femme fatale. Much of the experience of watching this film involves trying to solve the riddle that she presents both to us and to Collins. Indeed, one of the key elements of this film that aligns viewers with Collins's point of view is that we join him in trying to figure out how much sympathy we should have for Fay, while at the same time remaining wary of her potential dangers. Fay is also an unusual femme fatale in that she does not seem to be the primary architect of the scheme in which she ensnares Collins. Instead, that would be the man she calls Uncle Bud (Bruce Dern), though he is not her uncle, and he isn't named "Bud." He is identified as an ex-police detective, but exactly who he is remains a cipher. His entire life seems to consist of cooking up get-rich-quick schemes, while convincing others to carry out those schemes and take most of the risks that they involve. Fay seems fully aware that it is a bad idea to get involved in Bud's schemes, but she seems to go along almost out of sheer exhaustion, weakened too much by alcoholism and widowhood to have the will to resist. The relationship between Bud and Fay thus makes Fay as much a victim of Bud as she is a manipulator of Collins. That Uncle Bud has so much success manipulating them both suggests a characteristic that is often found in the world of Thompson's fiction: In a world of ultimate meaninglessness and moral uncertainty, anyone willing to choose a course and stick to it has a track to power over others.

The Uncle Bud scheme that lies at the center of this film involves a plot to kidnap the young son of a rich local family and to hold him for ransom, a plan that runs into several snags and undergoes several revisions. Collins doesn't like the plan from the beginning, but he wants to please Fay and Bud, essentially the only people he knows in the world at this point. He thus goes along with the plot but tries to rearrange the plan to make it less dangerous for the boy. Bud, meanwhile, starts rethinking the plan in order to blame everything on Collins while cutting Collins out of the ransom money. Thus, we have the typical noir plots and counterplots, creating a paranoid atmosphere in which it seems that no one can trust anyone.

One very Thompsonesque complication that occurs along the way involves the introduction of an additional character who makes little contribution to the plot but does add subtle hints to the atmosphere of vaguely defined corruption and perversion that pervades the film (and much of film noir). This character, Doc Goldman (George Dickerson), meets Collins early in the film and immediately sizes him up as an escaped mental patient. The doctor offers to take Collins in, offering him food and shelter (and nearly freeing him from the clutches of Fay and Uncle Bud). The doctor never does anything overtly problematic to Collins and seems superficially well-intentioned, but (as played by Dickerson) he exudes a sense of moral ambiguity that suggests he might be up to no good. Thus, Payne (reading the novel) sees the doctor as "well-intentioned,"[4] while Ebert (reading the film) believes that the doctor's "concerned and kindly manner . . . masks sexual desire" for Collins.[5] However, while it is true that Dickerson's performance adds an air of potential menace to Goldman's character that is not directly expressed in the novel, the texture of Thompson's fiction is such that readers know to suspect everyone they meet in his pages.

In any case, Collins flees the doctor's home and winds up back with Fay and the kidnap plot. Once the boy is kidnapped, however, more complications arise. A diabetic who depends on regular insulin injections, the boy falls into a diabetic coma and seems on the verge of death. Fay and Uncle Bud at this point seem unable to deal with the situation, but Collins, who has seemed to be basically well-meaning throughout, now rises to the level of hero as he breaks into Doc Goldman's office, steals some insulin, and administers it to the boy, saving his life. Later, Collins proves himself able to outwit Uncle Bud, leading to Bud's death at the hands of the police. As Payne notes, Collins does not unravel morally and psychologically like the characters who are most associated with Thompson's work. Indeed, the novel and film both end after Collins reaches what Payne sees as an "affirmation of moral certainty," giving his life a demonstrable purpose at last by sacrificing himself in doing the one thing he knows will save the lives of both Fay and the kidnapped boy.[6] Thus, McCauley has seen Collins as a "true savior—rather than a deluded savior like Lou Ford of *The Killer Inside Me* or Nick Corey of *Pop. 1280.*[7]

Polito, however, cautions against simplistic readings of the novel's ending. He agrees that the film depicts Collins's last sacrifice as a noble, even Christlike gesture.

At the same time, he suggests that the essentially identical ending of the novel is presented with more nuance, allowing for an interpretation of Collins's final sacrifice as "at once heroic and the culmination of all his childish, infantile impulses."[8] After all, the film ends as Collins, having been shot by Fay because she thinks he is about to kill the boy, quietly and poignantly drifts into death. In the novel, though, the dying Collins recalls Fay having earlier mocked him by comparing to a dog. Then, in a Thompsonesque touch of weirdness, he barks like a dog as he dies. Eliminating this final touch might be the film's biggest compromise, its greatest concession to Hollywood propriety.

After Dark, My Sweet was unable to attract a substantial audience when it was in theaters, but it did attract some critical praise. Meanwhile, its reputation has grown over the years. Reviewing the film fifteen years after its initial release, Roger Ebert gave the film four stars (his highest rating). He declared the film to be "one of the purest and most uncompromising of modern films noir," noting in particular the ending, which he describes as "inevitable, heroic, sad and flawless." All in all, Ebert describes *After Dark* as a classic example of film noir, noting how it checks all the boxes for the definition of a film noir. That observation is a crucial one. This film, thanks largely to its roots in Thompson's fiction, has some seemingly unusual touches, but most of the ways in which it goes beyond the original noir cycle are entirely consistent with what the original noir films might have done had the Production Code and prevailing social attitudes allowed it. In this sense, *After Dark* is a quintessential neo-noir, illustrating well the ways in which neo-noir films deviate from the original noir cycle without really challenging the premises upon which that cycle was based.

Because of the overt threats to the health and even life of a child, *After Dark, My Sweet* probably could not have been made during the reign of the Production Code in Hollywood. Otherwise, though, it remains largely within the scope of the original noir cycle. Kidnappings (of adults) often occur in film noir, while the various plots and counterplots among the three co-conspirators in this particular kidnap plot are absolutely quintessential film noir. Collins lacks the extreme mental instability of Thompson's more extreme protagonists, such as Lou Ford; he's really more of a hard-luck drifter, somewhat in the mode of Tom Neal in *Detour*. Fay might lack the single-minded devotion to the manipulation of others that is often associated with the femme fatale, but this character, in fact, is often endowed with moral ambiguity and with a background that to some extent supplies reasons for her actions that are beyond her control—think Norma Desmond in *Sunset Boulevard*.

All in all, then, *After Dark, My Sweet* is a typical neo-noir film in the sense that it borrows enough from film noir that those borrowings are obvious, lending the film an air of nostalgia for the original noir cycle. Its source in Thompson's fiction also has a certain nostalgic aspect, especially given that the film was made during a resurgence of interest in Thompson's fiction. All in all, while *After Dark* is already less extreme and more directly filmable than most of Thompson's novels, this film adaptation does trim away some of Thompson's rough-hewn weirdness, keeping the film within the same general territory covered by other neo-noir films of its era and avoiding any direct challenge that might change the way we view the original noir cycle.

Chapter 11

The Neo-Noir Lost Man: *The Man Who Wasn't There*

(2001, Directed by Joel and Ethan Coen)

Beginning with the innovative neo-noir film *Blood Simple* (1984), the brothers Joel and Ethan Coen have established themselves as leading makers of neo-noir film. Virtually all of the Coens' films contain some noir elements, though their use of noir motifs is particularly striking in *The Man Who Wasn't There*, a black-and-white film whose protagonist (and voiceover narrator) is a classic noir lost man and whose classic noir plot is even set in 1949, during the heyday of film noir. *The Man Who Wasn't There* employs its numerous noir motifs, respectfully, even nostalgically, and it does very little to make us reassess the way we think about noir. At the same time, this highly innovative film uses well-known tropes in creative ways that make it anything but a work of slavish imitation.

Barber Ed Crane (Billy Bob Thornton) is the protagonist and title character of *The Man Who Wasn't There*. He supplies the film's voiceover narration and is otherwise absolutely central to the impact of the film. As indicated by the title, he is a true lost man, his life so empty that it is hardly a life at all. In addition to his empty and sexless marriage, he finds his job as a barber unrewarding and even oppressive. He keeps cutting hair, but it keeps growing back, a kind of futility that is symbolized (perhaps over-obviously) in the film by the barber pole that keeps turning, sending its stripes spiraling upward, yet never actually going anywhere. Then again, Crane is virtually affectless and seems to have little enthusiasm for anything. He hardly even reacts when he learns that his wife Doris (Frances McDormand) is having an affair with her boss, Big Dave Brewster (James Gandolfini).

The Man Who Wasn't There is a virtual compendium of film noir plot motifs, involving adultery, blackmail, murder, courtroom drama, unjust criminal convictions, and a general sense of anxiety and doom—all conveyed with a twist through the Coens' distinctive ironic style. The individual noir film of which it is most reminiscent is clearly *Double Indemnity*, though it draws more directly upon James M. Cain's original novel of that title than on Wilder's 1944 film. Not only do many elements of *The Man Who Wasn't There* recall *Double Indemnity*, but the Coens even signal their debt to Cain's novel by having the department store that Brewster manages and where Doris works as an accountant be called Nirdlinger's Department Store, a sort of nod to noir fans, who might know that, in Cain's original novel, *Double Indemnity's* famed femme fatale is named Phyllis Nirdlinger, rather than Phyllis Dietrichson.

The Man Who Wasn't There conducts a thoroughgoing critique of the emerging consumerist society of postwar America. The Cranes have spent their lives chasing the American Dream, and the ultimate emptiness of their lives suggests the emptiness of that quest—a suggestion that is typical of noir film. Granted, the American economy is booming in the film, but the lack of enthusiasm for the rewards brought by this boom is quite clear in Crane's opening voiceover, which tells us that he and Doris live "in a little bungalow," complete with "an electric ice box, a gas hearth, and a garbage grinder built into the sink. You might say I had it made." You might say that, but Crane clearly wouldn't. Meanwhile, when Crane then tells us about Doris's job at the department store, he announces that she gets a 10 percent discount on whatever she buys at the store, as if this fact is crucial to her being. But what she buys, he tells us, are "nylon stockings, make-up, and perfume," a list that suggests not only her superficiality but possibly also the superficiality of consumerism in general.

The Man Who Wasn't There is pervaded by an air of greed and corruption that is typical of noir film. However, unlike most noir films, it is set, not in a large city, but in the small town of Santa Rosa, California.[1] It thus suggests that corruption occurs, not just in big cities, but even in the small towns that have so often been idealized in American mythology. However, as is often the case in noir films, the action of this film is the result not of a well-crafted criminal scheme, but of a series of missteps and miscalculations. This action is set in motion when would-be entrepreneur Creighton Tolliver (Jon Polito), comes to town looking for investors in what he bills as the revolutionary new technology of dry cleaning. As I have pointed out elsewhere, dry cleaning was not really that novel in 1949, but Tolliver's scheme is very much in keeping with the opportunistic spirit of American capitalism at the time.[2] Meanwhile, Tolliver's plan to get rich from advertising seems a bit sketchy from the beginning, though it seems surprisingly attractive to the normally stolid Crane, who dreams of making so much money off the plan that he can abandon his despised work as a barber.

The problem is that Crane doesn't have the $10,000 that Tolliver is looking for, so he conceives a scheme to blackmail Big Dave over his affair with Doris, a scheme that ultimately leads Big Dave to murder Tolliver (erroneously thinking he is the blackmailer) and leads to Crane's killing of Big Dave (in self-defense). Then Doris is wrongly convicted of Big Dave's murder, subsequently committing suicide in jail, while Crane is ultimately convicted (wrongly) of the murder of Tolliver. In short, *The Man Who Wasn't There* is filled with precisely the same sort of events that filled the original noir films, though it probably contains more such events than any of those original films. In addition, as is typically the case with neo-noir films, *The Man Who Wasn't There* moves beyond the original noir films in ways that are directly related to the removal of the restrictions of the Production Code. For example, Doris's suicide is treated much more frankly than it could have been under the Code. Moreover, we eventually learn that, at the time of her suicide, she had been pregnant (by Big Dave), a detail that would certainly have been forbidden under the Code.

The Man Who Wasn't There often takes elements that were typically unstated in the original noir films to a new, more overt level, even when not directly related to Code restrictions. For example, while it is clear that the Cold War nuclear arms race made important contributions to the air of tension and anxiety that pervades the original noir cycle, the Cold War was seldom mentioned openly in those films. Yet *The Man Who Wasn't There* foregrounds this topic early on as a character reads a newspaper report of a Soviet A-bomb test. Meanwhile, the strangest aspect of this film is probably the flying saucers that either appear or are mentioned several times, reflecting the fact that the 1949 setting of *The Man Who Wasn't There* was a peak time of popular anxiety over UFOs in America. At one point, we even observe Crane reading a magazine article entitled "Mysteries of Roswell, New Mexico," in reference to the famous 1947 incident in which a UFO supposedly crashed near the town. Even the flying saucers, then, help to establish the historical context of the film, while also adding still another element of the air of American paranoia that was so crucial to the texture of the films of the original noir cycle.

The Coens also add some of their own signature quirkiness to the noir matrix of *The Man Who Wasn't There*. For example, the inclusion of courtroom drama in the film is not uncommon in the original noir films. However, there is surely nothing in those original films that can quite match the scene in which Freddy Riedenschneider (Tony Shalhoub), the expensive defense attorney who is recruited by Ed to defend Doris in her murder trial, announces his plan to create reasonable doubt in the minds of jurors by employing a version of the Heisenberg uncertainty principle (though he can't actually recall Werner Heisenberg's name, attributing the principle to some German guy named "Fritz something or other"). It is, in fact, quite clear that Riedenschneider doesn't really understand the uncertainty principle at all—he is presumably relying on the fact that the jury won't understand it either, so that the argument might just confuse them enough to create the uncertainty he hopes for.

Riedenschneider never gets to try out this strategy because Doris commits suicide before he gets a chance to try it on the jury. Meanwhile, the scene in which he explains this strategy is one of the most visually striking in the entire film. Marked by extreme expressionist lighting, it takes place in a large jail visitation cell that is essentially in darkness, except for one section that is illuminated by a bright overhead light that allows Riedenschneider to pace about as if performing on stage in a spotlight. Meanwhile, light also comes through a barred window, casting a pattern of shadows on the floor of the room in what might be seen as an exaggerated version of the "venetian blind" effect so common to film noir. In short, this scene replicates visually much of what happens in the events of the plot, taking a well-known noir trope and pushing it to an extreme, but not in a way that would challenge the way we have tended to see that trope in the original noir films.

In the wake of Doris's death, Crane's life goes from bad to worse, again possibly exaggerating the bad luck experienced by so many noir characters. Floundering in his attempt to find a new direction for his life, Crane first pays a visit to an apparently fraudulent medium in an attempt to communicate with Doris in the afterlife. Then, he takes another obviously misguided turn when he becomes fascinated with local teenager Rachel "Birdy" Abundas (played by fifteen-year-old Scarlett Johansson). Having earlier heard Birdy playing the slow second movement of Beethoven's Piano Sonata Number 8 ("Pathétique"), Crane now develops an obsessive interest in her playing, which suggests to him "some kind of escape, some kind of peace."

Beethoven's sonatas—including passages from Sonatas 14 ("Moonlight"), 15 ("Pastorale"), 23 ("Appassionata"), 25, and 30, as well as "Pathetique"—provide a crucial part of the soundtrack of *The Man Who Wasn't There*, which is somewhat ironic, given Crane's lack of affect and Beethoven's reputation for emotional intensity in his music. However, the mismatch between the music and the film's central character effectively highlights the emotional emptiness of Crane's life, while also helping to explain why he becomes so fascinated by this music, which might provide something that he so sorely lacks. Crane himself, however, doesn't seem to understand the music at all, finding it peaceful, rather than intense. Indeed, it is clear from the beginning that Crane knows absolutely nothing about music—so much so that, when he first hears Birdy playing "Pathetique," he assumes that it might be her own composition.

Given Crane's complete ignorance of music, it is clear that things will not end well when Crane decides to dedicate his life to managing and promoting her musical career. Crane denies (even to himself) that there is anything sexual in his attraction to Birdy, which he claims is purely based on an aesthetic appreciation of her playing, though it is virtually impossible not to suspect that he is fooling himself. The problem, though, is that Birdy is not actually a particularly gifted musician, even though Crane seems to think she is an absolute genius. Moreover, she is not even especially interested in a musical career, participating in Crane's plan mostly because she doesn't seem to want to disappoint him.

Crane takes Birdy to an elite piano teacher in San Francisco, only to have him imperiously decline to take her own as a pupil after hearing her play. "Nice girl," the teacher declares, "however, stinks." On the drive home to Santa Rosa, Birdy thanks Crane for trying to help her but admits that she didn't really want to be a professional concert pianist in the first place. Then she reveals that she might have misread him as much as he misread her. "You know what you are?" she asks him. "You're an enthusiast." Crane's central characteristic seems to be lack of enthusiasm, of course, though he has seemed enthusiastic about Birdy—so much so that she assumes he will welcome her further in an attempt to thank him even more by trying to perform oral sex on him while he is driving. The shocked Crane recoils in horror, fighting her off and losing control of the car, which careens off the side of the mountain road on which they are driving. In one of the film's strangest moments, we see the car flying through the air in slow motion, accompanied by Crane's typically (but here, surprisingly) affectless voiceover, in which he makes it clear that he assumes he is about to die: "Time slows down right before an accident, and I had time to think about things. I thought about what an undertaker had told me once: that your hair keeps growing, for a while, anyway, after you die. And then it stops." And then he continues to muse on why this process might happen, until we see a shot of him lying unconscious in the wreck of the car.

While we hear this voiceover, we also see a hubcap that has come loose in the wreck as it rolls along the ground in a way that recalls a hat that similarly blows away in a prominent dream sequence in the Coens' *Miller's Crossing* (1990), a gangster film that draws strongly upon the fiction of Dashiell Hammett and contains strong noir elements. In this case, though, the loose hubcap suddenly transforms into a flying saucer and zooms off into the sky, perhaps recalling the circular images of *Detour*.

A sudden cut takes us to the porch of Crane's bungalow, where he sits smoking one of his trademark cigarettes. A salesman approaches him, hoping to interest him in having his driveway paved with "tar macadam." Then, just as we are attempting to figure out how we got back to this point, Doris suddenly pulls into the driveway, jumps out of the car, and dispatches the salesman. The hard-drinking Doris then enters the house and pours herself a cocktail then sits on the couch to drink it, while Crane sits at the opposite end of the couch, emphasizing the distance in their marriage. The scene, though, is simply a sort of dream sequence, which ends as the screen cuts to blackness, out of which the flying saucer again appears, then transforms into a round examination mirror strapped to the forehead of a doctor who is rousing Crane into consciousness so that he can be arrested for murder.

The film then briefly returns to courtroom drama, as Riedenschneider defends Crane, who has now been charged with the murder of Tolliver. Riedenschneider's defense this time relies on attempting to win the sympathy of the jury by convincing them that Crane is a prototypical "modern man," whose existential predicament is much like their own. Surprisingly, the tactic seems to be working, until Doris's brother disrupts the proceeding by attacking Crane, leading to a mistrial. When Crane is retried, he can no longer afford to pay Riedenschneider, so he gets a less inventive lawyer and is convicted and sentenced to death, which he accepts with his customary passivity, despite the fact that he was completely uninvolved in Tolliver's murder.

Now *The Man Who Wasn't There* shifts into something of a prison drama, with Crane awaiting execution on death row. He passes the time by writing his story for publication in a men's magazine, presumably providing the source for the movie we have just seen. There is one last moment of strangeness as we see Crane walking, as if in a trance, out of his prison cell and into the yard outside, there to encounter a

Figure 11.1. Ed and Doris Crane (Billy Bob Thornton and Frances McDormand) in a dream sequence in *The Man Who Wasn't There*. USA Films/Photofest © USA Films

flying saucer. It is, however, simply another dream sequence. Crane is then awakened and taken to the electric chair to be executed (despite the fact that executions in California at the time would have been carried out via the gas chamber). The screen cuts to black as Crane dies.

Crane's fate demonstrates the sense of doom that often pervades noir films, with Rudolph Maté's *D.O.A.* (1950) perhaps providing the most obvious example. It also recalls the many noir films in which unfortunate lost men are accused of crimes they didn't commit, perhaps most notably Hitchcock's *The Wrong Man* (1956). However, the most direct predecessor to the ending of *The Man Who Wasn't There* is surely *The Postman Always Rings Twice*, in which both the 1934 James M. Cain novel and its 1946 film noir adaptation end as protagonist Frank Chambers (played by noir superstar John Garfield in the film) also writes his story while awaiting execution (in the gas chamber), having been wrongly convicted of murdering his femme fatale lover Cora (Lana Turner in the film). As it turns out, Cora was accidentally killed in a car crash in which Chambers had been the driver, an event that obviously parallels Crane's crash with Birdy (though Birdy suffers only a broken collarbone). A more direct parallel is that both Chambers and Crane accept their wrongful convictions because of other things they had done without getting punished.

This film shows the Coens as true masters of noir, able to include many elements that might at first seem out of place in a film of the original noir cycle while at the same time producing a film that looks and feels like a genuine noir film. After all, even its seemingly excessive elements, such as the flying saucers and the Heisenberg-citing defense attorney, are no stranger than the drug-induced hallucinations of *Murder,*

My Sweet (1944) or the glowing atomic briefcase that features so prominently in Robert Aldrich's *Kiss Me Deadly* (1955). Even the motif of Birdy's would-be career as a concert pianist has something of a noir precedent in still another James M. Cain novel: the daughter of the title character of Cain's *Mildred Pierce* (1941) aspires to be an opera singer, though the 1945 film noir adaptation of that novel eliminates that motif. And nothing in *The Man Who Wasn't There* is quite as bizarre as the brawl with artificial body parts in a mannequin factory at the end of Stanley Kubrick's film noir *Killer's Kiss* (1955). All in all, *The Man Who Wasn't There* pushes noir motifs about as far as they can without spilling over into revisionary noir.

Chapter 12

The Revisionary Noir Lost Man: *The Killer Inside Me*

(2010, Directed by Michael Winterbottom)

Jim Thompson's 1952 novel *The Killer Inside Me* remains the best-known of his novels, though it is also one of the more extreme ones, perhaps rivaled in its exploration of violence and psychopathology only by his later novels *Savage Night* (1953) and *Pop. 1280* (1964).[1] It is thus a good illustration of the reasons why Thompson's novels were never adapted to film during the original noir cycle. At the same time, it is no surprise that, after the collapse of the Production Code made it thinkable to bring Thompson's fiction to the big screen, *The Killer Inside Me* was both one of the first Thompson novels to be adapted to film and one of the hardest to adapt faithfully. Thus, the 1976 adaptation, which showed little in the way of graphic violence and only hinted at just how psychopathic Ford might be, was not at all successful. Polito called it a "car wreck" of a movie and noted that Thompson himself (who died in 1977) was horrified by it.[2] However, Michael Winterbottom's 2010 adaptation is much more faithful and a much better film.

Were an unwitting and uninitiated reader to pick up and start to read a copy of *The Killer Inside Me*, having no idea what to expect, they would immediately be plunged into a classic noir setting as the first-person narrator describes having pie and coffee at a late-night diner. We will eventually learn that this narrator is Deputy Sheriff Lou Ford. He seems an affable sort, joking with the waitress (a newcomer to town) that he doesn't need to carry a gun or other weapons because Central City has so little crime. As he leaves the diner, he accepts the thanks of the "Greek" proprietor for helping to set the man's once-arrant son onto the straight and narrow. Ford responds with a barrage of clichés, which (at first) seems to suggest that he might be a bit shy and uncomfortable with praise. The deputy, it would seem, is an all-around good guy. However, as Ford steps out into the "cool West Texas night," his thoughts suggest that the clichés were a puzzling form of unprovoked hostility. Then he finds a bum waiting for him on the street as the chapter ends.

In the second chapter, in a flashback to three months earlier, Ford is assigned to run an apparent prostitute, Joyce Lakeland, out of town. When Joyce talks back to him with surprising defiance, Ford becomes enraged and feels his "sickness" (which he has apparently been attempting to suppress for some time) coming on. He then viciously beats the woman, though he stops short of seriously injuring her at this point. She herself seems to have a perverse streak that makes her actually enjoy the beating, though Ford's violence, especially against women (though also against men), will escalate to a deadly level of brutality as the novel proceeds. Meanwhile, this chapter ends as we loop back to the end of the first chapter. The bum innocently asks Ford for a handout, and Ford (his sickness having been fully released by months of sadomasochistic sex with Joyce by this time) responds by grinding a burning cigar into the man's hand, obviously relishing this opportunity to inflict pain. By this time, even before he embarks on a string of brutal murders, it is clear that Ford is not your typical protagonist and that we are likely to be traveling into shocking territory.

Ford as it turns out, is a genuine psychopath who has engaged in disturbing behavior since his childhood—with hints that his physician father might have been a psychopath as well, though perhaps with more control over his impulses. Part of the problem with the 1976 adaptation was that Lou Ford was played by Stacey Keach, an actor with a sinister aspect that led him to be cast, a few years later, as the sadistic private detective Mike Hammer in a television film and then a television series based on the fiction of Mickey Spillane. But a key element of Lou as a character in the novel is that he conceals his violent and perverse tendencies by looking so innocent and harmless. For that reason, the casting of baby-faced Casey Affleck in the role for the 2010 remake seemed quite promising, especially after Affleck's impressive Oscar-nominated performance as Robert Ford in the noir-inflected Western *The Assassination of Jesse James by the Coward Robert Ford* (2007).[3] That promise of potential faithfulness to Thompson's novel is largely fulfilled in Affleck's harrowing performance in *The Killer Inside Me*, even if his periodic voiceover narration is not entirely able to capture the tension of Lou's narration in the novel, which brilliantly reflects the violent rage that seems on the verge of erupting from beneath his affable exterior at any moment. The rest of the film is surprisingly faithful to the original novel as well, including a number of graphic scenes of violence, much of it sexual. Indeed, director Winterbottom has said in interviews that fidelity to the original was one of his key goals in making the film.

This faithfulness to the original means that *The Killer Inside Me* can be a highly uncomfortable viewing experience—probably more uncomfortable than the novel itself, largely because we can actually see the violence on the screen.[4] A great deal of this violence is directed at women, who here have none of the power and agency of the classic femme fatale character. There are, in this film, only two important female characters. Jessica Alba plays the prostitute Joyce Lakeland as very much the ravishing beauty that she is described as being in the novel—as opposed to the rumpled and aging whore she appears to be as portrayed by Susan Tyrell in the 1976 film, where her contrast with the seemingly wholesome schoolteacher Amy Stanton (Tisha Sterling) is quite stark. In the 2010 film, Kate Hudson plays Amy in a way that places her much closer to Joyce in character. Indeed, Lou is struck (as he is in the novel) by the extent to which they remind him of each other. Some of that might be his own projection, of course, but the one thing the film seems to suggest is that both women are willing to tolerate Lou's sexual violence (though it appears that Joyce genuinely enjoys the pain he inflicts, while Amy is merely willing to tolerate it as the price of being with him). Then again, it is not clear how much of the women's compliance is filtered through Lou's distorted perceptions and thus presented to us inaccurately. In the cases of both women, though, this compliance makes Lou's treatment of them seem *more* horrifying, rather than less, the physical violence extending to psychological domination. Meanwhile, Lou does not hesitate to murder men as well as women, but he murders the men relatively quickly, such as by gunshot or strangling and does not appear to particularly relish. But he appears to murder both Joyce and Amy by beating them to death with shocking brutality. Granted, we learn in a plot twist that Joyce actually survived the beating, but then he murders her *again*, just before he is himself killed. There is, in fact, an inevitability to Lou's ultimate demise, and one can feel his fate closing in on him from the very moment his long-dormant "sickness" is triggered by the first sight of Joyce Lakeland.

All of this brutality is conveyed in a film that is extremely well crafted. For one thing, given the focus on character, it is crucial that the film is extremely well acted. But the film has extremely high production values throughout. It is well lighted and beautifully shot, its elaborate set dressings evoking its early-1950s Texas setting in a way that seems almost too gorgeous, setting the film starkly apart from the typical film of the original noir cycle, which added to the noir atmosphere with low-key lighting and rough-hewn cinematography. Music was also key to the creation of atmosphere in the original noir cycle, typically through the use of ominous (original) jazz-inflected soundtracks. With rare exceptions—such as several noir Westerns or *Reign of Terror* (1949, aka *The Black Book*), set during the French Revolution—the original noir films were set in a time contemporary with their making and release, so that creating period atmosphere was not really an issue. Made more than half a century after the setting of the film, *The Killer Inside Me*, on the other hand, effectively creates a 1950s atmosphere both visually and through the use of actual popular music from the era or slightly before. Much of this music tilts toward the blues, though it also includes country and western tracks intended to evoke the Texas setting, such as Al Petty's "Steel Guitar Wobble" and other steel guitar music. Particularly crucial is Spade Cooley's "Shame on You," which actually dates back to 1944 but definitely has a 1950s feel, reminiscent of the better-known music of Hank Williams Sr.[5] This song appears on the soundtrack during the film, is briefly at one point sung by Lou himself, and then accompanies the apocalyptic ending.[6]

This use of so much recognizable music, much of it upbeat, combines with the seemingly excessive visual artistry of *The Killer Inside Me* to create a conflict between the film's style and content, producing a sort of Brechtian estrangement effect that signals to viewers that they should be thinking about the meaning of this film in a critical way. This aspect of the film sets it apart from the original noir cycle, which was typically characterized by a remarkable synchrony between noir style and noir content. Here, though, one finds none of the expressionistic light-and-shadow effects or heavily stylized exchanges of snappy dialogue that characterize the typical film of the original noir cycle, while the content is darker than that of any film in the original noir cycle.

The Killer Inside Me is a hard film to love, thanks largely to the fact that so many of its scenes are simply unpleasant to watch. On its initial release, some critics were outright dismissive of the film as a total failure, as was the case with A. O. Scott of *The New York Times.*[7] Among the film's initial critics, even those who appreciated the film's artistry tended to fall short of praising the film overall. Roger Ebert's review of the film was fairly negative, largely based on his sense that Ford, as played by Affleck, "remains a vast empty lonely cold space," leaving viewers little with which to connect.[8] But this emptiness, of course, is precisely the point to Ford and the key to what makes him such a frightening character. Though intelligent and well- (though self-) educated, Ford believes in nothing, loves nothing, and has no moral compass whatsoever. One gets the sense that there is almost nothing he wouldn't do, to the point that it comes as no surprise that he ultimately destroys himself—but in an apocalyptic ending that also takes out as many other people as possible, while destroying the home in which he has lived his entire life and in which he was first exposed to perversion.

The 1950s have been the object of more cultural nostalgia than any other decade, based partly on a recognition that so many important aspects of later American culture (such as television and rock 'n' roll) were still in their infancy. But 1950s nostalgia also depends on the notion that American society at that time was itself younger, simpler, and more innocent than it would soon become. This memory, of course, is selective and was furthered by idealized contemporary representations such as television sitcoms. But this picture partial and elides many aspects of the 1950s that were deeply oppressive for large numbers of people who were, on the basis of race, gender, or class, excluded from many of the positive aspects of life in the America of the 1950s. The brutality of *The Killer Inside Me* sheds particular light on gender inequities and misogynistic tendencies during this period, though other aspects of inequality in America are also addressed, but in more subtle ways. Highlighting racism during this era is clear, ethnic condescension in the way Lou regards "the Greek" Pappas (Ali Nazary) and the Greek's son Johnnie (Liam Aiken). Lou will eventually murder Johnnie in an act made to seem even more heinous by the rather simple-minded trust that Johnnie places in Lou.[9] It is important to remember, though, that we receive information about Johnnie from Lou's point of view, so it is impossible to know how simple-minded he might really be or how much of his depiction is due to Lou's racist assumption that Johnnie's ethnicity makes him less intelligent. Meanwhile, the local rich capitalist Chester Conway (Ned Beatty) looms in the margins of *The Killer Inside Me* as a corrupt and sinister figure. Again, his negative characterization might be treated as a reflection of Lou's view of him, given Lou's suspicion that Conway had been responsible for the death of Lou's adoptive brother. However, the other characters view Conway with suspicion as well. In addition, capitalist figures tend to be treated negatively throughout the fiction of Thompson, a former member of the Communist Party who maintained certain leftist leanings despite his disillusionment with politics in general by the 1950s.

The original noir films have been widely noted for their presentation of the dark side of the American Dream, a presentation that stood in stark contrast with official Cold War images of American righteousness and prosperity. However, whatever the specific content of the imagery in *The Killer Inside Me*, the general air of perversion and corruption that pervades the film goes so far beyond anything in the original noir cycle that the seriousness of the social critique in the original cycle is called into question. Indeed, what has often been seen as an exposé of the dark underbelly of American society in the original noir cycle suddenly looks almost more like a cover-up, the tameness of the material allowed by the Production Code throwing a blanket over the truly darkest aspects of America.

The original noir films have their crazed killers, of course, and the killings even sometimes have a sexual element to them. Probably the best example here would be the sinister Harry Powell (played by noir icon Robert Mitchum) in Charles Laughton's *The Night of the Hunter* (1955). But even in this film, which is extreme enough to be often considered a horror film, the violence is mostly just hinted at, without any of the kinds of graphic scenes we see in *The Killer Inside Me*. In addition, *The Night of the Hunter* includes some of the most striking (and most stylized) expressionist visuals in all of the original noir cycle, creating an effect of artistry that tends to make the perverse violence seem stylized and artificial, while Powell is also made less threatening by the fact that he is ultimately killed by a kindly little old lady (played by one-time silent film star Lillian Gish).

The contrast between the bright surface of American society as depicted in official visions and dark depths of American society as probed by *The Killer Inside Me* is striking, much more striking than the same contrast in the original noir films. Meanwhile, Lou himself embodies this same disparity in the stark contrast between his harmless-looking external appearance and the vicious killer that lurks inside him. Indeed, this contradiction is one of the key reasons why he is such an effective character—and why the casting of Affleck in the role was so much more effective than the casting of Keach in the 1976 film.

All in all, the extreme nature of *The Killer Inside Me*, a film set in the 1950s and based on a well-known novel from the 1950s, can be taken both as a criticism of the sanitized memories that so often feature in nostalgic representations of the 1950s and as a criticism of the limited nature of such appraisal that is contained in the original noir cycle, suggesting that these films weren't violent *enough* to fulfill their apparent mission. Yet the film's extreme violence can be interpreted in the opposite way as well. In a contemporary review, Peter Bradshaw, gave the film only 3 of a possible 5 stars, largely because he found the film's ultraviolence unpleasant to watch.[10] Ultimately, though, he had a great deal of praise for the way this violence is portrayed in the film, which he saw as a "seriously intentioned movie, which addresses and confronts the question of male hate and male violence in the form of a nightmare." In particular, Bradshaw saw the film as a critique of, rather than a glorification of, the misogyny and sexual violence that it portrays. Moreover, he sees the film as a powerful critique of the way violence, including sexual violence, is so often represented in Western culture. For him, this film is "confronting the audience with the reality of sexual violence and abusive power relations between the sexes that cinema so often glamourizes. *Here*, the movie is saying, *here* is the denied reality behind every seamy cop show, every sexed-up horror flick, every picturesque Jack the Ripper tourist attraction, every swooning film studies seminar on the shower scene in *Psycho*. Here. This is what we are actually talking about."

Here, of course, the film is walking a difficult line. Other films that have critiqued the glorification of violence by showing brutality so extreme that surely no one would find it glorious have fallen afoul of the fact that audiences are so conditioned to glorified violence that they automatically parse it as entertainment, rather than as critique. One thinks, for example, of Oliver Stone's *Natural Born Killers* (1994), one of the few noir films produced during the peak years of the neo-noir cycle that critically confronts the noir tradition in a mode more typical of the noir-inflected films of the twenty-first century. However, the critique of noir is oblique and merely implied in this film, which was more directly intended as a critique of the representation of violence in the contemporary mass media. Unfortunately, the representation of violence in this film (accompanied by a full array of fancy postmodern filmmaking techniques, such as embedded parodies of specific genres) was widely interpreted as spilling over into the glorification of violence, however unintentional.

The Killer Inside Me, though, eschews fancy techniques and presents its stomach-turning violence in a way that would seem to be virtually impossible for any healthy viewer to find entertaining. Clearly not a mere exploitation film, its complexities bear considerable examination. But it is also a film that suggests the reexamination of the original noir films as well, asking whether these films were really effective as a means of social critique or whether they ultimately did more to hide than reveal the dark side of American society.

Chapter 13

The Revisionary Noir Lost Man:
You Were Never Really Here

(2017, Directed by Lynne Ramsay)

The title of Scottish director Lynne Ramsay's *You Were Never Really Here* makes it sound almost like a more radical follow-up to the Coens's *The Man Who Wasn't There*. The films are not directly connected, but this suggestion is not entirely off the mark. In Ramsay's film, the protagonist is a man named "Joe" (Joaquin Phoenix) who has virtually been erased as a human being because of a lifetime of trauma, leaving him in a broken condition that seems far more extreme than the lifeless predicament of the Coens's Ed Crane. By the time of the film's action, Joe has been pushed into a life as a professional rescuer of lost or kidnapped girls (apparently specializing in rescuing the victims of sex trafficking). He employs brutally violent methods to rescue these girls from their own trauma, but in tracking them down, he acts as a sort of private detective. Indeed, the plot of *You Were Never Really Here* is a classic noir detective story: detective seeks missing person and uncovers a web of corruption among the rich and powerful. However, the violence with which Joe goes about his work, combined with the extremity of both his own psychological condition and the situation from which he rescues young Nina Votto (Ekaterina Samsonov), pushes this film well beyond anything found in the original cycle of noir films, which suddenly seem much less dark and cynical in comparison.

As the film begins, he has just completed such a rescue, though it takes a while for that to become clear. Indeed, it is at first not clear what is going on in this scene at all. All we can tell for sure is that some undefined violent event has just happened, while certain elements of the scene even tend to suggest that Joe might be the bad guy in this event. This confusing opening scene thus sets the stage for the violence and epistemological uncertainty of the rest of the film.

Meanwhile, the exact terms of Joe's trauma are also not specified, but it is clear that he suffered as a boy at the hands of an abusive, authoritarian father and that he has subsequently had a number of traumatic experiences serving in the military (in Afghanistan) and in some form of law enforcement (apparently the FBI). He bears the marks of those former experiences both in the extensive physical scars on his hulking, battered, pain-ridden body and in the mental scars that drive him into suicidal ideation and sudden flashbacks so vivid that he sometimes seems to confuse them with present-day reality. Yet we see almost everything in this film from Joe's point of view, so his unsteady mental condition introduces a significant amount of jittery, interpretive uncertainty into the film.

This uncertainty is carefully supported by certain technical aspects of the film, such as its highly effective soundtrack. As Sheila O'Malley puts it, "Jonny Greenwood's score hums and pulses underneath, creating an atmosphere of nerve-jangling tension and dread. The sound design is a living nervous breakdown."[1] A key example of the role of the soundtrack involves the song "Angel Baby" that is played as Joe breaks into a sex club for his initial rescue of Nina, much of the sequence is shown via surveillance camera footage, giving it an extreme sense of realism that conflicts with the almost dreamlike nature of this song and other aspects of the sequence. "Angel Baby" is a sweet-seeming love song, recorded in 1960 by Rosie and the Originals, a girl group whose lead singer was fifteen years old at the time. At first glance, the song seems diegetic, perhaps designed to create atmosphere in this establishment, emphasizing the innocence of the underage girls that it apparently specializes in offering to wealthy clients. The song, though, creates conflicting effects, adding a note of extra anxiety to this tense sequence. In some ways, the lyrics and melody of the song conflict strongly with the depravity of the club and the action on the screen; at the same time, this contrast serves to make the club seem even creepier, thus reinforcing the sense of its depravity. To add to the uncertain effect of this song, it occasionally skips or repeats and seems to be playing at about the same level everywhere in the club, raising the possibility that it might not be diegetic, after all. In addition, given Joe's psychological condition, it is also possible that this song simply sounds inside his head whenever he is in the key stage of rescuing a girl. The real point, though, is that we just can't know, adding to the film's overall sense of Joe's uncertain purchase on reality.

Joe also has an uncertain sense of his own identity. Kyle Turner, amid a discussion of the importance of music in the film, suggests that, whenever Joe is in action, "he seems to disassociate entirely." "I'm just a hired gun," Joe says at one point, and he is indeed essentially reduced to his function in that capacity (though he tends to prefer the brutality of a ball peen hammer as a killing weapon, having learned the effectiveness of that tool from his abusive father). The film does, however, add some touches of humanity to Joe's existence, including the obvious tenderness he shows toward Nina (even if he finds it difficult to express). Joe's human side can also be seen in his relationship with his elderly mother (played by Judith Roberts), who lives with Joe and who seems to be struggling with the early stages of dementia—though

Figure 13.1. Nina Votto and Joe (Ekaterina Samsonov and Joaquin Phoenix) in *You Were Never Really Here*. Amazon Studios/Photofest © Amazon Studios

she might also be struggling with the effects of having been abused by Joe's father in her own right. Joe attempts to take care of his mother as best he can, and they share some tender moments in the film, making the moment in which Joe finds her murdered by Joe's enemies all the more powerful. Yet any attempt to view this scene as pure pathos is disrupted when Joe finds the killers still present, then kills one and mortally wounds another, lying beside the second dying victim and weirdly singing along with him as the radio plays Charlene's banal 1977[2] pop ballad "I've Never Been to Me," in which a woman of adventure urges a wife and mother not to abandon her conventional domestic life.

You Were Never Really Here is an emotionally complex film that constantly surprises, sometimes veering into dark comedy or just plain weirdness at what conventionally would be truly tragic moments. Joe himself even occasionally shows a sense of humor as he jokes around with his mother concerning Alfred Hitchcock's 1960 noirish slasher film *Psycho* (though Joe seems to enjoy it more than does his mother). Hitchcock's classic famously features a troubled relationship between Norman Bates (Anthony Perkins) and his mother that ironically comments on that of Joe and his mother. Norman's unstable psyche clearly makes him a forerunner of Joe, as well, though the many classic noir elements of *You Were Never Really Here* point toward numerous other predecessors as well. Martin Scorsese's *Taxi Driver* (1976)[3] has probably been mentioned most often in reviews of the film—and the connection between these two films was even used in the marketing for *You Were Never Really Here*. There are obvious similarities in the plots of these films, both of which involve the violent rescue of a young girl from sex work. O'Malley, though, has also noted the many parallels between *You Were Never Really Here* and the classic film noir *The Big Sleep* (1946), in which Humphrey Bogart's Philip Marlowe has to rescue a somewhat older young woman from a somewhat sanitized version of sex trafficking.[4]

Indeed, a comparison between *You Were Never Really Here* and *The Big Sleep* makes it clear that the former is a revisionary noir film. Bogart's version of Marlowe seems somewhat tougher than Dick Powell's Marlowe in *Murder, My Sweet*, but he has nowhere near the potential for explosive violence that is a crucial characteristic of Joe. Marlowe is also sane and stable and seems to be a pillar of emotional strength in comparison with Joe. He is anything but a lost man. And it would certainly be hard to imagine Marlowe clubbing someone to death with a hammer. In addition, there is no comparison between the overtly sordid underworld of perversion and corruption into which Joe's work takes him and the one into which Marlowe moves in *The Big Sleep*—and in ways that go beyond even the dark worlds of the post-Code neo-noir films. In addition, as Sue Thornham has argued, Ramsay's film, while drawing upon certain well-established narratives of white masculinity (narratives that she notes are crucial, in particular, to *Taxi Driver*), actually challenges these narratives and essentially rewrites *Taxi Driver* to reveal its complicity with these narratives. These narratives are also relevant to the entire noir phenomenon, whose heroes tend to be prone to the same sorts of masculine violence that Thornham discusses. In particular, Thornham draws upon Karen Lury's study of the representation of children in film to suggest that narratives such as *The Big Sleep*, *Taxi Driver*, and *You were Never Really Here* all share a representation of "city-wide corruption and sexual exploitation, and another white girl who cannot really be saved" as well as "a central focus on a solitary and violent white man whose threatened masculinity—the site of anxiety for the film—is bound up with a nostalgic sense of national as well as individual identity. In all of them, the heroic quest which should restore this identity is, as Lury argues, bound up with the protagonist's 'desire to possess and control the sexuality of a little white girl.'"[5] However, according to Thornham, these sorts of narratives of masculine violence depend on a construction of the human subject as male, a construction that *You Were Never Really Here* thoroughly dismantles and revises.[6]

Meanwhile, a close look at Ramsay's film also shows that it dismantles the narrative of a damaged white man restoring his manhood by rescuing a threatened little white girl. Leigh Singer, in fact, concludes that this film is "a fascinating upending of the traditional heroic, or even anti-heroic journeys, where, in Ramsay's words, 'instead of having this big set piece about vengeance, it was about impotence.'"[7] Indeed, a look at the plot of the film shows just how thoroughly it disrupts conventional heroic narratives. At first, Joe seems as if he might be a coldly efficient professional. As he prepares to rescue Nina, we see him purchasing exactly the items he will need in a regular hardware store, almost McGyver-like (though he also carries a gun, just in case). He then carries out the rescue in what seems to be a rather conventional professional outing for him. However, things turn nasty when agents working for

Governor Williams of New York (Alessandro Nivola) later snatch the girl from Joe, shooting Joe in the face and nearly killing him in the exchange. In his work, Joe seem careful almost to the point of paranoia, but in this case his normal precautions turn out to be insufficient.

By the end of the film, Williams's men have killed virtually everyone Joe knows (including his handlers and his mother, as well as Nina's state senator father). After the death of his mother, Joe gives her a touching watery burial filling his pockets with rocks so he can join her, then changing his mind, unloading the rocks and shooting back to the surface, as if coming back from the dead. Meanwhile, this whole burial sequence is shot with such excessive artistry—reminiscent of the underwater "burial" of Shelley Winters's character in the film noir *The Night of the Hunter* (1955)—that the reality of the whole scene is called into question, given the uncertain texture of the whole film.

Ultimately, Joe does track Nina to Williams's country estate, which he stealthily enters with the intention of rescuing the girl. What follows is a climactic scene at Williams's home that is the climax, not just of the plot, but also of the film's epistemological uncertainty. Joe seems to get past Williams's security rather easily,[8] though reality and imagination are thoroughly entangled at this point. For example, a scene in which we see Williams preparing, possibly for sex with Nina, probably comes from Joe's imagination, even though Joe is not even present. As Joe looks for Nina in the home, we again hear "Angel Baby" playing, which further confuses our understanding of this song. The way it plays on the soundtrack here (louder in some rooms than others) makes it seem as if the song is really playing in the house. Is it the theme song of Williams's sex trafficking ring? Yet other aspects of this sequence suggest that this song is primarily intended to confuse our ability to distinguish between fantasy and reality, thus perhaps replicating the uncertainty that Joe experiences every day.

In a key moment, Joe locates Williams, only to find him dead on the floor with his throat cut. Joe seems to have a sort of breakdown, after which he rips off his shirt and wanders through the house, vaguely looking for Nina. When he sees his recently buried mother sitting calmly on a couch inside the house, then sees himself sitting opposite her, it is obviously his own imagination at work. He hears a strange, pounding noise, sees a vision of himself as a child, then finds Nina, sitting as if in a trance at a table eating with her bloody fingers from a dinner plate, a bloody razor lying next to her plate. The pounding noise morphs into discordant string music. Joe reaches out and strokes Nina on the shoulder, presumably to comfort her, but it is also possible that he is simply trying to determine if she is really there. Both he and we, at this point, are a little unsure of the reality of what we are seeing. Then Nina attempts to comfort *him*. "It's okay, Joe," she tells him.

In this crucial sequence, then, *You Were Never Really Here* clearly disrupts the narrative of *Taxi Driver*, a narrative that has been widely recognized to have been something of a rewrite of the problematic narrative of John Ford's classic Western *The Searchers* (1956), in which another damaged white male protagonist (played by John Wayne) rescues a young white girl from sexual captivity at the hands of a presumably savage ethnic Other. In Ramsay's film, however, the "savage" captor is a rich white figure of authority, while Nina is anything but a passive victim. Meanwhile, Joe shows a great deal of vulnerability. In a very real sense, Nina and Joe save each other, such as it is, thus disrupting the polarity of those earlier narratives in terms of race, class, and gender.

The film then immediately cuts to a scene in a diner, where Joe and Nina are having milkshakes. However, as opposed to the seedy diners seen so often in film noir, this one, though modest, is clean, well-lit, and wholesome looking. That is, it looks wholesome until Nina goes to the restroom, leaving Joe alone in their booth, where he takes out his gun and blows his head off. No one reacts, and Nina returns to awaken Joe from sleep, the shocking suicide having been just a dream (or a fantasy so vivid he lost consciousness). This whole unsettling sequence, though, makes the important point that the future of these two traumatized individuals remains extremely uncertain. The film seems to end on a positive note, as Joe agrees with Nina's reassuring declaration that "it's a beautiful day." Still, all we really know is that, at least for the time being, they have each other. With both her parents dead, Nina can now look to Joe as a sort of surrogate father. However, in keeping with the complexities of relationships in this film, Nina does not now assume the role of Joe's daughter. Instead, she becomes a sort of surrogate for his dead mother, each of them thus playing the role of both mirror image of the other and substitute parent for the other, defeating any attempt to view their relationship in conventional binary terms. Noir films have often been noted for their blurring of conventional hierarchies, but *You Were Never Really Here* performs a radical disruption of the narratives of heroic masculine violence that can be found in many films of the original noir cycle, thus encouraging us to rethink the implications of those narratives.

Chapter 14

The Revisionary Noir Lost Man: *Uncut Gems*

(2019, Directed by Josh and Benny Safdie)

Vincent Brook begins his study of the impact of Jewish émigré directors on the development of film noir by noting that directors such as Fritz Lang, Billy Wilder, Otto Preminger, Edgar G. Ulmer, Fred Zinnemann, Robert Siodmak, Curtis Bernhardt, Max Ophuls, and John Brahm have received a significant amount of attention in terms of their status as refugees but have received almost no attention with the regard to the Jewishness of their work, an omission that Brook's book (first published in 2009) is designed to rectify.[1] This list of directors is an impressive one, and to it one might add Jewish actors (such as John Garfield, Edward G. Robinson, and Kirk Douglas), writers (such as Herman Mankiewicz and Abraham Polonsky), composers (such as Bernard Herrmann and Erich Wolfgang Korngold), cinematographers (such as Stanley Cortez and John Alton), and producers (such as Mark Hellinger and Dore Schary), all of whom made major contributions to film noir. Yet Jewishness was seldom a major issue within the films themselves, no doubt partly because many Jewish filmmakers (and film executives) were wary of inadvertently triggering anti-Semitic backlash against the industry. When Jewishness was an issue in film noir, it was typically addressed somewhat obliquely, as in the critique of Nazism in Orson Welles's *The Stranger* (1946) or the critique of anti-Semitism in Edward Dmytryk's *Crossfire* (1947). As a result, Josh and Benny Safdie's *Uncut Gems* (2019) is striking both for the extent of its emphasis on Jewish life and culture and for the way the Jewishness of its characters and milieu is foregrounded in the film. As Michael Koresky puts it, "It's an exceedingly Jewish movie, and, in this era of movie product lacking cultural specificity and homogenized for prime international export, that's a good—even shocking—thing."[2] When combined with its genuinely new take on the noir lost man and its presentation of the world of New York's Diamond District as a compelling setting for noir action (not to mention a somewhat quirky emphasis on the game of basketball), *Uncut Gems* clearly qualifies as a revisionary noir film.

The protagonist and point-of-view character in *Uncut Gems* is New York gem dealer Howard Ratner (Adam Sandler), who qualifies as a lost man in almost every way. His jewelry business seems to be struggling, though his money troubles are apparently due primarily to his addiction to gambling, which has gotten him into debt to dangerous loan shark Arno Meradian (Eric Bogosian), who just happens to be married to the sister of Dinah Ratner (Idina Menzel), Howard's estranged wife. Meanwhile, the main plot of the film revolves around Ratner's grand (but somewhat sketchy) scheme to get rich quick by acquiring a gigantic rare black opal at a cut rate from a diamond mine in Ethiopia. Meanwhile, even this motif has a Jewish twist because the Ethiopian miners are Jews. It quickly becomes clear that Ratner's personal life is in tatters as well: in the process of becoming divorced from Dinah, he is living with his much younger mistress Julia De Fiore (Julia Fox), who also happens to work in his jewelry shop (and with whom he also has a problematic relationship).

Fox's performance is one of the highlights of the film—and she has since become something of a social media sensation, buoyed by a viral video highlighting her pronunciation of the film's title. Meanwhile, her character plays an important role in the film, though she tends to function mostly as a reflection of certain aspects of Ratner's character—largely because he is so firmly situated as the film's point-of-view character that we tend to see her as he sees her (which is very much as just another of the showy trinkets that he loves to acquire as signs of his success). Julia seems genuinely to care about Ratner but might be excessive in her willingness to put up with his sometimes-abusive behavior and his insecurities—as when he goes ballistic over her flirtation with the singer Weeknd (played by himself), though she is apparently only trying to close a sale of jewelry to him.

Ratner's tendency to make questionable personal decisions and disastrous financial choices eventually bring the film to a stunning ending when he is suddenly shot and killed by Phil (Keith William Richards), one of Arno's goons, just as a winning bet seems on the verge of making everything better. Yet this sudden and shocking ending has actually been set up and made almost inevitable by virtually everything that has come before in the film. Indeed, within the first few minutes of the film, Phil has already become infuriated at Ratner, yelling at him, "You're dead!" In this sense, Ratner is very much a typical doomed noir lost man, almost along the lines of Frank Bigelow (Edmond O'Brien) in *D.O.A.* (1950), who begins the film by announcing that he has just been murdered, or Joe Gillis (William Holden) in *Sunset Boulevard* (1950), who begins his voiceover narration as we see his own body floating face down in a swimming pool.

What is different about Ratner is the open focus on his Jewishness. Ratner's Jewish background figures directly in scenes such as the one in which he and his extended family (including Arno) sit down together for a Passover Seder, during which Ratner and his mother (she in Hebrew, he in English) recite the ten biblical plagues sent by

Figure 14.1. Howard Ratner (Adam Sandler) in *Uncut Gems*. A24/Photofest © A24

God to Egypt, which nicely rhymes with the sufferings of Ratner throughout the film. Ratner himself calls attention to his Jewishness several times, as when (relieved that his recent colonoscopy showed no signs of the cancer that killed his father) he sardonically remarks, "What is it with Jews and colon cancer? I thought we were the chosen people." At one point when their relationship is on the rocks after the Weeknd incident, Julia gets Ratner's name tattooed on her hip to express her love for him. He's touched but points out that now she won't be able to be buried with him, tattoos being taboo for Jews. Other characters also call attention to Ratner's Jewishness, as when his black associate Demany (LaKeith Stanfield) refers to him early in the film as a "crazy ass Jew." More subtly (and more importantly), *Uncut Gems* engages in an active dialogue with a number of stereotypes concerning what Jews experience in America. Ratner is a brash, loud, vulgar Jew, thus coming close to enacting a variety of negative Jewish stereotypes. As Jamie Lauren Keiles notes, this film is daring in its willingness to explore "whatever rough edges survive among American Jews."[3]

Uncut Gems was clearly a personal project for the Safdies. The film grows out of their own Jewish background, as well as their experience as the sons of a father who worked in the Diamond District when they were growing up. But its gritty noirish texture is also very much an extension of their earlier films, especially *Good Time* (2017), which is something of a noir heist film that features a lost man (played by Robert Pattinson) who resembles Howard Ratner in that his every attempt to make things better only ends up making them much worse. At the same time, the sordid, low-rent world of *Good Time* also makes it a revisionary noir, in that its unfortunate characters aren't disappointed by the American dream because they are so far outside the loop that their dream was already a nightmare.[4] Ratner, on the other hand, has very large dreams that seem to derive directly from the classic American dream narrative of immigrant opportunity and upward mobility.

Because of Ratner's status as a businessman, *Uncut Gems* engagesge directly with the system of American capitalism, his travails suggesting that there might be something inherently cruel and unsavory about the capitalist quest for profit. Koresky thus suggests that the film can be seen as "an expression of the inherent masochism of American entrepreneurship."[5] Of course, entrepreneurs are, in many ways, the new American heroes, often visualized as daring disruptors and risk takers, a cross between gunslingers and pirates but supposedly operating in a legal range (though often very close to the edge of that range). Of course, Ratner is very much not the ideal image of the heroic entrepreneur. He does make money, though he makes it by selling garish, kitschy trinkets to rappers and basketball stars; he also uses it to purchase showy, vulgar items that might impress others in his world but that don't exactly radiate taste and class. As Keiles puts it, "The wealth he accrues is not a tasteful kind of wealth but the type of striving, transcultural excess that shows up all across the ethnic upper classes: track lighting, Lucite, Sub-Zero fridges, sectional sofas in bizarre configurations."[6]

The black opal that figures so prominently in *Uncut Gems* is a fascinating object in its own right, sometimes presented as having almost mystical powers, perhaps along the lines of the commodity fetish, as discussed long ago by Karl Marx. Garnett, for example, is convinced that the gem has the power to help him play better. At one point, Ratner waxes poetic on the antiquity of the gem, then the camera seems to veer inside the opal, where it records a fast-motion montage sequence of the entire history of planet earth. The sequence is a bit heavy-handed, though there is reason to believe that it might be presented at least partly as a suggestion that Ratner might be putting too much faith in the gem, especially when it is combined with an early sequence in which the camera also veers inside the gem, encountering a sort of psychedelic wonderland, again suggesting almost mystical powers. Then, the sequence transitions into a shot inside Ratner's colon as he undergoes that colonoscopy. We are thus perhaps signaled early on that everything Ratner touches turns to shit.

On the other hand, the opening sequence inside the opal is mirrored by another sequence at the end of the film that shows the camera appearing to zoom through the bullet hole in the face of the murdered Ratner and then to soar about inside his body, which also turns out to be a CGI wonderland. This flight then morphs into a shot of a black starry sky, as if to suggest that Ratner has perhaps gone to heaven. Alternatively, this scene might be seen to suggest that even the vulgar and undisciplined Ratner contains wonders, that he is made (as Carl Sagan might have said) of "star stuff." This sequence thus becomes the mirror image of the opening sequence inside the opal, which began with wonders and ended with a shot of what Mikhail Bakhtin would have called the "grotesque body," while this final scene begins with an image of the grotesque body and ends with wonders.

Given the Cassavetes-like realism of most of the film, the artifice of the film's three CGI sequences seems particularly intrusive, demanding interpretation, while supplying no information that might make a definitive interpretation possible. The scenes are not especially impressive or well-crafted and certainly do not represent the state of the art in computer animation, no doubt partly because the film's $19 million budget is minuscule compared with the budgets of large CGI blockbusters. Still, these scenes need not have been included at all, so it seems likely that they are significant, and it is not entirely unreasonable to imagine that these sequences are meant to suggest that there *might* be a dimension to Ratner's life (and perhaps to life in general) that is nobler than the seediness of the material we see in the film.

One thing these sequences do for certain is add just a bit of noir strangeness, somewhat in the mode of the mysterious box in *Kiss Me, Deadly* (1955) or the drug sequence in *Murder, My Sweet* (1944). But this film recalls classic noir films in other ways as well. For example, the opal is something of a Hitchcockian MacGuffin, a device that helps to drive the plot but seems to have far more emphasis put on it than it really deserves. Perhaps the classic case of such a device in noir is the supposedly jewel-encrusted bird statue in *The Maltese Falcon* (1941). Indeed, Koresky compares the opal with that statue, as well as with the doomed treasure in the noir-inflected Western *The Treasure of the Sierra Madre* (1948).[7]

Granted, the gem does lead to an economic windfall—after a number of twists and turns, Ratner sells it to basketball star Kevin Garnett (played by himself) for $175,000, having supposedly bought it under the table from the miners for $100,000,[8] then bets that money on Garnett's next game. In one of the film's gestures toward realism, this pivotal game is the seventh game of the NBA's 2012 Eastern Conference semifinals (won by Garnett's Boston Celtics over the Philadelphia 76ers[9]), and the scenes featuring this game consist of actual footage from the game's television coverage. The Celts win the game, and Ratner wins a lucrative parlay, but only after a highly dramatic sequence in which Ratner confronts Arno and this thugs as the game goes on. Unfortunately, Ratner is killed by Phil before he receives the payoff, which could have gotten him out of trouble with Arno.

In addition to Garnett, other "real" people appear in the film, some of whom were essentially plucked by the Safdies off the streets of New York, such as twins Marshall and Ronald Greenberg, Jews who work in the Diamond District and who play Ratner's pawnbrokers in the film. Brothers Mitchell and Stewart Wenig appear as a hapless pair attempting to collect money that Ratner owes them, Mitchell having been spotted by the Safdies years earlier in a Tribeca diner. Even actors with much larger roles—such as Fox and Richards, both New Yorkers[10]—were acting for the first time in a feature film. In addition, the film also adds to its New York feel (and it is certainly a New York movie as much as a Jewish movie) by incorporating some well-known New York personalities, such as Mike Francesa, a prominent sports commentator who plays Ratner's bookie. Perhaps the most striking of the film's "real" characters is Wayne Diamond, an outrageous figure who is well-known in certain circles of New York society and who essentially plays himself as the high roller who befriends Julia at the casino where she places Ratner's bet on the Celtics-76ers game.

Diamond's character (described by another character in the film as "a cartoon") is so over-the-top that he adds a note of noir strangeness to the film, but most of the other "real" people in the film adds to its sense of gritty realism—and especially to its sense of *New York* realism. At the same time, the film does address a broader context. For example, its main Jewish characters might be very New York, but its Ethiopian miners provide a reminder of the global reach of the Jewish diaspora—and that there are *Black* Jews. The latter is important because the interactions between Ratner and the film's African American characters, which center on basketball (another personal enthusiasm of the Safdies) addresses what has been a long and sometimes complex relationship between these two prominent American ethnic minorities. One recalls here the crucial role, outlined by Michael Rogin, played by blackface in the historical process through which Jews inserted themselves into American culture partially through an appropriation of black cultural energies in complex ways that allowed Jews to proclaim themselves white. Focusing on the seminal 1927 film *The Jazz Singer* (prominent in film history as the first "talkie"), Rogin outlines the centrality of Jews to the development of the American film industry, while at the same time insisting that "every transformative moment in the history of American film has founded itself on the surplus symbolic value of blacks, the power to make African Americans stand for something besides themselves."[11] For Rogin, the plot of *The Jazz Singer* (in which little Jakie Rabinowitz becomes the jazz singer Jack Robin in order to escape the European Jewish culture of his father and thereby become a real American) provides an allegory of the importance of the entertainment industry to the cultural and economic assimilation of Jews in America. *The Jazz Singer* includes a striking scene in which star Al Jolson dons his famous blackface, thus allegorizing the phenomenon through which African Americans supply cultural energy, while Jewish performers like Jolson become stars and Jewish entrepreneurs like the Warner Brothers become rich.

Uncut Gems does not address the film industry directly—and involves the entertainment industry only via the sequence involving The Weeknd. Instead, this film substitutes basketball, which might be considered an entertainment industry—and one that is dominated almost entirely by Black performers. Thus, Demany (puzzled by Jews who love basketball, which Demany seems to regard as Black territory), asks Ratner, "What the fuck is it with you Jewish niggas and basketball, anyway?" This question, Koresky suggests, might as well have been addressed to the Safdies themselves.[12] But Ratner has a ready answer when he proudly (and accurately) boasts that a Jewish player, Ossie Schechter of the New York Knickerbockers, scored the first goal ever in the NBA back in 1946. Nevertheless, Jewish players have been fairly rare in the NBA, though the league has had a number of Jewish owners and executives, from high-profile owners such as Mark Cuban and Jerry Reinsdorf all the way up to current NBA commissioner Adam Silver. In short, however "Black" it might seem, the NBA resembles the rest of the American entertainment industry in that Black talent has typically been managed by white (often Jewish) executives.[13] In short, *Uncut Gems* addresses, via its basketball motif, the historical interrelationship between Jewish Americans and African Americans in some interesting ways.

Uncut Gems is typical of lost man noir in its focus on the personal tribulations of a deeply flawed male protagonist. The plot is also not unusual in that it involves a disastrous play for quick wealth. But the film goes far beyond most noir films in the intense realism of its emphasis on the New York Diamond District milieu of this protagonist—and especially on the Jewishness of this character and his life. In so doing, *Uncut Gems* also reaches beyond the specificity of its setting to address larger issues involving Judaism and ethnicity. Such emphases make this film an excellent example of revisionary noir because they call attention to the underrepresentation of Jews in the films of the original noir cycle, which was especially significant given the contributions of Jewish actors, executives, and filmmakers to the making of those original films.

Part III

WOMEN IN NOIR FILM

INTRODUCTION: WOMEN IN NOIR FILM

The original film noir cycle appeared at a time when gender roles in American society were in great flux, partly because of the role played by women in entering the workplace to substitute for men who were away at war and partly because of the sweeping changes in American society as a whole. And, while second wave feminism is generally seen as beginning with the women's movement of the 1960s, it is also clear that the beginnings of this movement were already taking shape in the 1950s. It is not surprising that the changing roles of women in American society in the 1940s and 1950s were reflected in American culture in a number of ways. It is also not surprising that film noir, one of the edgiest forms of American cultural production in the 1940s and 1950s, would also be one of the places in which the changing roles available to women would be reflected most clearly. In this case, the figure of the femme fatale—a strong, capable woman who is typically more than an intellectual match for the men she encounters—was clearly a step forward in the portrayal of the agency of women in American film, even if the typically amoral (or even downright evil) nature of the femme fatale made this advance a problematic one.[1]

Barbara Stanwyck's Phyllis Dietrichson, in Billy Wilder's *Double Indemnity* (1944) set a high standard for women in film noir, remaining to this day perhaps the best-known example of the film noir femme fatale. Later films, such as Joseph H. Lewis's *Gun Crazy* (1950)—with Peggy Cummins as Annie Laurie Starr and Wilder's *Sunset Boulevard* (1950)—with Gloria Swanson as Norma Desmond—would help the femme fatale character to evolve in some very interesting directions. *Double Indemnity* and *Sunset Boulevard* will be discussed in detail in this section.

Michael Curtiz's *Mildred Pierce* (1945) features another of the most important representations of women in film noir. Here, the title character (probably the most important female noir protagonist) is played by screen legend Joan Crawford, who won an Oscar for the role. Mildred is the faithful and hardworking wife of an unsuccessful husband, Bert Pierce (Bruce Bennett). She has devoted her entire adult life to this marriage; when it breaks down, she resolves to make it on her own and to give her daughters the things they need, beginning by finding a job as a waitress. Eventually, though, Mildred parlays this first job into a career as a successful restauranteur, along the way marrying the (now poor) scion of an old, wealthy family, Monte Beragon (Zachary Scott). When flirtations flare between Monte and Mildred's spoiled daughter Veda (Ann Blythe), a sort of young femme fatale in training, Veda and her mother become estranged. Ultimately, the whole story turns to tragedy.

Otto Preminger's *Fallen Angel* (1945) features Dana Andrews as Eric Stanton, an on-the-make drifter who gets stranded in the sleepy California town of Walton, lacking the $2.25 bus fare that would take him on to San Francisco, his intended destination. In Walton, he goes into Pop's Diner, where he encounters the eponymous aging proprietor (played by Percy Kilbride), who wiles away his days sick with love for his young employee, Stella (Linda Darnell). The dazzling Stella, in fact, seems to be a romantic target of many of the town's men, but she is no naïf waiting for love. In fact, the cynical, tough-talking Stella (the femme fatale of the piece) doesn't appear to believe in love at all. She just wants someone to marry her and provide her with a home so that she can stop working in the diner and have her own life. Stanton, who purports to be a formerly successful New York PR man, immediately falls for Stella and begins to employ all of his skills in an attempt to win her over. Recognizing what she wants, he manages to get her to agree to marry him on the condition that he come up with the money to buy a house and get a start in their new life together.

Given that Stanton can't actually even afford bus fare, this promise predictably leads to tragedy—in some very noir ways. The single-minded Stella and the fallen Stanton are classic noir characters, just as the Walton-San Francisco nexus provides some classic noir settings, while the mixture of romance, cynicism, corruption, and violence provides some classic noir thematics. It is also typical of film noir that the conniving Stanton and the gold-digging Stella are both rather sympathetic figures whose cynicism is appropriate to the world in which they live. Stella, in fact, is the real center of this film, and her depiction as a strong woman who knows what she wants and pursues it doggedly and honestly, refusing to be distracted by the longings of any of her lovesick suitors, is indicative of the kinds of female characters often found in film noir. That her dreams are so modest and pedestrian only makes her predicament more poignant, serving as a reminder of the limited opportunities open to women in 1940s America.

Charles Vidor's *Gilda* (1946) is a true classic of film noir. It is also the film that made Rita Hayworth, who plays the title character, the top sex symbol in Hollywood in the late 1940s. Gilda herself is one of the most famous of all femmes fatales, and she is complex character, as much victim as villain. In a sense, Gilda is almost pure sex object—except that she is not only in on her objectification, but largely in control of it. In many ways, she exemplifies woman as object; in many others, she exemplifies Judith Butler's notion of the performance of gender. She just happens to choose, for her own purposes, to perform a role of woman-as-conventional-sex-object. She's strong, she's wily, she's fierce, she's pitiless, treating men as objects as well and using them at least as much as they use her. In fact, if the film has a flaw, it's that male lead Johnny Farrell (Glenn Ford) seems completely out of his league with Gilda, partly because the serviceable but unimposing Ford is so overshadowed by Hayworth. Yet Gilda is also vulnerable and sweet at her core, acting more out of her own hurt and loss than any genuine malice. In short, she's a collection of feminine stereotypes, but a very interesting and complex collection whose own contradictions point out the contradictions in those stereotypes themselves. Perhaps the most memorable moment in this film is Hayworth's ultrasexy performance of "Put the Blame on Mame," with its central suggestion that all of the world's disasters are ultimately caused by conniving women. Just a little interpretive twist, though, and it's a critique of the way men have so often tried to blame things on women unfairly.

The year 1946 also saw the release of another woman-centered noir featuring one of Hollywood's most glamorous leading ladies. However, Hedy Lamarr, the star of *The Strange Woman*, was continually pushed to the margins of Hollywood, partly due to never overcoming the stigma of having appeared in the "shocking" European film *Ecstasy* (1933) as a teenager and partly due to never fully overcoming her Austrian accent. But Lamarr was resourceful and brilliant, as well as beautiful (one of her ideas provided a key technological basis for the later development of Bluetooth and Wi-Fi technologies), so she decided to form her own production company, which would make films in which she could star without dealing with the usual Hollywood nonsense. That effort was not notably successful, but *The Strange Woman* is actually a gem, no doubt partly due to the fact that Lamarr nabbed fellow Austrian ex-pat Edgar Ulmer (who had himself long been exiled to the margins of the film industry) to direct. The result is a noir film set in a New England town, mostly in the 1830s, though the town has much of the texture of the Wild West about it. That setting alone makes the film an unusual noir film, but noir it is, with Lamarr's Jenny Hager serving as a particularly interesting femme fatale, partly because she is also the protagonist and not simply a dangerous woman who brings *down* the protagonist. She's also a complex figure: absolutely ruthless in her willingness to exploit men to help her get beyond her difficult beginnings in life, Hager can also be generous and kind, while her backstory at least provides an explanation from her ruthlessness. The film has a bit of a hokey ending, but up until then it's a solid noir, despite the historical setting. And Lamarr is mesmerizing on screen, as usual.

Completing the trio of femme fatale noirs from 1946, Lana Turner is also mesmerizing in Tay Garnett's *The Postman Always Rings Twice*, based on James M. Cain's 1934 novel. The second half of this film gets a bit bogged down in legalistic maneuvers and excessive plot twists, but the first half is classic noir, dominated by Turner as the sultry Cora Smith, a classic example of the femme fatale who is driven by an American ideology that has taught her she can't possibly be happy unless she's rich. She's also a classic example of the femme fatale as siren: a poor girl who has never had anything going for her but her looks, she uses those looks to good effect to reel in drifter Frank Chambers (John Garfield), who just happens by the roadside diner and gas station that Cora runs with her aging husband Nick (Cecil Kellaway). Cora then induces Frank to help her kill Nick, unleashing a series of unintended consequences that ultimately dooms them all.

Just as Cora is a complex character who is both victim and villain, the crime-doesn't-pay message of this film is more complex than it first appears. For one thing, the legal system itself is represented as corrupt and heartless. Frank's impending execution for a crime he didn't commit after he earlier escaped execution for one he did, is thus not a simple case of poetic justice: it also suggests that, in modern America, it is simply impossible for individuals to beat the system—especially unconnected working-class individuals like Frank and Cora.

Jean Negulesco's *Road House* (1948) is another female-centric film that revolves around singer Lily Stevens (Ida Lupino), who is brought in from Chicago by roadhouse owner Jefty Robbins (Richard Widmark) to entertain the patrons at his establishment, located somewhere near the Canadian border. It turns out, however, that Robbins has a habit of recruiting female singers as sexual targets, but Stevens turns out to be a match for him. Not only does she repel his advances, but she begins a relationship with the roadhouse's manager, Pete Morgan (Cornel Wilde). The smarmy Robbins concocts a plot to frame Morgan and have him sent to prison, so that he can have Stevens for himself. Stevens, though, is still a match for him and ends up shooting him down in self-defense, while evidence surfaces that will clear Morgan. *Road House* is an interesting drama with some very effective rapid-fire noir dialogue, though Lupino's musical performances as Stevens are a highlight of the film, as is the depiction of Stevens as a strong, independent female who can very much take care of herself. Widmark, meanwhile, delivers another strong performance as a psychopathic character with a mad giggle, repeating (in a slightly toned-down form) the persona he had created a year earlier in *Kiss of Death*.

In Byron Haskin's *Too Late for Tears* (1949), Lizabeth Scott—who often plays the (relatively) good girl in noir films—gets to be the villain, even though she is at least partly the victim of circumstances. When a satchel containing $60,000 literally falls into the laps of Scott's Jane Palmer and husband Alan (Arthur Kennedy), he wants to turn it into the cops, but she wants to keep it to make their lives financially easier. After all, she still bitterly remembers her own difficult childhood. As she herself puts it: "It wasn't because we were poor, not hungry poor at least. I suppose it was worse, far worse. We were white collar poor, middle-class poor. The people who can't quite keep up with the Joneses and die a little every day because they can't." The money, as it turns out, was meant as a blackmail payment to the smarmy Danny Fuller (Dan Duryea), who inevitably shows up to retrieve the money. Jane (apparently by accident) shoots and kills Alan, then she intentionally poisons Fuller to get him off her back. She tries to kill Alan's sister Kathy (Christine Miller) as well, so by this time it is no real surprise when we learn that she apparently killed her first husband as well. She escapes to Mexico with the loot and then accidentally falls to her death as the Mexican police, tipped off by the brother of her first husband (played by Don DeFore), close in. A bit sloppy around the edges, this film still effectively presents Jane as a surprisingly deadly villain—but also as a victim of the American middle-class drive for upward mobility.

The File on Thelma Jordon (1950), directed by Robert Siodmak, is a classic case of a film noir built around a femme fatale character, in this case the character of the title, played by Barbara Stanwyck, one of the greatest enactors of the femme fatale role. The plot is simple: Jordon conspires with her shady boyfriend Tony Laredo (Richard Rober) to murder her Aunt Vera (Gertrude W. Hoffmann) and inherit a fortune for the two of them. What's worse, in order to assure herself of getting away with the murder, she connives to begin an affair with Assistant DA Cleve Marshall (Wendell Corey), precisely so that she can count on Marshall to sabotage the prosecution should she go to trial. Marshall is a classic film noir character: he is not evil, just restless and bored with his marriage, which makes him easy pickings for Jordon, who has all the wiles of the typical femme fatale, if not all the ruthlessness. The plan thus works like a charm—except that Jordon has a change of heart in the end. She shocks Marshall by confessing the entire plot, then leaving him behind as she goes away with Laredo to enjoy the fruits of their deceit. Then, suddenly overcome by guilt, she intentionally causes their car to crash. Laredo is killed, and she is mortally injured. Before she dies, though, Jordon confesses to all her crimes, though she does not finger her accomplice (Marshall), saying she will not identify him because she loves him. Nevertheless, Marshall is left a broken man as the film ends, his life shattered and his career ruined.

In Roy Rowland's *Witness to Murder* (1954), the protagonist spots a murder being committed in another apartment across the way, but then has trouble convincing the police that the murder even occurred. The film is thus strikingly similar to Hitchcock's much admired *Rear Window*, which was released later in the same year. However, *Witness to Murder* features a female protagonist, played by noir goddess Stanwyck, introducing some additional gender-related themes. For example, though the police detective investigating the case is a bit sweet on Stanwyck's character, it is clear that he initially dismisses her account of the crime because of her gender. The film also includes another common noir theme in that the killer (played with delightful menace by George Sanders) is a former Nazi. But what really makes this one a great noir film is the outstanding cinematography of John Alton, which is so effective that many true fans of noir might find that *Witness to Murder* is actually *better* than *Rear Window*, though the latter obviously has a loftier reputation in film history.

Women in Neo-Noir Film

Given that neo-noir film arose at about the same time as the women's movement of the 1960s, it should come as no surprise that women were often represented in interesting new ways in neo-noir films. Thus, roles other than that of the femme fatale became more available to women in neo-noir film, even though the figure of the femme fatale remains absolutely crucial to the genre.[2] A landmark film such Lawrence Kasdan's *Body Heat* (1981), which will be discussed in detail in this section, mimics *Double Indemnity* in many ways—so many that it is clearly not a revisionary noir. But the mismatch between its femme fatale (Kathleen Turner's Matty Walker) and its lost-man point of view character (William Hurt's Ned Racine) is far greater than that between Phyllis Dietrichson and Walter Neff—partly because Ned is more hapless than Walter and partly because Matty is even more ruthless and nefarious than Phyllis. Similarly, the femme fatale of John Dahl's *The Last Seduction* (1994)—Linda Fiorentino's Bridget Gregory—is always several steps ahead of the male characters she encounters. That film is also discussed in detail in this section. Both Matty and Bridget go well beyond the original femmes fatales in the way they so explicitly use sex as a tool of manipulation, then actually triumph and are not punished for their nefarious ways. Neither, however, really seems to go beyond the original noir films in ways that would make us understand those films differently.

Body Heat and *The Last Seduction* participated in a wave of "erotic thrillers" that was one of the key elements of the representation of women in neo-noir film. These two films were part of a wave of neo-noir "erotic thrillers" that also included such films as *Body Double* (1984), *Fatal Attraction* (1987), *The Hot Spot* (1990), *Shattered* (1991), *A Kiss Before Dying* (1991), *Unlawful Entry* (1992), *Malice* (1993), *Indecent Proposal* (1993), *Sliver* (1993), and *Disclosure* (1994). In general, though, the revision of noir conventions in these erotic thrillers is fairly weak, consisting mostly of things the original noir films might have done if not for the limitations dictated by the Production Code—especially sexual things. As Kate Stables puts it, the 1990s femme fatale might have been summed up by the declaration of Madonna's Rebecca Carlson in *Body of Evidence* (1993): "That's what I do—I fuck."[3]

Meanwhile, neo-noir films featuring women have continued to appear in the twenty-first century. Brian DePalma's *Femme Fatale* (2002) is overtly linked to the original noir cycle, both in its title and in the fact that the majority of its action turns out to be an extended dream sequence that is partly inspired by a viewing of *Double Indemnity* on the part of its title character (played by Rebecca Romijn). However, most of the film doesn't really look or feel all that much like film noir, and the film certainly doesn't engage *Double Indemnity* or other original noir films in any kind of critical dialogue. Meanwhile, while Romijn's character is both seductive and formidable (and an international jewel thief), she really does little to revise our understanding of the original femme fatale characters. Thus, while it is true that the film's use of *Double Indemnity* is so gimmicky as to weaken any nostalgia effect, this film is clearly better regarded as neo-noir, rather than revisionary noir.

Deon Taylor's *Fatale* (2020) also calls attention to its central femme fatale character (and almost gives away its central plot twist) via its title. That character herself breaks some decidedly new ground relative to the femme fatale characters in the original noir cycle. As played by Oscar-winning actress Hilary Swank, Val Quinlan is not only a femme fatale but also a police detective, which would never happen in the original noir films. The film's male lead, played by Michael Ealy, is Derrick Tyler, a successful sports agent whose seemingly wonderful life is disrupted by marital troubles that lead him to even worse troubles when he takes a business trip to Vegas, then hooks up with Quinlan, having no idea that she is a police detective or that she is from Los Angeles, where he lives. After Tyler returns to L.A., Quinlan is assigned to investigate a break-in at his home, which sets in motion a series of twists and turns that are made significantly more serious by the fact that Quinlan is not a woman to be trifled with and cast aside, having more than a little bit of Alex Forrest in her character. She is also a strong character who is perfectly capable of carrying out her own plots, rather than simply to lure a man into doing it for her (though she does that too). This film also goes beyond anything in the original noir cycle in that Tyler is Black, while Quinlan is white, but race is essentially treated as a nonissue in this film (which in itself might be seen as a step forward). All in all, though, this film's updates to noir motifs do relatively little to revise our understanding of the original noir cycle.

Women in Revisionary Noir Film

The roles played by women in revisionary noir film have extended well beyond what is seen in neo-noir film, though many of these films have simply involved a greater frankness in the exploration of certain sexual themes. For example, it seems appropriate to consider at least one film from the erotic thriller cycle of the 1980s and 1990s—Paul Verhoeven's *Basic Instinct* (1992)—to be a revisionary noir film mainly for this reason, largely for its explicit treatment of sexuality, including lesbian sexuality. At the same time, its central female character, Catherine Tramell, is extremely intelligent and well educated, giving her tools for the manipulation of men that go well beyond her considerable physical charms. This film also introduces a sort of metafictional wrinkle by having femme fatale Catherine Tramell (Sharon Stone) be a novelist who uses her noirish encounters as fodder for her fiction. Finally, some of the narrative twists in *Basic Instinct* revise the narrative conventions of film noir in unusually strong ways.[4] It is discussed in detail in this section.

A number of recent noir films qualify as revisionary because their treatment of specific social issues is so significantly updated beyond what is found in the original noir cycle that they ask us to rethink the treatment of those same issues in the original noir films. *Basic Instinct*, for example, is joined by films such as Jane Campion's *In the Cut* (2003), David Fincher's *Gone Girl* (2014), Steve McQueen's *Widows* (2018), and Emerald Fennell's *Promising Young Woman* (2020) in presenting female characters as smart, independent, and capable, with considerable agency (though that agency is often—but not always—put to ill use). To this list one might add Ridley Scott's stylish *The Counselor* (2013), which adds to the legacy of noir films involving Mexico or the US-Mexican border[5] but is probably most interesting for its particularly sexy, efficient, and ruthless femme fatale (played by Cameron Diaz), who emerges triumphant from a web of schemes that leaves most of the characters played by the film's high-profile cast addition dead by spectacular means. *Gone Girl* and *Promising Young Woman* are discussed in detail in this section.

Finally, one might also note films such as Karyn Kusama's *Destroyer* (2018), which features Nicole Kidman as a Los Angeles police detective, and John Patton Ford's *Emily the Criminal* (2022), which features Aubrey Plaza in the title role as a young woman struggling so mightily to pay off her student loans that she is driven into crime, where she ultimately achieves a lucrative career. In a sense, the female characters in these revisionary noir films do very much what the women in the original noir films attempted to do, but they go so far beyond those original films that they highlight the severely limited way the original noir films were able to portray women. It is not entirely clear whether this sort of revision makes the original noir films seem more daring or less daring in their portrayal of female characters, but it is fairly clear that these newer films can at least open up a debate on such questions. Meanwhile, it is not insignificant that many of these revisionary noir films were directed by women,[6] a phenomenon that promises to expand in the future.[7]

Chapter 15

Women in Film Noir: *Double Indemnity*

(1944, Directed by Billy Wilder)

Double Indemnity was described by Raymond Durgnat in his survey of film noir as "perhaps the central film noir, not only for its atmospheric power, but as a junction of major themes."[1] James Naremore, meanwhile, agrees that *Double Indemnity* is "a definitive film noir and one of the most influential movies in Hollywood history."[2] Indeed, the film contains numerous classic noir elements, though it is also the case that some of these elements became classics because of the influence of *Double Indemnity* on other films. The film itself was a groundbreaking effort that barely made it past the Code censors, and then only after significant revisions. Directed by Billy Wilder and based on a 1943 novella of the same title by hardboiled writer James M. Cain, *Double Indemnity* is built on a classic scenario in which femme fatale Phyllis Dietrichson (Barbara Stanwyck) lures the greedy-but-weak insurance salesman Walter Neff (Fred MacMurray) to his doom as part of her own plan to kill her husband and make off with his insurance money. Indeed, Stanwyck's Phyllis is perhaps the best known femme fatale in all of film noir. The story itself is not all that remarkable, but the execution—from the script by Wilder and Raymond Chandler to the performances by Stanwyck, MacMurray, and Edward G. Robinson to the music of Miklós Rózsa and the camerawork of John Seitz—is superb.

Like so many noir films, *Double Indemnity* begins at the end, as a dying Walter Neff (Fred MacMurray) speaks into a Dictaphone, telling the story that will then be enacted in flashback on the screen, finally bringing us, at the end, back to the point where Neff, mortally wounded, staggers into the offices of his employer, the Pacific All-Risk Insurance Company, to dictate his story. That story, as it turns out, is quintessential film noir. If anything, the film is even darker and more cynical than

Figure 15.1. Phyliss Dietrichson and Walter Neff (Barbara Stanwyck and Fred MacMurray) secretly meet in a supermarket in *Double Indemnity*. Paramount Pictures/ Photofest © Paramount Pictures

the original novel. However, the film, taking full advantage of its medium, is also much campier and more theatrical than the novel. Many of the scenes are classics of visual suggestiveness—like the one in which Phyllis walks slinkily down a transparent stairway wearing a honey of an anklet, looking every bit as dangerous as she is (even though shown only from the knees down), while Walter waits below ogling, the camera clearly representing his point of view. The scenes in which Walter and Phyllis furtively meet in a Los Angeles supermarket, surrounded by neat rows of commodities, are visual masterpieces as well, hinting (but only hinting) at a possible symbolic association between their criminal activities and the ethos of modern consumer capitalism.

Such scenes might be described as visual double entendres; double entendre also being crucial to the rapid-fire dialogue that helps to make *Double Indemnity* so truly memorable. This dialogue, far more interesting than any in Cain's novel, is in fact more reminiscent of the verbal energies of Chandler's novels. For example, Walter first sees Phyllis as she stands on a balcony at the top of that stairway, wrapped only in a towel, having just come in from sunbathing. The towel hangs tantalizingly (as if carefully arranged that way), seeming just on the verge of falling down to reveal her left breast. Insurance salesman that he is, Walter immediately reminds her how unfortunate it would be were something untoward to happen while she is not "fully covered." "Perhaps I know what you mean," she says. Something clicks behind both their eyes, whirs inside both their heads, and the two are off to the races in a mad rush toward adultery, deception, and murder. Much of the rest of their dialogue is like a dangerous and delirious dance, each trying to one-up the other in elliptical suggestiveness, their conversations mirroring the way in which their relationship is both a torrid romance and a bitter competition.

This dialogue can be highly entertaining, but this film has a lot to say beyond the dialogue. For example, we should not underestimate the extent to which the Nirdlinger/Dietrichson residence is a dream home, particularly an *American* Dream home. But it is a middle-class dream, a modest dream, a far cry from the mansions into which Philip Marlowe wanders in *Murder, My Sweet* or *The Big Sleep*. The reason it is like so many other homes in Los Angeles is because it epitomizes what people come to Southern California hoping to achieve. That it is presented in both the novel and (more effectively) in the film as a fake and manufactured goal—something people have been programmed to want rather than something that meets any real needs—is precisely the point. Even if they achieve this dream, what do they really have? Indeed, one reason why *Double Indemnity* is widely viewed as the quintessential noir film is the extent to which exemplifies the cynical attitude toward the American dream that is typical of film noir in general.

One reason the film is more effective than the novel in this sense is the way in which it turns its critique inward, making *Double Indemnity* itself (and, by extension, Hollywood in general) an example of the commodified falseness that it so effectively critiques. For example, the lighting and shadow effects for which film noir in general are justifiably famous are here used so extensively as to call attention to themselves. If the classic film noir visual is the pattern of light and shadow cast on a wall by light shining through a Venetian blind, then the classic example of this effect is the Dietrichson living room when Neff first walks into it, a pattern that suggests the world of shadowy morality into which Neff is about to be plunged but that also suggests careful composition. As Neff enters the living room, the shadows of the Venetian blinds fall not only on the opposite wall but on him, suggesting that he is about to become a part of what goes on here. Meanwhile, his own shadow is also cast on the opposite wall, suggesting that he, too, will contribute to the shadowy misdeeds that are to come.

If the visuals of *Double Indemnity* are self-consciously composed, then the dialogue is even more so. Not so much realistic as expressionistic, this dialogue (like the lighting) is designed to create a mood, but also to call attention to its own manufactured quality. It is a kind of hardboiled poetry, not only more Chandler than Cain, but also more Brecht than Ibsen, more melody than meaning, in a modern American version of the Shakespearean dialogue rejected so forcefully by Tolstoy because "nobody talks that way." Among other things, the intentional artifice of such conversations suggests the hands of the makers: surely audiences are meant to delight to such lines as the creative products, not of Walter and Phyllis, but of Wilder and (especially) Chandler, with Cain in the background. At the same time, the artifice of these lines suggests the inauthenticity, not only of the relationship between Walter and Phyllis, but of the characters themselves. They speak prefabricated lines that are not their own because they are prefabricated subjects, produced by a consumer capitalist culture that turns out row after row of hollowly inauthentic individuals, as interchangeable as the rows of canned goods on the shelves of the supermarket that is, tellingly, the preferred meeting place of the two murderous lovers. It is not for nothing that Phyllis is willing blithely to exchange Mr. Dietrichson for Walter or Walter for Nino Zachette, or that Walter is also willing to change horses in midstream, jumping from the treacherous Phyllis, to Lola, her young and presumably innocent stepdaughter.

Amid all these superficial relationships, the film also provides, for contrast, a reminder of what a more authentic relationship might be. For Walter, in the film, not only attempts to carry on problematic love affairs with Phyllis and then Lola, but also has a sort of bromance with Barton Keyes (Edward G. Robinson), the head claims investigator at Pacific All-Risk. Indeed, Walter is wont to answer Keyes's gruff barbs by announcing, "I love you too," even as he habitually lights matches (with a suave flick of the thumb) for the ignition of Keyes's phallic cigars, in a gesture the homoerotic implications of which are quite clear. Then again, as Johnston points out, Keyes can also be seen as a father figure to Walter.[3]

Keyes's dialogue is itself hardboiled, but the exchanges between Walter and Keyes are relatively straightforward and realistic when compared with those between Walter and Phyllis, indicating a much more candid understanding and stable bond between the two male characters. This dialogue, however, has a richness of its own: Naremore sees it as the kind of dialogue that one might find between two screenwriters at a story conference, with Pacific All-Risk Insurance Company subbing for Paramount and the insurance industry standing in for the film industry, a suggestion that shifts much of the film's obvious critique of capitalism into a more subtle critique of the film industry and of its complicity with capitalism.

The hyperconscientious Keyes is in many ways the opposite of Phyllis, but in the world of film noir, such oppositions seldom exist in the form of simple good versus evil. For Keyes is also a hollow man. His devotion to his duty is almost inhuman, though that devotion does seem to be to his own personal code rather than to the company, for which he expresses a certain contempt. Meanwhile, Keyes, as the minion of a powerful corporation, can be brutal in his treatment of the little people with whom he comes into contact. Thus, in the early scene in which he dismisses a claim by truck driver Sam Garlopis (Fortunio Bonanova) as fraudulent (because of evidence that Garlopis intentionally set his truck on fire), Keyes seems to take genuine (sadistic) pleasure in humiliating the man, despite the latter's protestations to poverty and hardship. Keyes is at his most human in his clear, somewhat fatherly, affection for Walter, to the point that this affection clouds the claims man's usual sharp judgment, leading him to conclude that Walter could not possibly be involved in a plot to murder Dietrichson and collect the insurance. Nevertheless, when Keyes is confronted with the fact of Walter's guilt, his affection for his younger colleague does not dissuade him from the swift performance of his subsequent duty. He refuses even to let the wounded Walter die quietly, insisting on calling the police and an ambulance, though, as the film ends, it appears that Walter may die before this "help" arrives.

Walter is, in many ways, the quintessential film noir lost man. He thinks of himself as cynically wise in the ways of the world, yet, at every turn, he faces circumstances that are beyond his capacity to manage. Compared to Phyllis, he is a true naif; his proclivity for calling her "baby" throughout the film contains a grim irony that merely highlights her superior ruthlessness and sophistication—an irony that is, in fact, reflected in Walter's own voice. In many ways, Keyes is even more naïve than Walter, however savvy he may be in the maneuvers used by policyholders in their attempts to extract payment from the insurance company. After all, Keyes seems to know very little about life beyond the insurance business. Once, he tells Walter, he nearly married, but took the precaution of having the woman investigated beforehand. What he found led him to conclude, as Walter summarizes it for him, that "she was a tramp in a long line of tramps." This long line, for Keyes, apparently includes all women, so he now avoids them, sticking to the masculine world of business, whereby he manages to avoid the disasters that befall Walter when the latter becomes ensnared in Phyllis's web. The final scene, in which Keyes looks down on the fallen Walter, now so helpless that *Keyes* has tos light a match for *him*, thus doubly emphasizes Walter's demise, while at the same time merely reinforcing the true helplessness he has experienced throughout the film. Meanwhile, the circular narrative structure of *Double Indemnity* (like so many other noir films) reinforces this sense of helplessness. The characters merely spin their wheels, travel in circles, and get nowhere, verifying their own lack of any true direction in life.

At first glance, the politics at stake in *Double Indemnity* are sexual ones. Andrew Dickos sees the film as emblematic of a certain strain of noir films in which "fierce sexuality identified with the female image reinforces the misogyny behind the male construction of such a dangerous woman who clearly threatens the power of her male rivals." For Dickos, the femme fatale in such films is able to lead the male protagonists to their dooms largely because they assume that, as males, they will be able to establish a position of dominance in their relationships with these dangerous women. "The 'tragic' error such men make, recurrent throughout the tales of *femmes fatales*, is in their attempt to control, to tame, the female image that at once arouses and threatens them."[4]

It is certainly the case that, in *Double Indemnity*, Walter seriously miscalculates his ability to handle Phyllis. He, at least initially, thinks of her as a woman, a wife, accustomed to being confined to the domestic sphere, though he also recognizes in her a fellow transgressor against conventional norms of behavior. He, a man of the world who is constantly out and about selling insurance to all different sorts of people, is confident that he understands the workings of the world better than does Phyllis. For her part, Phyllis is perfectly aware of his condescension and uses it to her advantage—though one might also argue that she herself miscalculates her ability to manipulate Walter. From the very beginning, their relationship is more a contest for power and control than of genuine romance. Little wonder, then, that it all comes to such a bad end, with each delivering a fatal gunshot to the other.

It is important, however, to recognize the careful construction of the Walter-Phyllis relationship not as an aberration, but as a typical result of life under modern capitalism, where the prevailing ethos of each-against-all dictates that all relationships between individuals are also contests between competitors. As opposed to the relationship of Walter and Keyes, which is figured as something of a throwback to earlier times, this relationship is purely commodified, purely instrumental, like every other product of modern capitalism as figured in the film: each partner is in it only for the profit that can be gained, not out of any sort of genuine feeling for the other.

Such interpretations are subtly reinforced by numerous elements of *Double Indemnity*, as in Neff's reference to the mass-produced, soulless décor of the Dietrichson home or in the frequent use of mechanical and industrial metaphors in the language of the text. It is, for example, not insignificant that the murder plan centrally involves a train, trains having functioned since the nineteenth century as key metaphors for capitalist modernization. In this case, of course, the use of the train rhymes with the language of Neff's narration, which often uses mechanical or industrial metaphors. Indeed, as William Luhr has pointed out, machine metaphors permeate the text, suggest a certain deterministic view of reality as a giant machine that, once set in motion, cannot be stopped by human intervention.[5] Meanwhile, as Naremore points out, Phyllis Dietrichson herself is a thoroughly commodified sexual object, even if she has actively participated in her own commodification. Compared with Phyllis Nirdlinger in the novel, he notes,

> The character portrayed by Barbara Stanwyck is much more blatantly provocative and visibly artificial; her ankle bracelet, her lacquered lipstick, her sunglasses, and above all her chromium hair give her a cheaply manufactured, metallic look. In keeping with this synthetic quality, her sex scenes are almost robotic, and she reacts to murder with an icy calm.[6]

Naremore sees *Double Indemnity* as a particularly grim condemnation of modern American society, arguing that the only other Hollywood feature from the same time period to treat the "theme of industrial progress with greater despair and sophistication was Orson Welles' *The Magnificent Ambersons*."[7] Indeed, notes Naremore, both of these films were so negative in their diagnosis of the impact of modern industrial capitalism on the lives of individual human beings that both had to have their endings changed—Welles's film when the studio reshot the ending behind his back and Wilder's film when he agreed to change the original ending (which saw Neff executed in the gas chamber) in order to placate the censors implementing the Production Code.

Most critics have felt that *The Magnificent Ambersons* was diminished by its changed ending (which tacked an essentially happy—and very discordant—resolution onto a film that otherwise moves irrevocably toward doom and disaster), though most critics (supported by Wilder's own statements on the matter) have tended to see the somewhat lighter (though still dark) ending to the released version of *Double Indemnity* actually to be an improvement. Naremore is not so sure, however, guessing that a final vision of Walter being killed by a coldly impersonal modern arm of the state would have won sympathy for him, while making the book's critique of modern American capitalism all the more powerful.

However, Naremore grants that this critique is already quite powerful, focusing on the specifics of Los Angeles as a sort of ultimate embodiment of modern American society, as "a dangerously seductive Eldorado—a center of advanced capitalism, instrumental reason, and death."[8] For Naremore, what was truly controversial about the film, especially in the original version, was the way in which the gears of modern America turn relentlessly, carrying Walter to his death as if on an assembly line in the culminating gas chamber sequence.[9] Both Chandler and Wilder grew up in Europe, and Naremore suggests that they were able to critique Los Angeles so effectively because they viewed it with the eyes of outsiders.

As James Paris (who puts great emphasis on the unprecedented nature of *Double Indemnity*) notes, of Wilder, "Perhaps it took a European who had lost an entire world to see life with such a bittersweet sense of irony."[10] And yet, at the same time, Paris also captures something else important that should never be neglected when speaking of *Double Indemnity*—the exhilarating sense that one is encountering, while watching the film, a truly wonderful work of art. As Paris puts it, "What in Cain's novel seems merely sordid is converted by Wilder's magic touch into something rich and strange."[11] One thinks here of nothing more than that crucial moment in Wilder's *Sunset Boulevard* (1950) when young, wide-eyed Betty Schaefer remarks of the artificiality of a street that has been constructed on the Paramount lot as a movie set, then declares it her favorite street in the world. In this sense, *Double Indemnity* captures not only the sordid reality of the contemporary American dream (and of the Hollywood dream factory), but also the glorious promise of dreaming in general.

Chapter 16

Women in Film Noir: *Sunset Boulevard*

(1950, Directed by Billy Wilder)

Sunset Boulevard enjoys a somewhat uneasy position within the noir canon, partly because it is informed throughout by a humor (however dark) that is rare in a noir film. However, with the great noir director Billy Wilder at the helm, the great noir cinematographer John F. Seitz (who shot Wilder's *Double Indemnity* and *The Lost Weekend*) behind the camera, and a narrative structure that provides the ultimate in flashback technique, *Sunset Boulevard* clearly qualifies as a noir film. Like many such films, we are guided through its story by the voiceover narration of the male protagonist (in this case screenwriter Joe Gillis, played by William Holden), but this film is clearly dominated by the figure of one-time silent film superstar Norma Desmond (Gloria Swanson), who is herself an unconventional femme fatale, though she is a femme fatale, nevertheless. Desmond's story provides us not only with telling commentary on the gender politics of aging but also the biting commentary on the film industry for which this film is so well-known.

Sunset Boulevard begins with a classic noir opening sequence, as if to direct viewers to view the film in that context. It opens on a shot of a somewhat rundown-looking sidewalk, with a brief musical cue that echoes Miklós Rózsa's theme music for *Double Indemnity*. The camera then slowly moves downward, revealing that "SUNSET BOULEVARD" is painted on the curb. However, the gutter next to the curb looks grimy, littered with leaves. Desmond lives in Beverly Hills, but the condition of this gutter and this sidewalk suggests that it is a decaying Beverly Hills, and not the iconic rich Beverly Hills of the popular American imagination. Thus, given the popular image of Beverly Hills as a haven for those who have realized the American dream to its fullest, the setting itself already suggests that the American dream might not be all that it is cracked up to be.

The camera next pans onto and down the boulevard itself, showing lots of marred, cracked, and broken pavement. This is far from a golden avenue to paradise. It is, in fact, the road to death, as we realize when the camera suddenly shows a detachment of police racing down the boulevard, identified by Gillis's voiceover as belonging to the homicide squad. Further, Gillis explains that a murder has been committed at one of the big mansions along the way, one that belongs to a once-famous Hollywood star. Wilder then gets in a bit of news media critique (anticipating the main subject matter of his *Ace in the Hole* a year later) when he has Gillis announce that he is going to explain the truth behind the events leading to this murder before the press can get to the story and distort it.

We see the body of the murdered man floating face down in the pool adjacent to the mansion, though it will still be a few moments before it becomes clear that this is the body of Gillis himself, who is thus posthumously narrating the events leading up to his own death. In this sense, he becomes a particularly overt example of the doomed men who so often populate noir films. That this sort of narration is not literally possible is no problem, of course—this is a Hollywood film, not reality. This posthumous narration thus serves as a constant reminder that what we are watching is a constructed fiction, a product of the very Hollywood system that the film is so directly about. But this motif also destabilizes our interpretation of the film, introducing an element of cognitive dissonance that runs throughout, often creating a strange sort of black comedy but always threatening to disrupt the kind of immersion in the narrative that is usually the goal of Hollywood films.

As Gillis begins to tell his story, we learn that he is a not-so-successful screenwriter who is struggling mightily to make ends meet, among other things trying to evade the repo men who are attempting to take his new car, on which he has been unable to make the payments. He tries to sell his latest movie idea (essentially a noir film set in the world of professional baseball, of all things) to Paramount, but fails when junior script reader Betty Schaefer (Nancy Olson) points out that the story is basically just a trite rehash of *Hunger*, an 1890 novel by Norwegian Nobel Prize–winner Knut Hamsun. Growing more and more desperate, Gillis drives down Sunset Boulevard with the repo men in hot pursuit; then, to make matters worse, he has a blowout, causing him to have to pull into the nearest driveway.

The driveway, of course, leads to the mansion we saw at the beginning of the film, which happens to be the home of Norma Desmond, who lives in the ritzy, but decaying edifice with her "butler," Max von Mayerling (Erich von Stroheim), who turns out also to have been her first director back in the silent film days, as well as her first husband. Gillis stashes his car in the garage, where he notices a huge foreign car with a 1932 license plate. The mansion is impressive, but it is also clearly in a state of disrepair. "It was a great big white elephant of a place," says Gillis in his voiceover, "the kind crazy movie people built in the crazy twenties."

Desmond mistakes Gillis for an undertaker who has been called to the mansion to ply his trade. The decidedly sinister-like von Mayerling takes charge of Gillis and sends him upstairs, calling out to him, "If you need any help with the coffin, call me." Desmond then guides Gillis to the dead body, which has been placed on a massage table in front of a fireplace, because "he always liked fires, and poking at them with a stick." She immediately starts describing the kind of coffin she wants, while at the same time already haggling over the price. She slowly uncovers the body—which turns out to be that of a chimpanzee. Taken aback, Gillis decides to beat a hasty retreat from this house of madness. But then he suddenly recognizes Desmond and notes that she "used to be big." She immediately—and theatrically—responds (in one of the film's most famous moments), "I *am* big. It's the pictures that got small."

Desmond then launches into a diatribe about how the coming of sound degraded the stature of film as an art form, producing arguments that are actually not insane at all, echoing the well-known concerns of silent film legends such as Charlie Chaplin. At the same time, despite her complaints about the way in which "words" have diminished the visual medium of film, it turns out that she herself has been working on a screenplay for years. When she discovers that Gillis is a screenwriter, she then decides to enlist his help in whipping her script for biblical-era temptress Salome into shape so that she can make a comeback by starring in it.

Desmond's idea of a film featuring Salome is probably not a bad one, given that biblical epics were about to become all the rage in American film. One could argue, however, that she is too old to play the role. One also wonders whether Desmond could adjust her acting style to 1950s norms. That style is highlighted in the film by Swanson's bravura performance, playing Desmond as a woman who goes through real life with the exaggerated movements and facial expressions of a silent screen actress. These exaggerations, of course, were necessary in silent film because of the absence of dialogue; Desmond has access to words (and uses them almost to excess) but adds the excessive nonverbal gestures, nevertheless, creating an absurd effect. This aspect of Swanson's brilliant performance helps to convey the sense that Desmond is a woman who is not only living in the wrong time but who has lost the ability to distinguish between fiction and reality.

Viewed as a film noir character, Desmond is clearly this film's femme fatale, the dangerous "bad" woman set against the film's "good" woman in the person of Betty Schaefer. It's an almost classic noir use of paired female characters, except for the unusual age difference between the two. Swanson was fifty-one in 1950, which is not really all that old, though she was significantly older than Nancy Olson, who was twenty-two at the time. Desmond is also, if one gets beyond the aplomb and the excess, still quite an attractive woman, but that aplomb and excess are hard to get beyond. Still, Desmond is clearly presented as a woman who became rich and famous as a young woman valued for her sexual charms and who is now having a great deal of trouble coping with being older. Within the context of film noir, she is not just an aging film actress: she is an aging femme fatale.

Part of the perception of Desmond as old has to do with Swanson's performance. She doesn't really look old, but her costuming and the power of her performance convey a *sense* of being old, of having been passed by. Viewing Desmond from the perspective strictly of her age also casts a new light on the various other femmes fatales in film noir, giving their actions an extra note of desperation. Aware that they have the sexual charm to manipulate men to do their bidding, perhaps they are also aware that they will have this sexual charm for a relatively short time. But Desmond's predicament, while cast specifically as that of a silent film star unable to make the transition to sound, also says a lot about ageism in Hollywood in general, especially where women are concerned.

This motif, of course, also says a lot about the status of women in American society as a whole, and one of the aspects of *Sunset Boulevard* that makes it a genuine classic is the way in which it so effectively employs the Hollywood film industry as a microcosm of the larger society of which it is a part. Thus, James Naremore sees *Sunset Boulevard* (along with Wilder's *Ace in the Hole* a year later) as a "savage critique of modernity" in the mode of many noir films, which clearly suggests that the mismatch between Desmond and contemporary reality is at least partly the fault of the latter.[1] Of course, Desmond and Gillis seem mismatched as well, and many have found the way she makes him a virtual prisoner—both as a writing partner and (apparently) as a sexual one—to be a key sign of her mental instability. Her treatment of von Mayerling might fit in this category as well, and it is clear that both of these relationships are, as much as anything, a matter of power in which Desmond seeks to exert control, thus compensating for the fact that so many other aspects of her life seem *out* of control.

For his part, Gillis rebels against Desmond's control and flees the strange house, in the midst of a New Year's Eve party. He returns, however, when he gets word that Desmond has attempted suicide due to his departure. This suicide, of course, can be taken as another sign of her mental instability, but it might also be interpreted as a calculated tactic designed precisely to induce Gillis to return. Gillis then settles into the role of kept man, working with Desmond on her (apparently) dreadful script, submitting to her advances, and letting her outfit him in a lavish new wardrobe. In the meantime, however, he also establishes a clandestine collaboration with Schaefer, as they try to make one of his original stories into a viable screenplay, meanwhile reigniting some of his former desire to be a legitimate creative artist. Predictably, the two establish a romantic relationship as well, so that Gillis's relationship with Schaefer mirrors his relationship with Desmond in multiple ways, but with the power dynamics reversed. Perhaps sensing these parallels, Desmond finds out about the relationship and attempts to intervene, eventually causing Gillis to confess his role as kept man and to send Schaefer away.

Eventually, Gillis packs his things and stalks out of Desmond's mansion, disgusted at the demeaning role into which he has been forced there. Desmond follows him out of the house, screaming for him to stop, then shoots him when he refuses to do so. Mortally wounded, he staggers into the newly refurbished pool, bringing us back to the beginning of the film. Gillis then weirdly narrates the discovery of his body by the police and the subsequent arrival of reporters and newsreel cameras. When those cameras arrive, Desmond appears to have finally become unhinged altogether, believing the newsreel cameras to be part of a Paramount crew come to begin the filming of *Salome*. The film ends as Desmond, now believing von Mayerling to be famed director Cecil B. De Mille, dramatically descends the staircase and thrusts her face into the camera lens. Famously, she is ready for her closeup.

Of course, Desmond is not alone in this film in being unstable. Everything in *Sunset Boulevard* is somewhat destabilized by its strange narrative structure. Since Gillis presumably can't *really* be narrating the film from beyond the grave, he would seem to be the ultimate unreliable narrator. In that case, just how are we to interpret *anything* we are told or shown in this film. And this unreliability goes well beyond the posthumous nature of the narration. Gillis is, in fact, a rather bitter and unpleasant sort and his glib dismissal of Desmond as a pathetic, crazy woman should be taken with a bit of skepticism. The case of the chimp is typical of Gillis's attitude. However bizarre this motif might be, one can surmise that the chimp was a beloved part of Desmond's life and that its death should not be taken as a joke. Yet Gillis continually refers to it as a "dead monkey" and makes a bad joke of the fact that, when the real undertaker arrives, he actually treats the deceased ape with dignity and decorum. "He must have been a very important chimp," snarls Gillis. "The great grandson of King Kong, maybe."

We should also be cautious in assuming that Desmond's screenplay is as bad as it seems. After all, the only information we have about it (other than the fact that it seems excessively long) is what we hear from Gillis, who assumes it is terrible before he even starts reading it. He is, in fact, completely dismissive of the screenplay— which he describes as a "silly hodgepodge of melodramatic plots"—from the very beginning. He clearly *wants* it to be bad, perhaps out of jealousy. After all, given his own failures as a screenwriter, Desmond's success might make him look *really* bad. And, of course, there is also the possibility that Gillis might not recognize a good script when he sees one, given the apparently low quality of his own work.

Sunset Boulevard combines a compelling plot, dazzling performances, and thought-provoking subject matter to produce a classic commentary on the relationship between historical reality and the world of American film. This commentary, however, is complex enough that it allows for a variety of interpretations. For Robert Ray, for example, Desmond becomes a sort of allegorical stand-in for a film industry so caught up in its own values and conventions that it loses touch with the outside world. Desmond's downfall, for Ray, suggests the folly of ignoring the outside world.[2] In short, *Sunset Boulevard* warns that Hollywood needed to remain engaged with the rapidly changing American society that surrounded it at the beginning of the 1950s. In this sense, the film perhaps serves as a warning that Hollywood should not retreat from making politically relevant films, despite the Cold War climate of anticommunist hysteria that was just peaking in 1950.

Desmond's mansion, which is a virtual museum filled with artifacts from the Hollywood past, serves as a powerful visual representation of this aspect of the film. Desmond, with von Mayerling's help, has built her own little world in the huge, richly cluttered house. Almost every item in the house looks old and a bit rundown, evoking a lost past. Desmond's solipsism is particularly indicated by the hundreds of

Figure 16.1. Norma Desmond (Gloria Swanson) is ready for her closeup in *Sunset Boulevard*. Paramount Pictures/Photofest © Paramount Pictures

pictures of her that fill her house and by the weekly screenings of her own films that help her continually relive the past. At the same time, the shot of rats milling about in her initially abandoned pool remind us that this house is also a sort of mausoleum, as aspect that is reinforced by the fact that it also features a vintage organ at which von Mayerling's demented playing enhances the horror film vibe of the film.

Indeed, many aspects of the film make Desmond's mansion seem less like a regular house than like a *haunted* house, separating it from reality. More particularly, it is like a haunted house in a *movie*. It is a home that seems more like a movie set than an ordinary human dwelling. As J. P. Telotte puts it, "What the depth of *Sunset Boulevard*'s mise-en-scene ultimately reveals, then, is a world that has lost any real depth—a cinematic world that too easily renders its inhabitants similarly dimensionless, flat, leaves them, in perhaps a nice metaphor for the movie star, floating on a sheer surface."[3]

Even Desmond's friends seem to come from the world of movies rather than from the real world. When they come over for weekly bridge games, they seem to consist entirely of other aging film has-beens, including a cadaverous-looking Buster Keaton, played by himself. Keaton, of course, was one of the greatest of the silent film comedians, as was Charlie Chaplin, whose Little Tramp character (along with other characters from film history) Desmond imitates in the live shows with which she entertains Gillis. Even the great Keaton was never a big success in the sound era, however. Chaplin had more success in sound film, but nevertheless famously worried that sound was damaging film as an art form.

Importantly, Desmond is not the only character in *Sunset Boulevard* who seems to be immersed in the world of the movies. Gillis and Schaefer, though perhaps more up to date in their engagement with the film industry, nevertheless view the world through the optic of that industry as much as does Desmond. In one important scene, the two young writers speak to each other entirely in lines that are essentially parodies of famous lines from movies. There is also an important scene in which Gillis and Schaefer walk on the Paramount lot, strolling down a Potemkin street. Schaefer's comment is a perfect summary of America's love affair with the movies: "Look at this street," she tells Gillis. "All cardboard, all hollow, all phony, all done with mirrors. You know, I like it better than any street in the world."

This statement contains a genuine expression of love for the movies, but it also possibly contains an implicit criticism of the seductive power of the movies to replace reality with false images. In short, *Sunset Boulevard* is a highly complex film that contains a mixture not only of different moods and genres but also of different messages about the film industry, its role in American society, and the nature of American society itself. The film's central figure, aging femme fatale Norma Desmond, is one of the most fascinating characters in all of American cinema, and *Sunset Boulevard* is one of the most fascinating and complex of all noir films.

Chapter 17

Women in Neo-Noir: *Body Heat*

(1981, Directed by Lawrence Kasdan)

Lawrence Kasdan's *Body Heat* is a quintessential example of neo-noir film, partly because it was so self-consciously constructed to recall the original noir cycle, especially *Double Indemnity* (1944), of which it is a virtual remake. Indeed, *Body Heat* is largely a clever reconstruction, including almost all of the major elements of *Double Indemnity*, though slightly displacing most of them. It is, for example, set in South Florida at the beginning of the 1980s, rather than Southern California in the mid-1940s. *Body Heat* adds a few additional plot twists, but none that would be out of character in an original noir film. It also adds a few new atmospheric effects, such as the heat wave that keeps most of the characters drenched in sweat throughout most of the film. The most striking "revision" in *Body Heat* is its much more overt portrayal of sexual behavior, enabled by the collapse of the Production Code. Central to this portrayal is the role played by Matty Walker, this film's femme fatale. Ultimately, *Body Heat* gains much of its energy from its nostalgic look back at film noir, especially *Double Indemnity*, while doing nothing to engage the original noir cycle in a critical way.

Body Heat begins with a flurry of brief scenes that introduce most of the main characters. In the first scene, me meet attorney Ned Racine (William Hurt)—who plays essentially the same role in this film that Fred MacMurray's insurance agent Walter Neff had played in *Double Indemnity*. However, whereas Neff seems to be leading a lonely, spartan existence when he first meets femme fatale Phyllis Dietrichson (Barbara Stanwyck), *Body Heat* quickly establishes Racine as something of a womanizer in this first scene, which takes place in his apartment after he has just had casual sex with a woman in whom he seems to have no interest other than sexual. We next see Racine in the courtroom, where he seems a bit overmatched by Assistant District Attorney Peter Lowenstein (Ted Danson), thus establishing that

Racine's competence as a lawyer might be a bit questionable, a wrinkle not really present in *Double Indemnity*, where Neff is perfectly competent. Finally, a quick scene in a diner (a classic noir setting) establishes that Racine and Lowenstein are actually friends outside the courtroom.

In the film's first major scene, Racine spots Matty Walker (Kathleen Turner), this film's film fatale (and really its most important character).[1] Matty immediately grabs Racine's attention, and he sets out to try to seduce her, further establishing his predilection for casual encounters. The two then engage in an exchange of snappy, suggestive dialogue that is highly reminiscent of the first exchange between Neff and Dietrichson. After Matty has skillfully parried his initial pickup lines, Racine tells her, "I need tending. I need someone to take care of me, someone to rub my tired muscles, smooth out my sheets." "Get married," Matty tells him, to which he immediately quips, "I just need it for the night," causing her to do a spit take with the snow cone he has just bought for her. He seems to have scored a hit, and her subsequent half-hearted attempts to play hard to get barely slow him down as he barrels forward into a full-blown affair with her.

Of course, we will later realize that Matty has carefully engineered this early encounter—and their whole affair—in order to achieve the nefarious end of employing Racine to murder her husband for her. This affair is conducted mostly at the posh mansion Matty shares with her husband, shadowy "investor" Edmund Walker (Richard Crenna), who conveniently spends most of his time out of town to attend his mysterious business affairs. Meanwhile, the steamy love scenes that indicate the torrid nature of the affair are portrayed with a frankness that would not have been possible under the Production Code. These scenes helped to make an immediate star of Turner, who was performing in her first film and who quickly became known as one of Hollywood's sexist actresses. In 1995, *Empire* magazine named her one of the one hundred sexiest movie stars of all time, and it is safe to say that *Body Heat* contributed more to that ranking than did any other film. Indeed, while Racine is the principal point of view character in the film, it is very much dominated by Turner's performance as Matty, who breathlessly vamps (and camps) her way through the film in high film-fatale fashion, always a step ahead of Racine as she ensnares him in her plot to murder her husband and inherit his substantial wealth.

It is for good reason that Foster Hirsch, who sees *Body Heat* as the film that established neo-noir as a definite category once and for all, emphasizes Matty as the aspect of this film that makes it most remarkable. For him, Matty is a somewhat "modernized" version of the classic femme fatale, with "greater agency and initiative" than the typical femme fatale of the original noir cycle. In addition, he notes the clearly "performative" aspect of Matty's behavior—she is clearly always playing a role as she manipulates men by gauging their idea of the ultimate in feminine desirability and then acting out that idea. The result, for Hirsch, is that Matty is so skillful and so clever that it is difficult not to admire her artistry, even as we realize what a predator she is: "Matty is both a threat and a warning to the unwary male, but she is at the same time a figure whose sheer cleverness as a performer is meant

Figure 17.1. Matty Walker and Ned Racing (Kathleen Turner and William Hurt) in *Body Heat*. Warner Bros./Photofest © Warner Bros.

to elicit an approving smile."[2] Linda Ruth Williams agrees, identifying *Body Heat* as the beginning of a cycle of neo-noir "erotic thrillers," in which the female leads enjoyed unprecedented sexual freedom, often without being punished for it. Thus, Turner's Matty was the clear forerunner of such figures as Catherine Tramell (Sharon Stone) in *Basic Instinct* (1992) or Bridget Gregory (Linda Fiorentino) in *The Last Seduction* (1994).[3]

I also agree with Hirsch's assessment of Matty as a character, though I would suggest that the machinations of Phyllis Dietrichson in *Double Indemnity* can be quite entertaining as well. In addition, I would argue that the difference between Matty and Phyllis is not a fundamental one within their films and that would lead us to reassess our view of the femmes fatales of the original noir films. Instead, Matty's greater agency is largely a reflection of changing social norms between 1944 and 1981, so that Matty has the same relationship to what was regarded as "normal" feminine behavior in 1981 as Phyllis had to the same norm in 1944. The same might be said for the neo-noir femmes fatales that followed her, such as Trammell and Gregory. And it is, of course, their differences from the expected norm that make the femmes fatales stand out as characters.

Among other things, Matty's plotting is even more complex than Phyllis's. Her plot leads to Edmund's death slightly more than halfway through the film, but Matty's machinations are at this point only just getting started. Unknown to Racine, she forges a fake will for her husband, attributing its preparation to Racine. The will leaves half of Edmund's wealth to Matty and half to his young niece Heather (Carola McGuiness), which was, in fact, what Edmund had wished to do. But Matty has carefully prepared the will with a fatal flaw due to its violation of the basic legal principle of the "rule against perpetuities" (which serves, in this film, the same purpose as the insurance concept of "double indemnity" in *Double Indemnity*). Thanks to Racine's questionable reputation as a lawyer, the idea that he would have made such an error seems perfectly believable, especially as he himself, though shocked by the will, does not deny having prepared it.

Ultimately Matty's maneuvers will help to send Racine to prison for Edmund's murder, though she fails in her attempt to murder Racine himself, while succeeding in faking her own death. Meanwhile, the extent of Matty's plotting is only revealed after Racine does extensive research while in prison, discovering that Matty was not even Matty, but another woman by the name of Mary Ann Simpson, having stolen the identity of the real Matty Tyler to further her plan to marry and murder Edmund, and having meanwhile murdered the real Matty after she discovers the switch. We learn about most of this additional plotting (analogous to the revelation late in *Double Indemnity* of Phyllis's apparent murder of her previous husband as well) in an exposition scene in which Racine, now in prison, explains his theory to a skeptical police detective, Oscar Grace (J. A. Preston). Racine, it seems, has spent much of his time in prison trying to unravel the case, though he will not get the final piece of evidence he needs until slightly later than his talk with Grace. In short, the plot at this point becomes so tangled and complex that Kasdan felt someone within the film had to explain it to avoid confusing the audience altogether.

The complexity of the plot of *Body Heat* can be taken as a reference to the similarly complex plots of *Double Indemnity* and many other original noir films. *Body Heat* refers to those films in other ways as well, as in its jazzy soundtrack or the 1930s-style script of its opening and closing credits. Kasdan's film also includes a number of moments of oddly inserted moments of gratuitous strangeness, completely unrelated to the plot. At one point, for example, Racine observes a man in full clown makeup driving through the town. And, of course, there is Lowenstein's propensity toward dancing, as when he performs a full dance routine near the beach while waiting to meet with Racine.[4]

At times, *Body Heat* includes moments that comment on film noir in a way that adds a bit of humor, especially for knowing viewers. For example, in one scene, Racine and Matty have been summoned to a meeting to discuss the problematic will with Miles Hardin (Michael Ryan), Edmund's lawyer. Lowenstein, and Roz Craft (Lanna Saunders), Heather's mother, have also been called to the meeting. As the discussion begins to reach a crucial point, Hardin asks if anyone minds if he smokes. When no one speaks up, he takes out a cigar and lights it up. By this time, though, he has also triggered a chain of events in which, first, Matty, and then Roz and Racine take out cigarettes and begin smoking them. When Roz offers a cigarette to Lowenstein, though, he declines, saying, "I don't need my own. I'll just breathe the air." It's a funny moment in itself, but it is much funnier if one realizes that the films of the original noir cycle are notorious for the frequency with which their characters smoke, making this scene a sly and amusing nod to the noir roots of *Body Heat*.

At the same time, this amusing nod to the original film noir cycle is also something of an anachronism: the characters in this film smoke like they live in the time of *Double Indemnity*, not in the time of *Body Heat*, when widespread concerns over the health effects of smoking—emphasized in important reports from the US surgeon general in 1964 and 1972—had already begun to decrease the prevalence of smoking in American society. Some aspects of *Body Heat* would have never occurred in the original noir cycle, such as the fact that Grace, the principal police detective investigating the murder of Edmund Walker, happens to be a good friend of Racine, which seems odd in terms of conflicts of interest, but Grace is also an African American, which (especially in a Southern state) would seem much more likely in the 1980s than the 1930s. But, in addition to all the smoking, other aspects of *Body Heat* play with the fact that they would seem more at home in *Double Indemnity*, such as the nod to original noir in the 1930s-style hat that Matty gives Racine as a gift, or the times when the cinematography overtly mimics films noir, but now casting the famous parallel lines of shadow on the bodies of lovers. Meanwhile, one key anachronism is key to the whole feel of the film—the lack of effective air conditioning, so that even the wealthy Walkers don't seem to have decent air conditioning in their palatial home (and creating the constant heat and sweat that are so important in this film).

Body Heat's lack of firm attachment to its own historical period is crucial to what has been probably the most influential reading of the film, Jameson's centering of it as a key example of neo-noir as nostalgia film. For Jameson,

> Everything in the film . . . conspires to blur its official contemporaneity and make it possible for the viewer to receive the narrative as though it were set in some eternal thirties, beyond real historical time. This approach to the present by way of the art language of the simulacrum, or of the pastiche of the stereotypical past, endows present reality and the openness of present history with the spell and distance of a glossy mirage.[5]

For Jameson, *Body Heat*'s pastiche of *Double Indemnity* divorces it from its own historical moment and from historicity in general because it makes no attempt to engage its predecessor in a critical dialogue that would draw attention to the historical differences between the different time periods in which the films were made and set.

Building on Jameson's analysis, Carl Freedman notes both the similarities and the differences between *Body Heat* and *Double Indemnity*, arguing that this combination of imitation and revision makes *Body Heat* one of "the most purely and precisely neo-noir of all films."[6] For Freedman, the most important revision is "Kasdan's determined erasure of the whole problematic of labour, business and economic activity that is so important for *Double Indemnity*."[7] Freedman notes the importance to *Double Indemnity* of the fact that both Neff and Barton Keyes (Edward G. Robinson) are employees of the Pacific All Risk Insurance Company, spending much of the film simply doing their jobs—and doing them well. Racine, on the other hand, is self-employed in his own legal practice, but he spends very little screen time actually working as a lawyer, something at which he is also not very good (and something he professes not to enjoy). *Body Heat*, for Freedman, removes the interest in work that lies at the center of *Double Indemnity*, replacing it with an interest in leisure—especially of a sexual nature. After all, Racine's principal goal in getting involved in Matty's plot is to have lots of great sex and enough money never to have to work again. Ultimately, Freedman agrees with Jameson that *Body Heat* is essentially on vacation from history, which Freedman sees as closely congruent with the film's own "vacation ethos."[8] Thus, while *Double Indemnity*, clearly set in the late 1930s, "possesses a fine sense of its historical moment," *Body Heat* is only vaguely set at the beginning of the 1980s and even introduces intentional anachronisms.[9] Moreover, Freedman argues that the disengagement from history in *Body Heat*, as opposed to *Double Indemnity*, can be related to the fact that, in 1944, the tide of history was with the United States, which was on the rise as a world power, while 1981 was a time when American power seemed to be in decline, the tide of history having turned against the US, with the newly-installed Reagan administration about to make things much worse, giving American culture a good reason to retreat from history, even if unconsciously.

The point, of course, is not that Kasdan was intentionally retreating from history in writing and directing *Body Heat*. The point is that he and his film were participating in a sweeping cultural phenomenon in which so many neo-noir films (and other cultural artifacts) produced roughly between 1970 and 2000 drew upon the energies of the past, energies that were no longer available in the present. *Body Heat* thus serves as an excellent example of the way neo-noir films of this period often went beyond the original noir films in various ways, but without asking us to revise our views of original noir, which is treated with a nostalgic form of respect and admiration.

Chapter 18

Women in Neo-Noir:
The Last Seduction

(1994, Directed by James Foley)

The Last Seduction (1994) joins *Kill Me Again* (1989) and *Red Rock West* (1993) in a series of steamy neo-noir films directed by James Foley, all of which feature particularly conniving femme fatale characters.[1] However, Linda Fiorentino's Bridget Gregory/Wendy Kroy (the extent of her maneuvers is indicated by her double identity) is probably the only one of Foley's female characters who rises to the level of Matty Walker in *Body Heat* (1981), perhaps pushing the femme fatale envelope even further than had Matty. Indeed, Bren O'Callaghan, writing in 2013, suggests that Bridget still stood, at that time, as the unchallenged queen of noir bitchery.[2] *The Last Seduction* does not try as hard as *Body Heat* to signal its noir roots, perhaps because neo-noir had become so well established in the years between these two films and perhaps because *The Last Seduction* was identified as much with the erotic thriller craze of the 1990s as it was specifically with noir.[3] Besides her tendency to use sex to manipulate hapless men, Bridget, like Matty, is so deliciously evil that it is hard not to be amused and entertained by her, perhaps partly because these men are so completely overmatched by the much more interesting Bridget.

    The Last Seduction gets off to a quick start that really serves as a sort of prologue, as we see a woman who turns out to be Bridget mercilessly driving the crew of sketchy telemarketers that she supervises, immediately establishing her as tough, sarcastic, ruthless, and unscrupulous.[4] Then the film starts to cut between Bridget and a man we later learn to be her husband Clay Gregory (Bill Pullman), who is engaging in an illicit drug deal. Though he actually makes the deal successfully, he is clearly out of his element and collects his money only after the "real" criminals with whom he is dealing humiliate and make a fool of him. In fact, he is a fledgling medical doctor trying to make a few extra bucks by absconding with some pharmaceutical cocaine and selling it to street dealers. Within minutes, then, it is established that he is weak, cowardly, and corrupt. Before the opening credits (accompanied by an upbeat jazzy title track) have even completed, then, we've already learned a great deal about these two contrasting characters. We learn soon afterward that they are a married couple, while Clay slaps Bridget within seconds of joining her back in their apartment, telling us still more about his character—and giving her what she claims to be an excuse for taking off with the drug money while he is in the shower.

Cash in hand, Bridget decides to drive from New York to Chicago (where she has connections), but she first stops off in the fictional small town of Beston, near Buffalo, New York. She then decides to stay in Beston after her lawyer (apparently a former lover) advises her that she will be harder to find there than in Chicago, where Clay is likely to look for her. So she decides to settle in, getting a job at a local insurance company. Insurance, in fact, figures at several points in this film, again signaling us that *Double Indemnity* might be the film noir that provides the most relevant point of comparison with the original noir cycle. To disguise her identity, Bridget adopts the pseudonym "Wendy Kroy," which is derived from spelling "New York" backward, making us wonder is she is always as clever as she usually seems to be, especially after Clay quickly sees through the ruse.

If we are expecting small-town Beston to win Bridget over and cause her to change her ways, we'll be disappointed. She is not the type to be impressed by small-town charm, and she spends most of the film displaying her contempt for the town (which she sarcastically refers to as "Mayberry" at one point) and all the people in it—including local man Mike Swale (Peter Berg), whom she makes her "designated fuck" after picking him up in a bar with some sexually aggressive moves (both physical and verbal) that might have made Matty Walker blush. Indeed, Kate Stables compares the dialogue in this pickup scene with an exchange between Phyllis Dietrichson and Walter Neff in *Double Indemnity* to illustrate the much more overtly sexual language of the 1990s femme fatale in comparison with the classic femme fatale.[5]

Much of the fun of *The Last Seduction* is just waiting to see what clever trick Bridget/Wendy will come up with next to stay ahead of both Mike and Clay, who is still trying to track her down through much of the film to try to recover the drug money.[6] Indeed, Fiorentino plays the role with a clear, wise-cracking, eye-rolling comic touch, which is reinforced by the light-hearted musical cues that accompany many of her actions.[7] Indeed, this comic tone, going well beyond what is typically found in noir, allows us to enjoy most of Bridget's maneuvers, at least up to the killing of Clay, regardless of how reprehensible they might be. Of course, one reason we can forgive her for her various shenanigans is that the film is careful to delay the revelation of just how diabolical she really is. Another reason is that viewers with any familiarity at all with the original noir cycle will expect that she surely can't get away with it forever. Even the title of the film seems to suggest that Bridget's activities can't go on forever.[8] In fact, we are left wondering until the very end if she might have gone too far with her final betrayal of Mike (a much more sympathetic character

than Clay), only learning in the film's very last seconds that she has successfully destroyed all evidence that might have incriminated her. She then ends the film calmly
riding away in a limo, while Mike awaits trial for rape and murder.

That the hapless Mike is quickly won over by Bridget's sexual charms is not
particularly surprising, though it takes a bit more skill on Bridget's part to keep
him enthralled, despite the abusive way she treats him. Nevertheless, he balks at an
elaborate scheme she comes up with (or claims to come up with) to identify rich men
who are having affairs, spill the beans to their wives, and then have the wives pay
them to murder the husbands. The scheme seems a bit far-fetched, though Mike's
objections are mostly based, not on the low probability of success, but on the fact
that "murder is wrong," which Bridget regards as a hopelessly naïve attitude. In any
case, his reluctance only means that Bridget has to work extrahard to convince him,
partly by continuing to provide him with a once-in-a-lifetime sexual adventure and
partly by tricking him into believing that she has just successfully committed one of
these murders-for-hire on her own. She also convinces him that her next designated
victim is a particularly vile tax lawyer in New York City, though Mike is so blinded
by the sex that he is not especially hard to convince.

Mike, incidentally, is carefully depicted as something of a flawed, but well-meaning
bumpkin who is a perfect target for Bridget's sophisticated wiles. He is also stipulated
to be particularly in need of sexual reassurance at the time he meets Bridget, having
just returned to Beston from an especially humiliating misadventure in which he
married a woman in Buffalo, not realizing that she was transgender (and not exactly
having the mindset not to care). He keeps this experience a secret from everyone,
but the clever Bridget (always thinking several moves ahead) is able to discover the
truth and ultimately to use it against Mike at a crucial moment in the film. That moment occurs after Mike discovers that the "tax lawyer" is actually Clay and thus stops
short of killing him. Bridget then takes over and kills Clay herself by spraying mace
directly into his mouth, causing his air passages to close up and thus suffocating him.
Mike is stunned by this move, and it is surprising, but it would be even shocking if
it weren't the second murder we've seen her commit (and get away with) in the film.

Unlike Clay, Mike is basically a decent guy, if a flawed one. But he is also clearly
no match for Wendy, who outwits and manipulates him at every turn. The same
might be said for Clay, and Bridget gets rid of both of them at once by framing Mike
for Clay's murder, topping it off by also framing him for raping her (presumably to
make Mike look worse to juries and to make herself look like an innocent victim).
She is thus left not only with the original drug money but also with the money from
her husband's life insurance, in still another echo of *Double Indemnity*.

The fact that Bridget ultimately gets away with all her crimes would have never
been allowed under the Code, of course, though it is fairly common for the femmes
fatales of neo-noir to get away with their crimes. Indeed, it's almost as if Bridget
had been reading the old Production Code and decided to do everything she could
that the Code wouldn't have allowed the original femmes fatales to do, making this
film especially fun for those familiar with the original cycle of noir films. Certainly,

the film's sex scenes (though less steamy than those in *Body Heat*) would never have been allowed under the Code. But the most important way in which this film takes advantage of the absence of the Code is by making Bridget willing to go to extremes of evil that might have shocked even Phyllis Dietrichson. Like Phyllis, for example, Bridget uses her sexual allure to convince her boyfriend to murder her husband—but, in this case, she ends up committing the murder herself (and in a particularly gruesome way). And the main criminal scheme that she cooks up in the film is far more elaborate and diabolical than the typical film noir treachery—even though it would probably never have worked had it not been fueled by seduction.

The Last Seduction is a low-budget movie that went straight to cable, unable to find a distributor to put it in theaters, though a few enthusiastic reviews finally got it the attention it needed to get into theaters, after which it continued to receive positive reviews. Prominent critic Roger Ebert was one of those who championed the movie most enthusiastically, helping to ensure that the film would secure a durable place in the neo-noir canon, rather than essentially disappearing, like so many low-budget films do. Ebert gave the film four out of four stars and was especially impressed by Bridget, whom he describes as one of the great movie villains. For him, the film

> knows how much we enjoy seeing a character work boldly outside the rules. It gives us a diabolical, evil woman, and goes the distance with her. We keep waiting for the movie to lose its nerve, and it never does: This woman is bad from beginning to end, she never reforms, she never compromises, and the movie doesn't tack on one of those contrived conclusions where the morals squad comes in and tidies up.[9]

Indeed, there is no moral tidying up in this film. If anything, Bridget seems to get more and more evil as the film proceeds, remaining both unpunished and unrepentant. It might not quite be accurate to call her likable or even to say that audiences are likely to root for her, but she certainly holds our attention. Moreover, she has been read positively both by male critics who might perhaps have themselves been seduced a bit and by feminist critics who see her as a refreshing reversal of the tendency to see women as passive victims in film. Indeed, as Linda Ruth Williams notes, the general critical tendency has been to read murderous femme fatale figures such as Bridget Gregory or Catherine Tramell (Sharon Stone) in *Basic Instinct* (1992) as "unalloyed positive representations of sexual liberty and financial reward."[10]

In the case of Bridget, meanwhile, there are particularly overt reasons to read the character as a sort of feminist heroine. As Suzy Gordon points out, Bridget seems to have a textbook understanding of the kinds of harassment and exploitation frequently suffered by women, turning that knowledge to her advantage:

> Bridget deploys feminist discourses of male violence against women to ensure the success of her violent actions against men (she masquerades as a rape victim, claims she is a battered wife, and uses a can of mace to suffocate her husband, Clay (Bill Pullman)). . . . This fantasy of the violence women's sexual and economic independence does to

men is re-presented as a "feminist" empowerment in a world dominated by men's violence against women.[11]

To this list, one might add the fact that Bridget employs the narrative of workplace sexual harassment against Mike to win authority on the job at the company where they both work. In addition, Bridget is quite adept at enacting common stereotypical male visions of feminine behavior when it is to her advantage. Several times, for example, she pretends to be weak and helpless in order to get men to do what she wants—though Fiorentino plays these moments with an undisguised that seems designed to show contempt for the stupidity of the men she is beguiling. She is even able to play the role of happy homemaker when she "bakes" cookies as part of a ploy to shake the detective who is shadowing her for Clay—even though all she really does is reheat some store-bought cookies. Again, of course, all these ploys work because men are made especially gullible by her sexual charisma: they want to believe her claim to be a damsel in distress so that they can be her knight in shining armor and heroically come to her aid, a fact that she mercilessly uses against them.

Bridget Gregory goes beyond Phyllis Dietrichson or any other femme fatale from the original noir cycle in her more candid and aggressive sexual conduct and also in the fact that *The Last Seduction* can draw upon feminist discourses that simply were not available in the 1940s and 1950s. At the same time, these differences are conditioned by the removal of the Production Code and by social changes in society at large that we already know about without watching *The Last Seduction*. As a result, while this film pushes the envelope for the representation of women in noir film, it does not do so in ways that fundamentally change our understanding of the original noir films. Though made two years after *Basic Instinct*, *The Last Seduction* does not quite reach the level of that earlier film in revising our understanding of what a noir femme fatale can be.

Chapter 19

Women in Revisionary Noir:
Basic Instinct

(1992, Directed by Paul Verhoeven)

Basic Instinct was one of the most controversial films of the 1990s, though it is now a bit hard to remember how widely it was criticized at the time, with various groups declaring it homophobic, misogynistic, immoral, and exploitative. Groups along the entire ideological spectrum from "family values" advocates to LGBTQ advocates came out in numbers to protest against the film's offensive content. These controversies, though, only seemed to make the film more successful and influential, to the point that it is now difficult to appreciate how groundbreaking it was at the time, given the number of films that overtly tried to imitate it in the years that followed.[1] Using the film as one of her key examples of feminist filmmaking, Terri Murray calls *Basic Instinct* "a neo-noir masterpiece that plays with, and transgresses, the narrative rules of film noir," which is an accurate description as far as it goes.[2] However, in terms of the framework I am proposing in this volume, I would argue that the transgressive nature of *Basic Instinct* is so extensive that it moves beyond neo-noir and into the realm of revisionary noir, disrupting many of the fundamental ideas about gender that were built into the original noir cycle—and into patriarchal society as a whole.

Basic Instinct announces its unusual nature from its very first moments, involving a sex scene far more explicit than could possibly have been included in any film under the Production Code. But then it goes farther, as the woman, riding atop the man in cowgirl position, binds his hands with strands of silk—taking the scene into the realm of BDSM sex, though only in the lightest sort of way. Then, as the man orgasms, things take another turn as the woman reaches behind her, grabs an ice pick, and viciously stabs the man to death in a shocking turn to graphic violence. All the while, though, the woman's face has been hidden by her tousled blonde hair, thus disguising her identity and setting up the principal plot of the film, which will involve an investigation by the San Francisco police, led by Detective Nick Curran (Michael Douglas), into the murder we have just seen.

This investigation is made more sensitive by the fact that the murdered man was Johnny Boz (Bill Cable), who had been a minor rock star in the 1960s but was, at the time of his death, a prominent figure on the local cultural scene and a key financial supporter of the mayor's political campaigns. Oddly, this sensitivity does not prevent the police from assigning Curran to the case, despite the fact that he has something of a checkered past, having once been involved in a questionable shooting that still has Internal Affairs (IA) on his case. Indeed, the loathsome IA lieutenant, Marty Nilsen (Daniel von Bargen) seems to have it in for Curran, adding another complication to the plot. Curran is also still undergoing sessions with police psychiatrist Beth Garner (Jeanne Tripplehorn) because of that earlier shooting incident.

Nevertheless, the investigation seems to get off to a quick start when it turns out that Boz's girlfriend, Catherine Tramell (Sharon Stone), happens to be a writer of murder mysteries who, only a year before, published a novel in which the plot centered on a murder very similar to that of Boz.[3] When Curran and his partner, Detective Gus Moran (George Dzundza) go to interview Tramell, they encounter the character who made this film so special. Stone is not only dazzlingly gorgeous as Tramell, but she is also a distinctively new (and highly interesting) kind of femme fatale. Physically, she is a virtual embodiment of feminine sexual attractiveness. In almost all other ways, though, she defies patriarchal stereotypes of the feminine, often completely reversing conventional gender roles to take on characteristics that are normally considered to be masculine. Extremely intelligent and well-educated, she is a success in the normally male-dominated world of writing detective fiction. She is extremely independent, both emotionally and financially, having inherited a large fortune upon the deaths of her parents. And, of course, she is quite sexually liberated and open about how much she enjoys sex—but on her terms.

One key gender reversal, of course, involves the phallic ice pick that figures so prominently in the film. To employ that ice pick during sex, so that the woman can fatally penetrate the man, obviously calls for Freudian interpretations—so obviously that such interpretations probably add very little to our understanding of the film. All we need to do is note Curran's anxiety whenever he sees Tramell wielding an ice pick (which we see her do multiple times, but only literally on ice). After all, this clearly derives more from his threatened masculinity than from fear that she will suddenly stab him, especially given all the other figurations of gender in the film.

It is clear that Curran is immediately attracted to Tramell (as, presumably, is Moran, though the portly detective seems to recognize that Tramell is out of his league[4]). Sparks fly between Tramell and Curran, the latter clearly dazzled by her beauty, though perhaps taken back a bit by her sexual candor. For example, when asked about dating Boz, she calmly responds, "I wasn't dating him. I was fucking him." Noting her placid, but cold, demeanor, Curran asks her whether she is sorry that Boz is dead; she calmly responds, "Yeah, I liked fucking him." The lines of the

Figure 19.1. Catherine Tramell and Detective Nick Curran (Sharon Stone and Michael Douglas) in *Basic Instinct*. Tristar/Photofest © Tristar

plot are already falling into place in this initial meeting, which makes it clear that Curran suspects Tramell of murdering Boz but that his investigation of her is likely to be complicated by the sexual charge between them.

The investigation thus becomes a cat and mouse game in which more and more evidence begins to point to Tramell as Boz's killer, but in which she always seems a step ahead of Curran, carefully orchestrating their relationship, encouraged by her confident awareness that he finds her sexually irresistible. This awareness allows her to be completely in charge of their relationship and ensures that she will success-fully seduce Curran, despite the fact that their relationship is a huge violation of his professional ethics. Meanwhile, when they are in bed together, Tramell calls the shots and is often on top, including one very tense moment in which she seems to be reenacting the killing of Boz by tying Curran's hands during sex.

The gender dynamics of *Basic Instinct* are also complicated by the fact that Tramell is apparently bisexual and has a devoted lesbian girlfriend in the person of Roxy Hardy (Leilani Sarrell). The boyish-but-beautiful Roxy (one of two convicted murderers in Tramell's circle in the film) immediately senses that Curran might be a threat to her relationship with Tramell, so she tries to warn him off and then literally tries to murder him by running him down in Catherine's car (which at first makes it look as if Catherine might be the driver). In the event, it turns out that Roxy is the one who is killed, when her car runs off the road after a road battle with Curran (in his own car).

This incident would seem to restore Curran to a position of patriarchal power, having bested Hardy in a contest of automobiles, traditionally a realm of male dominance. However, this film refuses to allow Curran to occupy conventional male roles very comfortably. All we have to do is remember the earlier scene in which he followed Tramell in an extended car chase that provides some of film's most suspenseful moments, as Curran has one narrow escape after another while pursuing her on a winding road and then through city traffic, only to have her easily outdistance him. Granted, Tramell's Lotus Esprit is a superior vehicle to Curran's humble Dodge Diplomat, but Trammell seems to be the better driver as well, handily defeating the detective in a contest held on what would normally be considered an area of masculine dominance.

Tramell's ability to outdo Curran at traditional masculine activities is only one side of the equation. There are also a number of ways in which Curran displays behavior that is typically associated with the feminine within patriarchal societies. The most important form of this behavior has to do with his highly volatile, emotional responses to almost everything. He is constantly overreacting, bellowing and lunging at people, even with the slightest provocation. His behavior, meanwhile, seems even more histrionic when contrasted with the cool, unflappable demeanor of Tramell, who thus becomes the film's bearer of the traditionally masculine virtues of logic and self-control.

Basic Instinct, of course, is best remembered for a single scene in which Curran and a group of other police officials question Tramell in an interrogation room, ultimately catching a glimpse of a certain part of her anatomy as she crosses and uncrosses her legs while sitting in a chair wearing a short white dress with nothing underneath. However, this scene is more important for other reasons. It seems a classic scene of patriarchal power, as a group of men, fully backed by the full institutional power of the state, gather to question a lone, presumably vulnerable woman. It's also a classic enactment of the male gaze, as the men are clearly more interested in ogling Tramell than they are in getting information from her. However, Tramell is perfectly well aware of her mesmerizing effect on men, and she quickly reverses the apparent power dynamics, toying with the men and making it clear that she is very much in charge of the situation. The scene, in fact, becomes essentially comic as the men stumble over themselves, overwhelmed by her sexual power.

Not only does this scene give Tramell a chance to turn the tables on her masculine inquisitors, but it also sets up a later scene, in which Curran, now suspected of having killed his nemesis Nilsen (found with a bullet in his head), is interrogated by a number of police in that same interrogation room. Nick even echoes some of Tramell's specific answers from her earlier questioning, as when he asks whether they intend to charge him with smoking after he lights a cigarette and is reminded that there is no smoking allowed in the building. He is, however, unable to turn the tables on his questioners as Trammell had. More importantly, when Curran points out that he would never be so dumb as to kill a man with whom he had had a violent altercation earlier the same day, it is suggested that Curran might be trying to use the earlier encounter with Nilsen in the hope that it would make the police *believe* that he would never be dumb enough kill Nilsen after the two had had a fight earlier the same day. This exchange, of course, closely replicates Tramell's earlier suggestion that she would never be dumb enough to murder Boz in a way that corresponded so closely to a murder in her recent novel—though others, of course, find this correspondence to indicate that Tramell is, in fact, the killer. The effect of this correspondence is to create uncertainty: a great deal of evidence has seemed to point to Tramell, but Curran's situation now makes us question whether Tramell might really be innocent.

While *Basic Instinct* was, in many ways, unprecedented, it does invoke cinematic predecessors in several ways, as when many aspects of the film clearly participate in the noir tradition. In addition to numerous plot elements that are typical of noir film, there are multiple scenes in which we see the signature noir visual: lines of shadow projected as light shines through venetian blinds. Otherwise, as Robert Wood notes, the visual style of *Basic Instinct* is a "virtual reversal" of the typical noir visual style, prompting him to call it an example of "white noir." However, as Wood points out, the film is nevertheless similar to noir in the way it consistently privileges the visual over the verbal.[5] Even the casting of Dorothy Malone as Hazel Dobkins is a sort of allusion to noir. Dobkins is a woman who had murdered her family all the way back in the 1950s and who has struck up an unspecified relationship with Tramell after the writer consulted Dobkins as part of her research for a book. *Basic Instinct* was Malone's final film, which seems appropriately symmetrical, given that her casting here recalls the fact that her first film appearance was as a fetching bookstore clerk, who takes Humphrey Bogart's Philip Marlowe in out of the rain in the noir classic *The Big Sleep* (1946).

Perhaps the most specific nod to a predecessor in *Basic Instinct* involves the films of Alfred Hitchcock, most of whose films were perhaps a bit too glossy to be pure noir, but they certainly have many noir characteristics. Indeed, Hitchcock films such as *Shadow of a Doubt* (1943) and *The Wrong Man* (1956) are full-on noir. The most notable echo of Hitchcock occurs through the clear way in which Tramell's appearance and demeanor would make her the quintessential icy, sophisticated "Hitchcock blonde"—except that she is probably blonder, icier, and more sophisticated than any of the women in Hitchcock's films. Because of the San Francisco setting, there are a number of scenes that are visually reminiscent of Hitchcock's most respected film, *Vertigo* (1958), which is also set mostly in San Francisco. Finally, there are many elements of the Jerry Goldsmith's score for *Basic Instinct* that clearly echo the classic music of Hitchcock's films. Goldsmith has even said in an interview that Verhoeven encouraged him to try to replicate the style of the music in *Vertigo* when writing the score (Schweiger, n.p.).

Basic Instinct is also perhaps reminiscent of the films of Hitchcock in the way it is able to create suspense by manipulating audience expectations, first by piling up evidence that seems to point to Tramell as the killer in question. The film then slowly shifts to newly discovered evidence that seems to point more and more toward

Garner, who complicates the dynamic between Tramell and Curran by providing a third term. (Beth has, at separate times in the past, been sexually involved with both Tramell and Curran.) Of course, despite the fact that Tramell so thoroughly dominates this film, Curran is the point of view character and we tend to follow the evidence as he does. He thus also suspects Garner, then ends up shooting and killing her (replicating that other, earlier, problematic shooting in his career), thinking that she is reaching for a gun when she is really just reaching for her keys.[6]

The Garner-Curran relationship in the film is important partly because of its contrast with the relationship between Tramell and Curran. With Garner, Curran is much more in charge, something that is made clear in a scene in which they rekindle their sexual relationship, but only after he essentially starts to rape her, indicating the way in which Tramell is making him feel so disempowered that he needs to assert his patriarchal authority elsewhere. (Similarly, his road battle with Hardy might be taken as an attempt to compensate for his earlier car chase defeat at the hands of Tramell.) That such scenes reflect so badly on Curran is no doubt designed to make Tramell look better in comparison, so that his status as point of view character does not overwhelm her ability to function as the centerpiece of the film. Indeed, Curran is undermined so thoroughly that, even though he is the point of view character, the normal functioning of the male gaze is thoroughly disrupted. We might follow his lead in trying to interpret clues, but it is difficult fully to identify with him.

Our judgment of Tramell is then seemingly overturned at the end of the film when she and Curran appear headed for an ongoing relationship and are in bed together toward that end. Then the camera pans down slowly to show an ice pick under the bed. Most commentators on this film have taken this final scene as an indication that Tramell is the murderer, after all, and many feel that she is likely to murder Curran, as well.[7] On the other hand, Wood believes that Tramell has tossed the pick under the bed because she has decided *not* to kill Curran, thanks to his willingness to give up on having children together, something Wood sees as part of the film's reversal of "family ideology."[8] At the same time, all of the evidence that Tramell has committed *any* murders is entirely circumstantial, and everything that has happened in this film so far has warned us not to jump to conclusions based on circumstantial evidence, so that the solution to the various mysteries in this film is not entirely conclusive.

This denial of interpretive closure is still another way in which *Basic Instinct* goes beyond conventional noir. Still, *Basic Instinct* is primarily important for its depiction of Tramell as a ground- and rule-breaking femme fatale who dazzles every man she meets with her sexual charisma but also outshines them creatively, intellectually, and economically, all the while refusing to conform to traditional visions of feminine behavior, sexual or otherwise. This content is especially reinforced by the dynamic between Tramell and Curran, in which conventional gender roles are so often reversed (as is the traditional relationship between investigator and suspect). Such characteristics clearly make *Basic Instinct* an early example of revisionary noir, despite being released at the height of the neo-noir era.

Chapter 20

Women in Revisionary Noir: *Gone Girl*

(2014, Directed by David Fincher)

Gillian Flynn's 2012 novel *Gone Girl* is a genuine literary blockbuster, one that delivers considerable reading pleasure through its delivery of sordid (and not always consistent or believable) material through a complex and deftly fabricated narrative structure. In short, it is perfect material for film noir, a phenomenon that, as we have seen, is marked from the beginning by a sort of confrontation between modernist art and pop culture, while maintaining an uneasy relationship to both. It is not surprising that the book was adapted to film so quickly or that the resultant adaptation had so many of the characteristics that are normally associated with film noir. Nor is it surprising that the adaptation attracted an A-list director in David Fincher, noted for his own combination of high cinematic style with grim and violent content. At the same time, the film's noir characteristics are installed with a self-consciousness so extreme that the film becomes patently artificial, asking viewers to question every move in the process of the film's construction. Meanwhile, such questioning seems absolutely appropriate in a film whose characters self-consciously behave in artificial ways, constructing all sorts of narratives about themselves that are either questionable or patently untrue. In a film that so patently draws upon the noir tradition, such fundamental questioning inevitably asks us to reevaluate the use of the film's noir characteristics in the original noir cycle. Most centrally, the femme fatale in this film ultimately triumphs, gaining full control of her husband, thus calling attention to the fact that the original femmes fatales, however formidable, were typically punished, usually winding up dead or otherwise defeated.

Meanwhile, *Gone Girl* was on the cutting edge of a new form of literature that has come to be known as "chick noir," in which the tropes of "chick lit" are reformulated via the darker logic of film noir, now aimed first and foremost at a female audience. Flynn herself had already moved in this direction with her first two novels, *Sharp*

Objects (2006) and *Dark Places* (2009), and *Gone Girl* was quickly followed by such chick noir novels as Liane Moriarty's *Big Little Lies* (2014) and Paula Hawkins's *The Girl on the Train* (2015). Significantly, all of these novels have been adapted, either to film or to television miniseries. *Gone Girl* was the first of these novels to be adapted, its significant box office success helping to encourage the adaptation of other chick noir novels.[1]

Flynn's novel flaunts its sources in film noir by mentioning noir several times, as in an exchange between writer/teacher/bar owner Nick Dunne (Ben Affleck in the film) and his young girlfriend (and student) Andie Fitzgerald (Emily Ratajkowski in the film) discussing their secret relationship in the light of the highly publicized disappearance of Nick's wife Amy (Rosamunde Pike in the film): "God, it's like some bad noir movie," says Andie.[2] In response, Nick smiles to himself: "I'd introduced Andie to noir—to Bogart and *The Big Sleep*, *Double Indemnity*, all the classics. It was one of the things I liked best about us, that I could show her things."[3] A close reading of this passage shows that one of the attractions of Andie for Nick is that he feels empowered in their relationship, something he has never quite felt with the richer and better educated Amy. Meanwhile, the noir roots of the film are obvious as well, and the film as a whole is a faithful adaptation that maintains much of the feel of the novel, no doubt partly because it was scripted by Flynn herself.

Perhaps the most obvious noir aspect of *Gone Girl* is its presentation of Amy as a new sort of femme fatale. However, both the novel and the film (but especially the film) drew some criticism for the ways in which Amy's deceitful and manipulative behavior seemed to run against the grain of the "believe-women" ethos of the then-emergent #MeToo movement.[4] However, virtually *everyone* in this novel and film is deceitful and manipulative. Moreover, by centering Amy, this film breaks new ground with the agency of its femme fatale. Lota notes that the original noir films tended to be built around male alienation, however powerful their femmes fatales, but he argues that *Gone Girl* focuses on *female* alienation, resulting in the "use the figure of the *femme-fatale* to critique, not women themselves, but *noir*'s own gender logic, and by extension that of American society in general."[5]

The striking opening scene of the novel is carried over directly (though slightly condensed) into the film in a brief opening scene that also suggests Nick's sense of disempowerment in relation to Amy. The scene features Nick's voiceover narration (a common noir characteristic), which introduces motifs that will dominate the entire film. A dark screen gradually lightens until we see Amy's head, Nick's hand stroking her neatly combed blonde hair. "When I think of my wife, I always think of her head," says Nick in voiceover. His surprising next sentence, though, alerts us that all is not right in their household: "I picture cracking her lovely skull, unspooling her brains." Before we have time to digest the violent image that Nick has just given us, Amy turns her head to look up at him as he continues, revising his initial violent imagery to suggest that, by saying that he wants to "crack her skull," he really just means that he is curious about her thoughts: "Trying to get answers. The primal questions of any marriage. What are you thinking? How are you feeling? What have we done to each other?"

The questions Nick poses are the ones that drive the entire film, though they remain unanswered as we loop back to a repetition of this scene at the end, with the added question "What *will* we do?" suggesting that the two spouses will continue to be enigmas to each other as they move into the future. We can't really tell if this scene is an actual repetition of the scene at the beginning or whether it's the same scene and the rest of the film has been an extended flashback (with other flashbacks within that flashback), which would be a classic noir plot structure. It really doesn't matter, though: this is a film that can't be bothered with such details, which are often left hanging. Events in this film are presented for effect, not for verisimilitude. There are numerous points at which the plot is not terribly believable or when contrivances work suspiciously well, as when Amy fakes her kidnapping and rape at the hands of her old boyfriend Desi Collings (Neil Patrick Harris), then murders Collings and returns to Nick, the police buying her story absolutely without question. When Nick actually points out to one of the cops that some aspects of her story seem a bit fishy, he is simply told, "Can't you just be happy that your wife is home and safe?" And this moment, one of so many self-reflexive moments within the film pretty much sums up the film's own attitude toward problematic aspects of its narrative: it's fiction, anyway; just go with it.

This initial voiceover immediately centers Nick as the apparent main character of the film, something that will be reinforced by the quick disappearance of Amy from the present time of the film, initially leaving the central place in the film to Nick. Meanwhile, police suspicions about Amy's fate naturally and inevitably center on Nick as well, and much of the first half of the film involves their investigation, which gradually uncovers more and more evidence of Nick's apparent guilt. The film's plot is full of twists, turns, and surprises, however, and things are often (another typical noir characteristic) not what they appear to be. Just short of the halfway point, we find that Amy has, in fact, staged her own disappearance, and from here it quickly becomes clear that she has also carefully (and over an extended period) planted evidence suggesting that Nick has murdered her.

Thus, the "big reveal" in this mystery film occurs less than halfway through its runtime, leaving a segment as long as many noir films still remaining. That remaining segment, meanwhile, contains its own twists and turns, some of them quite shocking, as we follow Amy as she continues on the run, then commits a murder of her own (while framing her victim as her assailant), then returns to Nick (not, of course, to a happy reunion but to a battle of wills). By the end of the film, we have seen something that is part lost-man noir and part detective noir, driven mostly by the machinations of a chillingly crafty and cold-blooded femme fatale. In short, it combines all three of the major subcategories of film noir we have been discussing— and it does so quite self-consciously.

Gone Girl includes bits and pieces of other genres as well, as in the early flashback sequence in which we see (at least as she represents it in the fake diary she has left behind to implicate Nick in her "murder") the early courtship of Nick and Amy, neither apparently minding how unconvincing and insincere the other's snappy banter during this courtship really is. Such banter is typical of film noir as well; in this case, though, it is probably reminiscent more of romantic comedy (more chick lit than chick noir), and one gets the feeling that both Nick and Amy are acting out the roles of new lovers that they might have seen enacted in romantic comedy films (and perhaps not even good ones). The scene of their first kiss (amid a cloud of sugar), is just a bit too, well, sweet—not to mention wholly contrived.[6] Indeed, the actions of both characters have an inauthentic and calculated quality throughout the film, as if they are empty people with no real core personalities, simply performing personalities that they might have learned from fiction or film.

THE CHARACTERS OF *GONE GIRL*

However contrived the plot of *Gone Girl* might be, its most overt artificiality occurs in its characterization. Its two principal characters, Nick and Amy, are constantly acting, constantly playing roles, constantly constructing narratives. This behavior, to an extent, merely makes them products of the environment in which they live, in which the media is also constantly attempting to construct stories that will draw audiences. The media, especially television, is depicted as a tawdry and venal institution that values sensation and profit more than truth in reporting, continuing a war between film and television that dates back to the period of the original noir cycle.[7] In addition, Nick is an aspiring fiction writer, and Amy's whole life has been conditioned by the fact that her parents used (and improved upon) her childhood to produce a popular children's book series, giving her life a fictional feel from the very beginning. This fact perhaps also makes Amy especially self-conscious in her role-playing, as when she admits to having played the role of the "Cool Girl" during her original courtship with Nick, just as Nick admits in one of his television interviews that he originally won Amy over by pretending to be a better man than he really was.

Some of the other characters are much the same, as when Andie packages herself as a sweet, innocent young girl for the televised reveal of her relationship with Nick. Desi fits this pattern even better; acting as Amy's savior (and ultimately serving as her victim), he consistently displays a creepy affect that suggests a possible sinister side to his feelings for Amy.[8] And, of course, there is the white trash couple (played by Lola Kirke and Boyd Holbrook) who turn out essentially to be con artists who seem a bit simple-minded but then outflank the conniving Amy and rob her of all her cash. It is also significant that Kirke's character is very much the leader of this pair, echoing Amy's ultimate power over Nick. In addition, even the characters who seem relatively genuine, such as Nick's loyal twin sister Margo (Carrie Coon) and police detective Rhonda Boney (Kim Dickens), are more like stock characters lifted from popular culture than like authentic human beings, though they also reconfigure the "good girl" character from the original noir films. Finally, Tanner Bolt, Tyler Perry's

Figure 20.1. Ben Affleck and Rosamunde Pike during their initial courtship in *Gone Girl.* Twentieth Century Fox Film Corporation/Photofest © Twentieth Century Fox Film Corporation

showboat celebrity lawyer character (he likes to call himself Elvis), is also something of a stock character, yet he is also someone who is playing a highly theatrical role, working as much in the media as in the courtroom.

Archer suggests that the characters in this film are simply meant to serve a narrative function, not to be believable as human beings. For him, such characterization joins with the film's "self-conscious plot contortions" to "acknowledge its continuity with a cinematic narrative tradition: "The icy *femme fatales* and framed wrong-man stories in noirs and neo-noirs such as *Double Indemnity* (1944) and *The Last Seduction* (1994)," as well as the "ambiguities and machinations of a film like *Basic Instinct* (1992)."[9] One could name any number of cinematic predecessors, of course, and part of Archer's point is that *Gone Girl* seems to have been consciously constructed from familiar cinematic tropes, especially the tropes of noir.

CULTURAL COMMENTARY IN *GONE GIRL*

Archer notes that *Gone Girl* (in both the novel and the film) is "quite jokey about its own structure," which is something that it shares with many noir films.[10] However, the many self-reflexive gestures in *Gone Girl* go beyond those in the original noir cycle, while doing much more than adding entertainment value (though they do that). They can actually be taken as a key element of the film's considerable social commentary, which goes well beyond the obvious commentary on gender politics. In particular, the patent artificiality of the film and its structure serves as a commentary on late capitalist society itself. Overtly created in the image of the society within which it was produced, *Gone Girl* becomes a sort of overt demonstration of Jameson's dictum that postmodernism is the cultural logic of late capitalism, at the same time critiquing its own logic.

The original noir cycle grew out of anxieties related to memories of the Great Depression, then to World War II, and later to a postwar world informed by the threat of nuclear extinction in the midst of the rapid transformation of American society, including changes in the roles that both men and women were expected to play in this new society. Gender roles are still in question in *Gone Girl*, in which women are depicted as prominent and powerful members of the media and police, while masculinity is threatened and embattled. More specifically, the main action of *Gone Girl* specifically takes place amid the anxieties following the economic collapse of 2008, which is specified to have placed significant economic pressure on the Dunnes—even though (in point of fact) they seem to be living very comfortable lives in their nice suburban home. Indeed, the clearest sign of their financial difficulty is their large credit card debt, which was intentionally engineered by Amy to cast suspicion on Nick. Indeed, in this film, real economic pressures are mostly stipulated to add atmosphere, rather than represented in a realistic way, so that their inclusion in this film is as patently artificial as everything else.

This artificiality, however, does not necessarily lessen the impact of the film's social commentary. In fact, it might *increase* that impact. Among other things, it joins with the film's overall negative treatment of the media to suggest the way in which even something like this financial crisis, which ruined the lives of many and damaged the lives of many more, was essentially turned into a spectacle for (and by) the news media, especially television news. And yet, just by acknowledging the historical reality of the 2008 crisis, the film plants a seed that reminds us that the shiny surface of late capitalism obscures some very dark economic realities underneath. Meanwhile, the overtly metafictional construction of *Gone Girl* asks us to reexamine the often artificial structure of the original noir films, suggesting that they were telling us something very important about their contemporary American society through their own metafictional gestures.

Gone Girl revises our understanding of the original film noir cycle primarily through its centering of its femme fatale character, who emerges triumphant at the end, rather than being punished for her transgressions against masculine power. In addition, its patently metafictional structure, clearly meant as a commentary on late capitalist society in the wake of the 2008 financial crisis, also calls attention to the artificiality of the original noir films, themselves made amid the transformation of the consumer capitalist culture into its late form. This aspect of *Gone Girl* suggests that we should more carefully the dialogue of the original noir films with consumer and with capitalism as a whole, while also suggesting that the treatment of gender in film noir might be entangled with the treatment of capitalism. In this sense, the emergence of the original femme fatale can be taken as a cry of protest against the reification/objectification of women as an aspect of the commodification of every-thing under late consumer capitalism. However, the limited success of the original femmes fatales in carrying out their schemes (in relation to that of Amy Dunne) also suggests that Hollywood film, in the 1940s and 1950s, was quite limited in the extent to which it was willing and able to take on either capitalism or patriarchy as an object of direct critique.

Chapter 21

Women in Revisionary Noir: *Promising Young Woman*

(2020, Directed by Emerald Fennell)

Promising Young Woman, the debut film from British writer/director Emerald Fennell, is a highly topical work that deals with a number of important contemporary issues surrounding troubled relations between the genders at the beginning of the 2020s. A British/American coproduction, it is also a highly accomplished work of postmodern art that features impressive performances while participating in a number of different genres and keeping audiences on their toes with frequent, sometimes jarring, tonal shifts. It's also something of a puzzle film, keeping audiences engaged in an ongoing attempt to put together the clues it offers in order to figure out exactly what is going on, while leaving some important questions ultimately unanswered. Meanwhile, the film invites comparison with the noir tradition, which helps us to see that its title character is a very new kind of femme fatale.

Released near the end of 2020, *Promising Young Woman* was highly topical in its exploration of rape culture and the sexual objectification of women. *Promising Young Woman* also drew attention because of the impressive Oscar-nominated performance of British actress Carey Mulligan as Cassandra "Cassie" Thomas, the promising young femme fatale of the title—and the film's point of view character. Actually, "once promising" might be more accurate, because Cassie's life has been derailed due to the trauma caused by the rape of her friend Nina Fisher, a fellow medical student, seven years earlier. Unable to get any sort of justice for (or even acknowledgment of) what happened to her, Nina was eventually driven to suicide. Cassie, as conveyed by Mulligan's convincing and nuanced performance, was also seriously damaged by her friend's experience. Forced by this trauma to drop out of medical school, she now works in a coffee shop and lives at home with her parents. She seems to have no real direction in life, devoting herself primarily to seeking vengeance on predatory men—possibly to the extent of becoming a serial killer, though she remains relatable and sympathetic throughout.

The film gradually fills in details about Nina's experience, making it clear that she had not only been raped by fellow med student Alexander "Al" Monroe (Chris Lowell) while she was too intoxicated to resist, but that a number of Monroe's friends had watched the event and cheered Monroe on, regarding it as amusing entertainment. One of them even recorded the rape on video to be circulated as entertainment for his friends. Subsequently, Nina had sought action against her rapist, but both the school and police (and most of Nina's fellow students) concluded that the details of the crime were not clear enough to take action against Monroe that would likely end his career in med school and possibly send him to prison.

When we first meet Cassie at the beginning of the film, she herself appears to be helplessly drunk, slumped semiconscious on a bench in a club. Then, Jerry (Adam Brody), a "nice guy" who happens to be at the club with friends, offers to see Cassie home safely. He then suggests on the way that they stop by his place for a nightcap. There, he immediately sets about trying to take advantage of her inebriated condition. When she suddenly reveals that she is not intoxicated after all, Jerry freezes in shock and terror. Indeed, one repeated motif in the film involves the way in which men, confident and blustering when they think Cassie is helpless, crumple so easily into weakness (and even tears) when she reveals unexpected strength.

The end of this first encounter is particularly indicative of the way *Promising Young Woman* is constructed. For one thing, the film proceeds at an extremely crisp pace. The entire encounter in Jerry's apartment lasts just a bit over two minutes of runtime, and almost all of the major scenes of the film unfold in a similarly rapid manner, perhaps suggesting Cassie's sense of time and events unfolding around her at a dizzying pace. This pacing also creates a sense that we have observed a film that is packed with action, even though very little action actually occurs on screen. Thus, after we see Jerry's stunned reaction to the revelation of Cassie's sobriety, we don't actually see what happens next. Instead, the film immediately cuts to the opening title, presented in cheerful bright pink, on a screen decorated by pink hearts. Bright colors, especially pink, will be crucial to the very un-noir-like palette of this film.

The logic of much Hollywood film, of course, dictates that Jerry would be violently murdered by Cassie, an interpretation that is furthered by the fact that, after the cutaway from Jerry's face and to the film's title, the next thing we see is that title with the bright pinkish-red color of the letters beginning to run down the screen, perhaps like melting candy, though it is more likely that those who are familiar with certain types of films will interpret the running colors as emblematic of dripping blood. This reading, meanwhile, is enhanced as we see Cassie walking along the sidewalk with what is apparently a splash of blood running down her white blouse and another running down her leg.

It seems pretty clear at this point that we are meant to assume that Cassie has murdered Jerry in bloody fashion. At the same time, the film has yet to introduce

Nina's experience, so we have no way of knowing what might have motivated Cassie to undertake such violence. Moreover, we next see that, as Cassie walks along, she is messily eating a hot dog that is liberally dripping ketchup. Are the rivulets of red on her body and clothes really Jerry's blood, or are they actually just ketchup?

At the end of the film, it is still not clear whether Cassie has ever killed anyone, though we soon discover that she routinely picks up men much in the way she picked up Jerry. In fact, she keeps a journal of her numerous encounters with predatory men, complete with color-coded tally marks and a list of their names. We will never learn, however, just what this journal means or what the colors indicate. Such uncertainties abound in *Promising Young Woman*, again possibly indicating the uncertainty with which Cassie negotiates daily life in her traumatized condition, though one of the nuances of the film is that this condition does not render her helpless or inert.

Soon after the first scene with Jerry, Cassie experiences what might be taken as a parody of the typical Hollywood "meet cute" scene when Ryan Cooper (Bo Burnham), another former fellow student of Cassie's, happens into the coffee shop where she works. Ryan embarrasses himself by inadvertently insulting Cassie (for having such a lowly job), after which he invites her to spit in his coffee in retribution. To his surprise, she spits liberally into the drink; to her surprise, he accepts the coffee anyway and takes a big swig. She nevertheless turns him down when he asks her out, clearly preferring to limit her social life to her program of revenge.

Soon afterward, Cassie executes another club pickup by a purported "nice guy"— to whom she reveals that she does this sort of thing every week but whom it is fairly clear she *doesn't* murder. This encounter is a bit longer than the one with Jerry, but at five minutes it maintains the quick pace of the film. Within the next few minutes, Cassie has an awkward encounter with her parents on her birthday, gets asked out again by Ryan, and this time goes out to lunch with him. Ryan, now a successful pediatric surgeon, seems to be a genuinely nice guy, and there are signs that he is beginning to break through Cassie's protective armor with his boyish charm. But *Promising Young Woman* is not a film in which things happen in a simple fashion, and the Cassie-Ryan relationship will not proceed smoothly.

One sign of the complexity of *Promising Young Woman* is that Cassie seeks revenge, not only against abusive men, but also against the women who enable them. Just over half an hour into the film, we see the first of five sequences that are labeled with tally marks like those in Cassie's diary, sequences that each indicate a stage of Cassie's program of direct revenge against those who were involved in Nina's rape and its aftermath. In the first of these, Cassie has a luncheon meeting with her former classmate, Madison McPhee (Alison Brie), who has continually denied that Nina was raped ever since the actual event, perhaps because she now lives a comfortably affluent life as the wife of a successful man, with a social circle that still includes several people from med school. At the lunch, Madison suggests that Nina was at fault for being such a heavy drinker—even as Madison herself is in the process (with Cassie's encouragement) of getting falling-down drunk. Cassie then has a man she has hired for the purpose of taking Madison to a hotel room and putting her in bed. Madison wakes up not knowing whether she has been raped, thus presumably learning a lesson about vulnerability and helplessness, though Cassie, in a later meeting, ultimately assures a frantic Madison that nothing happened with the man, though she lets Madison twist in the wind for a considerable time. Most viewers likely believe Cassie's claim that nothing bad happened in that hotel room, but the film nevertheless leaves open just a bit of doubt, a doubt that one suspects might linger in Madison's mind as well. Meanwhile, it is not clear just what sort of traumatic effect this "lesson" might have on Madison going forward.

Brie plays Madison as a rather pretentious and unlikeable sort, which makes this episode a little easier to take, despite the obvious problem with the logic of Cassie's vengeance here, especially given the seed of doubt that has been planted concerning just what happened to Madison in that hotel room. After all, we have already been given a suggestion that Cassie might be a serial killer, so we are not really sure just what she might be capable of. The film's next numbered episode, meanwhile, is even more problematic, as Cassie ostensibly arranges for a teenage girl to be handed over to a gang of rowdy med students who live in the same dorm room where Nina had been raped. This girl, it turns out, is the daughter of Dean Elizabeth Walker (Connie Britton), the same dean who had failed to follow up on Nina's report of being raped years earlier. When Cassie pays a visit on Dean Walker to inform her that her daughter is now experiencing the same fate as Nina, there are some very tense moments when we are not quite sure whether Cassie is telling the truth, though she quickly assures the dean (and us) that the girl is quite safe and that Cassie has only constructed this episode to make clear to the dean just how easily bad things can happen to young women in our current culture.

Of course, the film presents no evidence that the girl is, in fact, safe, so we have to take Cassie's word for it. By this time, though, most viewers are probably invested in Cassie, thanks to Mulligan's winning performance of the character. Therefore (and especially in the absence of any evidence to the contrary), most viewers are likely to believe this later explanation and to conclude that the girl is safe. Moreover, most viewers are likely to be relieved to be able to believe that Cassie would not put a young girl in such danger.

In the third numbered segment of the film, Cassie pays a call on Jordan Green (Alfred Molina), a lawyer who had helped defend Al when Nina had attempted to bring charges against him. Indeed, Green appears to have worked for a law firm that specialized in defending men against such charges, largely by discrediting and intimidating their accusers. When Cassie arrives at Green's door, she tells him that it is his "day of reckoning," which (to her surprise) he appears to welcome. Indeed, when she speaks with Green inside, she finds that he is a contrite, broken man who has ceased to practice law out of guilt over cases such as Nina's. Unlike Dean Walker, Green even remembers Nina's name (or at least her first name). In this case, Cassie leaves without enacting revenge, apparently feeling that Green is already suffering enough. Then we find out that she has a hired thug waiting outside, but she calls him off. Thus, by demonstrating that she can show mercy, Cassie continues to win our sympathy. Moreover, the very fact that she has hired such a thug suggests that Cassie herself is not violent, adding to the suspicion that she has not actually killed anyone.

The positive arc of Cassie's characterization continues in the next scene, in which she pays a call on Nina's mother (played by Molly Shannon) at her oddly idyllic, all-American home, which serves as another example of visual settings in the film that seem a bit out of sync with the emotional subject matter of the film. The mother urges Cassie to move on and to stop lingering on Nina's tragic end. Soon afterward, Cassie is shown deleting the social media account she had been using to stalk her victims, then throwing away her notebook. The implication is clear: she has decided to take the advice of Nina's mother and to discontinue her project of revenge.

This change in direction also enables Cassie to rekindle her relationship with Ryan, after which the film transforms into what is essentially a romantic comedy— somewhat like the inserted flashback in *Gone Girl*. However, in keeping with the generally fast pace of *Promising Young Woman*, this entire segment lasts only seven minutes, a bit more than halfway through the film. This sequence includes such ultracute moments as Ryan's surprisingly adept lip-sync to Paris Hilton's "Stars Are Blind" in a pharmacy, intercut with subsequent classic rom-com moments of their growing attachment, accompanied by this same track. We then see the obligatory dinner with Cassie's parents, followed by the ultimate declaration of mutual love, after which Cassie seems to have found a road to happiness.

Just as we are beginning to believe that Cassie might have found true love and might be headed for some genuine recovery from her trauma, *Promising Young Woman* suddenly swerves in another direction, as the plot of the film continues to echo the emotional rollercoaster that is Cassie's continual experience. Madison shows up at the home of Cassie's parents, where Cassie reassures her that nothing happened with the man in the hotel room. Unfortunately, she also delivers to Cassie a phone containing a copy of the video of Nina's rape, Cassie having previously been unaware of the existence of the video. Then, as if that weren't bad enough, Cassie watches the video and discovers that Ryan had been one of the revelers cheering Al on during the rape. That relationship thus destroyed, Cassie resumes her program of revenge, moving the film into its deadly final stages.

The scene in which Cassie receives the video takes place in the living room of her parents' home, where the bizarre baroque décor—perhaps more at home at the Palace of Versailles than in a modern American suburban home (except for the portrait of a German shepherd over the fireplace)—possibly suggests the cluelessness of her parents. We've seen a few shots of the home before, and until this scene the décor seems only slightly odd, perhaps like something from the 1950s, suggesting that the parents may be out of step with the times. But this living room takes that motif to an entirely new level, to the point that one has to wonder whether what we are seeing is more symbolic than literal. I take it, in fact, as a sign of just how unreal and wrong the entire texture of life feels to Cassie, whose trauma makes it difficult to process the world around her in a normal way. She lives an uncomfortable, dreamlike

Figure 21.1. Cassie Thomas and Ryan Cooper (Carey Mulligan and Bo Burnham) lip-sync in a pharmacy during their courtship in *Promising Young Woman*. Focus Features/ Photofest © Focus Features

existence, in which nothing seems to be quite the way it should be, and this strange décor visually captures that fact.

Immediately after she views the video, we see a shattered Cassie staggering through a parklike area, on her way to confront Ryan at the hospital where he works. Music, as so often in this film, plays a crucial role here, as her walk is accompanied by the eerie lullaby-like "Once Upon a Time There Was a Pretty Fly." The otherworldly song feels perfect for Cassie's mood in this crucial scene, though its significance goes well beyond its mere sound. In particular, this song was originally used on the soundtrack of the classic 1955 noir horror film *The Night of the Hunter*, a film that we had earlier seen Cassie's parents watching on the television in their home. We even see a snippet from near the beginning of the film in which Robert Mitchum's blood-chilling, murderous preacher Harry Powell drives along in a stolen jalopy, talking to God about the offensiveness of women. Powell's misogny makes *The Night of the Hunter* a perfect noir companion to *Promising Young Woman* and the issues it raises.

Cassie breaks off her relationship with Ryan and meanwhile uses the video to coerce him into revealing the location of the bachelor party for Al's upcoming wedding. Then, in a fourth numbered segment, Cassie poses as a stripper and shows up at the party, eventually maneuvering Al into taking her upstairs to a bedroom where they can be alone. When Al realizes who she is, he panics and struggles with her, eventually suffocating her with a pillow. It is clear that Al regards her death as an accident, though the film leaves it for us to judge whether it should be regarded in this way. It also eventually becomes clear that Cassie, in fact, intended for Al to kill her: we learn, by the end of the film, that she has arranged for the police to be alerted to her death. As the film ends, police interrupt Al's wedding to arrest him for her murder, after having found evidence that Al and a friend attempted to burn her body to dispose of the evidence. (In one nice touch, Al is steered away in handcuffs by a woman police officer.) As the film ends, it is also given a final (very contemporary) touch as Ryan, attending the interrupted wedding, reads texts from Cassie that she has prearranged for him to receive at this time. Her final texted words to him, showing on his phone in the reddish-pink that has been a motif throughout the film, are:

You didn't think this was the end, did you?
It is now.
Enjoy the wedding.
Love,
Cassie & Nina
;)

This entire last sequence is accompanied by fitting music—Juice Newton's light-sounding 1981 Top-Ten pop ballad "Angel of the Morning"—which cleverly fits the moment with its theme of lack of remorse for previous "sins." Just as Al has shown no remorse for what happened to Nina, Cassie is not sorry for the way things turned out or for what she did to Al. Still, it is clear that she herself has experienced no lasting satisfaction from her program of revenge. The film then ends with one more clever musical twist as the soundtrack shifts soon after the beginning of the end credits from "Angel of the Morning" to "Last Laugh," a defiant hip-hop declaration of feminine power by Fletcher, a woman artist probably best known for her songs "I Believe You" (2018), released in support of sexual assault survivors, and "Undrunk" (2019), which perfectly fits the plot of this film.

The subject matter of *Promising Young Woman* is fairly typical of noir film, up-dated to the #MeToo era. The bright musical and visual textures of most of this film, though, are very unusual in a noir film, contributing to the film's careful suggestion of Cassie's traumatized mental state. Cassie's condition (and her status as the film's point of view character) helps to make her a very new kind of femme fatale and helps to make *Promising Young Woman* an excellent example of revisionary noir film.

Conclusion

This book has presented a survey of three different subsets of American noir film: films built on detective narratives, films featuring "lost" men, and films focusing on women. Within these three subsets, the films have been characterized (and essentially periodized) according to whether they participate in the original film noir cycle of the 1940s and 1950s, in the neo-noir cycle from the 1960s forward, and in the revisionary noir cycle of films that has appeared primarily in the twenty-first century. These period categories are explored via an introductory survey of noir film and introductory surveys of each of the three subsets. The period categories are then explored further via detailed discussions of a number of individual films in each subset and each period.

This book defines "film noir" very much as it is conventionally defined: films that employ a distinctive black-and-white visual style to deal with crime and corruption in ways that comment on the tribulations of life in an American society that has often failed to live up to its promise of prosperity and freedom. It also defines neo-noir in a fairly conventional way as a type of film that self-consciously resurrects the style and subject matter of the original noir cycle but extends them due to changes in filmmaking technology and in social attitudes—which led, among other things, to the collapse of the strict Production Code that governed Hollywood film in the original noir era. However, neo-noir film tends to look on film noir in a respectful, nostalgic way that does not ask us to reevaluate the original films. Therefore, this volume introduces the notion of "revisionary noir" to indicate films that go farther, pushing the boundaries of noir in ways that potentially lead us to change the ways we think about the original noir films and about the possibilities of the noir mode in general.

Notes

INTRODUCTION TO NOIR FILM

1. On Asian noir, see Lee.

2. For some general information on Nordic noir, see Creeber, Forshaw, and Nestingen.

3. In another classic article (first published in 1970), Raymond Durgnat traces the historical roots of film noir, while the article by Place and Peterson is a good brief introduction to film noir visual style.

4. The films of the Coen brothers in general are perhaps the ones that have most pushed the boundaries of noir most extensively, while remaining largely within the bounds of neo-noir. See my book *The Coen Brothers' America* for a survey of their films.

5. This is not to say that *no* specific external events impacted the rise of revisionary noir. For example, 9/11 and the 2008 financial crisis contributed to a rise in anxieties in American society as compared with the relatively sanguine 1990s. Social anxieties tend to fuel noir films.

6. See, for example, the book by Paula Rabinowitz.

7. On this phenomenon, see the concluding chapter to my book *Ulysses, Capitalism, and Colonialism* (169–87).

PART I: THE NOIR DETECTIVE FILM

1. Mandel, *Delightful Murder*, p. 134.

2. Mandel, *Delightful Murder*, p. 135.

3. In addition, a number of television series have been based on Chandler's writing or characters. Chandler himself also received screenwriting credit on five original noir films released between 1944 and 1951, most notably including *Double Indemnity* (1944). On Chandler and noir film, see Phillips.

4. Mandel describes Macdonald as a "follower" of Chandler, calling Macdonald "the most prolific representative of the creators of tough-guy private eyes" (37). Only a handful of film

adaptations have been made of Macdonald's many novels, the best of which are *Harper* and *The Drowning Pool* (1975), both featuring Paul Newman as private detective Lew Harper (Lew Archer in Macdonald's originals).

5. This shift might have been partly a nod to the fact that Chandler himself lived in England between the ages of twelve and twenty-four. But Chandler was, first and foremost, a Los Angeles writer.

6. As I note in *The Coen Brothers' America*, the Coens' *Miller's Crossing* (1989) is greatly influenced by the work of Hammett, so the Coens have covered both of these major hardboiled fiction writers (50).

7. One might compare here Villeneuve's 2017 film *Blade Runner 2049*, which is both a noir detective film and a science fiction film. However, this sequel to *Blade Runner* (1982) enters into dialogue more with that predecessor than with previous noir films as a whole. As a result, it should probably be considered a neo-noir film, rather than a revisionary noir.

CHAPTER 1

1. See Said, *Orientalism*.
2. Walker, p. 33.
3. Naremore, p. 61.
4. Palmer, p. 37.

CHAPTER 2

1. Dickos, p. 177.
2. Naremore, p. 234.
3. This portrayal, alas, is not a virtue of the novel. Chandler's homophobia has been noted many times, as when Palmer notes it in conjunction with the portrayal of Marriott and Amthor in *Farewell, My Lovely* (p. 82).
4. In both versions of *Farewell, My Lovely*, it is clear that Velma had been a prostitute. In *Murder, My Sweet*, with Code restrictions in place, this association is only implied.
5. Luhr, p. 81.
6. Spicer, p. 54.
7. Palmer, pp. 81–82.
8. Luhr, p. 78.

CHAPTER 3

1. Verevis, p. 315.
2. Jameson, *Postmodernism*, p. 19.
3. Jameson, *Postmodernism*, p. 20.

CHAPTER 4

1. Jameson, *Postmodernism*, p. 295.
2. Coughlin, p. 310.
3. Denzin, p. 75.
4. Chay, p. 93.
5. Berry, p. 89.

CHAPTER 5

1. Rumors that an Easy Rawlins television series was in development have circulated in Hollywood since early 2021, though the production of such a series does not appear to be imminent. Meanwhile, Washington and director Franklin did again work together on a noirish crime film with *Out of Time* (2003), a film that features two different interracial relationships without making race much of an issue—except in one scene in which an elderly white lady who might have been an important witness turns out not to be able to distinguish one Black man from another.

2. This same phenomenon informs Chester Himes's *If He Hollers Let Him Go* (1945), whose protagonist comes to Los Angeles to work at a shipyard during the war. This novel is one of the early works of Himes, perhaps the most important African American author of detective fiction prior to Mosley. However, *If He Hollers* is not, strictly speaking, a detective story in itself, though its style is reminiscent of the hardboiled tradition.

3. Monet is specifically identified as having a white father and a "Creole" mother. Mosley, incidentally, is the son of a Black father and white Jewish mother, while Beals is the daughter of a black father and white mother, so the principals have personal experience with the situation faced by Monet.

4. For a detailed discussion of the complex role of Monet's racial identity in the coding of this film, see Bastiaans.

5. Murphet, p. 33.

6. The opposition between Rawlins and characters such as Mouse and Albright is central to Flory's argument that this film uses the response of disgust to align audience sympathies with Rawlins and against these other characters in ways that potentially help audiences to recognize and reverse unconscious racist attitudes that have become habitual.

7. Mosley, p. xi.
8. Naremore, p. 249.
9. Naremore, p. 250.
10. E. Ann Kaplan, p. 307.
11. E. Ann Kaplan, p. 309.
12. Lott, pp. 167–68.

CHAPTER 6

1. Shoop, p. 210.
2. Miller, p. 234.

3. Gold, p. 210.

4. See Carswell for an application of Moraru's concept to *Inherent Vice*.

5. Of course, Lebowski, despite being a famously laid-back hippie type, is himself something of a Marlowe figure. On the important influence of Chandler on *The Big Lebowski* (1999), see Booker (*Coen Brothers*, pp. 61–74). On the links among Marlowe, Lebowski, and Sportello, see Carswell.

6. See, for example, Freer.

7. Among other things, while we tend to think of the "Reagan years" as his presidency from 1981 to 1989, *Inherent Vice* reminds us that Reagan was elected governor of California in 1966, so that, for Californians, the Reagan years begin much earlier.

8. On the role of Manson in the novel—and especially on the way Manson's female acolytes serve as emblems of female sexual availability in the counterculture, see Cook. Cook's claim that this motif demonstrates that Pynchon has been "suborned" by the modern California porn industry seems at best questionable, though. Granted, that industry does lurk in the background of the novel (and the film), but it also made intrusions even into the original noir films—as in the pornographic photo session with Carmen Sternwood, clad only in a "Chinese" robe, in *The Big Sleep*. In fact, one might argue that the Code-inflected hints at sexual conduct in the original noir films are much more pornographic than the free and easy sexuality we see in *Inherent Vice*.

9. Haynes, p. 6.

10. Haynes, p. 15.

11. The novel ends with a different scene of Sportello driving alone in a fog so deep that visibility is almost zero, cars able to move along (in a final moment of collective solidarity) only by following each other's taillights. But this fog also reinforces the film's sense of occurring at a transition point, possibly, miraculously into something truly new, possibly better. In the final sentence, Sportello waits "for the fog to burn away, and for something else this time, somehow, to be there instead" (Pynchon, p. 369).

CHAPTER 7

1. Bradshaw, *Under*, n.p.

2. Hans, n.p.

3. Tallerico, n.p.

4. Warren, n.p.

5. Jameson, *Political Unconscious*, p. 135.

6. Monroe's pool scene can be found on YouTube at https://youtu.be/i_r407KGp-o?si =7lUBE8EF7cKOUm-6.

7. Compare here the now-classic argument by historian Richard J. Hofstadter that there is a long-term strain of paranoia in American politics.

8. In another scene, Sam apparently collapses in a graveyard from having been drugged. Yet when he awakens, he is surrounded by liquor containers that hadn't been there before, suggesting that he really passed out from excessive drinking.

PART II: THE NOIR FILM LOST MAN

1. It should be noted that Betty Friedan's *The Feminine Mystique* (1963), one of the key manifestos of the women's movement of the 1960s, actually began as an article in *McCall's* magazine in 1957, the same year as the release of *The Incredible Shrinking Man*. Clearly, by 1957, the groundwork for the women's movement was already being laid, and American women were becoming less willing blindly to enact the stereotypes of proper feminine behavior being providing them by "role models" such as television's June Cleaver, Donna Reed, and Harriet Nelson. For their own part, American men, already beleaguered by the increasing pressures of corporate culture in the workplace, typically saw the rising women's movement more as a threat than as an opportunity.

2. Because of the investigations performed by Barton Keyes (Edward G. Robinson), *Double Indemnity* could also be considered a detective noir, illustrating how many noir categories it spans.

3. Silver and Ward, p. 228.

4. During this period, there was also a film adaptation of a short story by Thompson, entitled *This World, Then the Fireworks* (1997).

CHAPTER 8

1. David Coursen notes that, in *Detour*, "Ulmer is actually taking several American fantasies ('going West,' looking to Hollywood for success and happiness, finding freedom and happiness on the open road . . .) and performing unnatural acts on them, with devastating effects" (p. 19).

2. Despite the lack of recognition received in his lifetime, Ulmer's critical reputation has been steadily on the rise in recent years. See Isenberg and the collection of essays edited by Herzogenrath for examples of recent general criticism.

3. In this and other ways, the economic texture of the world of the film actually seems more reminiscent of the Depression years than of 1945, and it might be noted that the film was adapted (by screenwriter Martin Goldsmith) from his own 1939 novel.

4. Of course, Roberts might be an unreliable narrator and might not be telling the truth about the unlikely events he narrates.

5. Dickos, p. 186.

6. Coursen, p. 19.

7. Isenberg, p. 185.

8. Naremore, p. 149.

CHAPTER 9

1. Palmer, p. 59.

CHAPTER 10

1. Thompson did participate in the original noir cycle in one sense, apparently writing most of the screenplay for Stanley Kubrick's *The Killing* (1955), even though Kubrick was credited with writing the screenplay, while Thompson received a credit only for additional dialogue.

2. It might be noted, though, that at least one reviewer of the film on its initial release (Hal Hinson) complained that its visual style was a bit too slick and "fancy-pants" for the texture of Thompson's novel (Hinson, n.p.).

3. Polito, p. 372.

4. Payne, p. 103.

5. Ebert, "*After Dark*," n.p.

6. Payne, p. 100.

7. McCauley, p. 189.

8. Polito, p. 372.

CHAPTER 11

1. In the 2020 census, Santa Rosa had a population of nearly 180,000. But in the 1950 census, its population was only 17,000.

2. Booker, *Coen*, pp. 17–18.

CHAPTER 12

1. The extremity of *The Killer Inside Me* is such that Jamie Brummer has argued that it should be read within the context of the gothic novel, which Brummer argues helps us to understand its critique of the "cheery jingles, progressive propaganda, and comforting commercialism of America's dominant cultural narrative" (p. 211).

2. Polito, p. 497.

3. For a fuller discussion of Affleck's appropriateness for the role, see Jamieson.

4. For an extended attempt to understand why watching the film is more disturbing than reading the novel, see Gjelsvik.

5. Cooley was a prominent country artist of the period, though his music might have been chosen for this film partly because he was convicted of the 1961 murder of his wife, spending the remaining eight years of his life in prison.

6. The soundtrack also includes classical orchestral and operatic tracks, possibly to emphasize Lou's intellectuality. Indeed, at one point late in the film, Lou himself plays Bach on the piano in his home (though not especially well).

7. Scott, "Pulp," n.p.

8. Ebert, "*Killer*," n.p.

9. Greeks appeared in several films of the original noir cycle, serving as relatively noncontroversial markers of ethnicity. These characters are often treated with condescension, as with the mechanic Nick (Nick Dennis) in Robert Aldrich's *Kiss Me Deadly* (1955), whose murder is treated by protagonist Mike Hammer (Ralph Meeker) almost like the death of a beloved pet.

10. Bradshaw, "*Killer*," n.p.

CHAPTER 13

1. O'Malley, n.p.

2. This song was a commercial failure when released in 1977; a 1982 rerelease, however, became an international hit. Apparently, Ramsay's macho shipyard-worker father was a big fan of the song (Singer, p. 35).

3. Interestingly, *Taxi Driver*, along with Scorsese's *The King of Comedy* (1982), have both been mentioned as important predecessors to *Joker* (2019), for which Phoenix won a Best Actor Oscar—again for playing a psychically troubled character who (apparently) turns violent. See my book *No Joke* for a discussion of this film, which overlaps with *You Were Never Really Here* in a number of ways.

4. O'Malley, n.p.

5. Lury, p. 151.

6. Lury, p. 150.

7. Singer, p. 36.

8. Strictly speaking, we never see Joe engage with Williams's guards: we just see them lying bloody on the ground as Joe walks away from them carrying his hammer. It seems likely that they were dispatched by Joe, but this entire scene challenges our ability to make unequivocal conclusions.

CHAPTER 14

1. Brook, p. 1.

2. Koresky, p. 40.

3. Keiles, p. 38.

4. This observation holds even more for the young, drug-addled characters of the Safdies's 2014 film *Heaven Knows What*.

5. Koresky, p. 40.

6. Keiles, p. 40.

7. Koresky, p. 41.

8. Ratner tells Garnett that he paid $100,000, though it could well have been much less. Given that Ratner expected to sell the gem for at least $1 million, Garnett is perhaps justified when he complains that Ratner was exploiting the poor miners. The unsympathetic Ratner scoffs that the miners were so poor that $100,000 was worth "fifty lifetimes" to them.

9. This game was played on May 26, 2012, which does not exactly align with the Passover setting of the rest of the film, so there is a bit of dramatic license here.

10. Fox grew up partly in Italy but has lived the majority of her life in New York.

11. Rogin, p. 230.

12. Koresky, p. 41.

13. The Charlotte Hornets were the first NBA team with majority Black ownership, via an ownership group led by NBA legend Michael Jordan. However, in 2023, that majority share was sold to two Jewish investors, Gabe Plotkin and Rick Schnall.

PART III: WOMEN IN NOIR FILM

1. The figure of the femme fatale has been widely featured in critical commentary on film noir. See, for example, the book-length study by Silver and Ursini—who choose to move from the conventional French-originated term "femme fatale" to a straight English translation as "fatal woman" (Silver and Ursini, *Film Noir Fatal Women*).

2. See Covey for a survey of female-centered neo-noir films, focusing primarily on films featuring characters other than the femme fatale (on the basis of the fact that the femme fatale character had not changed all that much since the original noir films).

3. Stables, p. 175.

4. Another film by Verhoeven, 1995's *Showgirls*, could also be considered a revisionary noir, if only because of the extent to which it features sexually provocative nudity, something that made it the first NC-17 film to be widely distributed in mainstream theaters. Originally rejected by critics as a sort of soft-core pornography, the critical standing of this film has risen substantially in recent years. Any revisions to our understanding of the original noir films due to this film would probably be rather minor, though its representation of women goes beyond mere nudity. For example, its protagonist, showgirl Nomi Malone (Elizabeth Berkley), proves quite formidable in seeking violent revenge against a man who brutally rapes one of her friends.

5. Other films in this category include *Out of the Past* (1947), *Border Incident* (1949), *Where Danger Lives* (1950), and *Touch of Evil* (1958). It should also be added that Mexican film has a rich noir tradition of its own.

6. In addition, both *Gone Girl* and *Widows* were written or cowritten by Gillian Flynn, a key novelist in the phenomenon known as "chick noir"—noir novels written by women and centering on women characters.

7. The original noir films, of course, were almost exclusively directed by men, with the lone exception being Ida Lupino, who not only acted in several important noir films but also directed several films during the original noir period. One of these, *The Hitch-Hiker* (1953), is a noir classic. Female directors were only slightly more prominent in neo-noir, helming such relatively obscure films as Mary Lambert's *Siesta* (1987) and Katt Shea Rubin's *Stripped to Kill* (1987), and Karen Arthur's *Lady Beware* (1987). The most important female director of neo-noir was Kathryn Bigelow, who directed a series of films with prominent noir elements early in her career, though none are classic examples of neo-noir. These films include *The Loveless* (1981), *Near Dark* (1987), *Blue Steel* (1990), *Point Break* (1991), and *Strange Days* (1995).

CHAPTER 15

1. Durgnat, p. 47.
2. Naremore, p. 81.
3. Johnston, p. 94.
4. Dickos, p. 145.
5. Luhr, pp. 24–25.
6. Naremore, p. 89.
7. Naremore, p. 82.

8. Naremore, p. 82.
9. Naremore, pp. 82–83.
10. Paris, p. 21.
11. Paris, p. 21.

CHAPTER 16

1. Naremore, p. 93.
2. Ray, pp. 148–49.
3. Telotte, p. 152.

CHAPTER 17

1. Racine initially spots Matty as she exits an outdoor concert where an on-stage band is playing Sammy Fain's "That Old Feeling," a 1937 hit that has been used in many films since that time. This song is specifically about the experience of nostalgia and thus fits in nicely with this film's nostalgic look back at *Double Indemnity* and the original noir cycle.
2. Hirsch, pp. 182–83.
3. Linda Ruth Williams, p. 170.
4. Freedman interprets Lowenstein's dancing as a potential sign that he is gay, suggesting a homoerotic element to his friendship with Racine, something that rhymes with the similar element that many critics have seen in the relationship between Neff and Keyes in *Double Indemnity*. It should be noted, though, that Lowenstein dances somewhat in the style of Fred Astaire, who was at the peak of his stardom in the 1930s, thus linking back to the era in which *Double Indemnity* is set.
5. Jameson, *Postmodernism*, p. 21.
6. Freedman, p. 65.
7. Freedman, p. 66.
8. Freedman, p. 69.
9. Freedman, p. 71.

CHAPTER 18

1. For a colorful overview of this trilogy of films, see O'Callaghan.
2. O'Callaghan, p. 44.
3. Sharon Stone, based largely on her performance in *Basic Instinct* (1992), remained the queen of the 1990s erotic thriller, but *The Last Seduction* catapulted Fiorentino to a starring role in the big-budget, high-profile thriller *Jade* in 1995. That film, however, was a commercial and critical failure.
4. *The Last Seduction* doesn't really do much with the motif, but the world of telemarketing would seem to make a worthy addition to the traditionally seedy settings of noir film. Outside of documentaries, however, the film that has best utilized this world to date is not a noir film but the satirical science fiction horror film *Sorry to Bother You* (2018), directed by Boots Riley.

5. Stables, pp. 175–76.

6. But see also Thomson, who is decidedly unimpressed by Bridget, scoffing at her lack of imagination and noting that she never really gets anywhere, despite the seeming cleverness of her schemes.

7. See Butler for an extensive discussion of music in noir that uses *The Last Seduction* as a key example.

8. Alternatively, the title could be taken to suggest that, now that she has money, Bridget no longer has any interest in sleeping with men, but we probably shouldn't make too much of the title.

9. Ebert, n.p.

10. Linda Ruth Williams, p. 170.

11. Gordon, p. 215.

CHAPTER 19

1. One of the films clearly influenced by *Basic Instinct* was *The Last Seduction*. Perhaps the most overt imitation of *Basic Instinct* was the Madonna vehicle *Body of Evidence* (1993), though that film suffers from an inane script and a lack of on-screen charisma on the part of its star. More than a decade after its release, *Basic Instinct* also had a sequel, *Basic Instinct II* (2006), which again featured Sharon Stone as Tramell but was not well received.

2. Murray, p. 97.

3. Tramell publishes her novels under the name "Catherine Woolf," suggesting a link to the groundbreaking modernist novelist Virginia Woolf, whose writing transgressed all sorts of boundaries with regard to the representation of gender in fiction.

4. One could argue, though, that Tramell is out of Curran's league as well. As Wood notes, he is a virtual blank who "seems defined by his complete absence of individuating character-istics" (p. 44).

5. Wood, p. 46.

6. See Wood for a more detailed comparison of *Basic Instinct* with the films of Hitchcock.

7. See, for example, Becca Cragin, who believes that "we know from the opening scene that Catherine is the killer" (n.p.). As a result, Cragin also sees the film as less subversive of noir conventions than do I.

8. Wood, p. 50.

CHAPTER 20

1. See Thoma for a discussion of *Gone Girl* within the context of chick noir.

2. Ironically, in the novel, the *Amazing Amy* book series gives Amy a boyfriend whose name is Andy. Andy, though, is a very secondary character, essentially playing Ken to Amy's Barbie.

3. Flynn, p. 206.

4. For example, Dobbins argues that the novel's Amy has more depth, while the film's Amy is simply "a real Grade-A bitch. Horrible" (n.p.).

5. Lota, p. 168, his italics.

6. When Nick leads Amy into the cloud of sugar, it is hard not to suspect that he has made this same move before, a suspicion that is potentially reinforced when we see Nick (now married to Amy) essentially reenact the same move with his girlfriend Andie, though now with a snowstorm instead of sugar, while Amy (seemingly always a step ahead of her husband) secretly looks on in disgust. On the other hand, we only see this reenactment as part of one of Amy's later accounts, which might well have been fabricated by her, as (for that matter) might the sugar scene and many other scenes that appear on the screen via Amy's highly unreliable narration.

7. There is perhaps a special irony here in the fact that, before becoming a novelist, Flynn served as the television critic for *Entertainment Weekly*.

8. Archer notes the potentially homophobic implications of the casting of the openly gay Harris in this role (n.p.).

9. Archer, n.p.

10. Archer, n.p.

Bibliography

Anderson, Perry. *The Origins of Postmodernity*. Verso, 1998.

Archer, Neil. "*Gone Girl* (2012/2014) and the Uses of Culture." *Literature/Film Quarterly*, vol. 45, no. 3, Summer 2017, no pagination. (Available on-line at https://lfq.salisbury.edu /_issues/45_3/gone_girl.html. Accessed October 5, 2023).

Bastiaans, Aisha D. "Detecting Difference in *Devil in a Blue Dress*: The Mulatta Figure, Noir, and the Cinematic Reification of Race." *Mixed Race Hollywood*, edited by Mary Beltrán and Camilla Fojas, New York University Press, 2008, pp. 223–247.

Berry, Betsy. "Forever, In My Dreams: Generic Conventions and The Subversive Imagination in *Blue Velvet*." *Literature/Film Quarterly*, vol. 16, no. 2, 1988, pp. 82–90.

Booker, M. Keith. *The Coen Brothers' America*. Rowman and Littlefield, 2019.

Booker, M. Keith. *No Joke: Todd Phillips's* Joker *and American Culture*. University of Liverpool Press, 2023.

Booker, M. Keith. Ulysses, *Capitalism, and Colonialism: Reading Joyce After the Cold War*. Greenwood Press, 2000.

Borde, Raymond, and Étienne Chaumeton. *A Panorama of American Film Noir, 1941–1953*. 1955. Translated by Paul Hammond. City Lights Books, 2002.

Bould, Mark. *Film Noir: From Berlin to Sin City*. Wallflower, 2005.

Bradshaw, Peter. "*The Killer Inside Me*." The Guardian, June 3, 2010, https://www.theguardian.com/film/2010/jun/03/the-killer-inside-me-review. Accessed December 17, 2023.

Bradshaw, Peter. "Under the Silver Lake review—It Follows director bellyflops with ghastly noir." The Guardian, May 16, 2018, https://www.theguardian.com/film/2018/may/16 /under-the-silver-lake-review-david-robert-mitchell-andrew-garfield-cannes. Accessed November 30, 2023.

Brook, Vincent. *Driven to Darkness: Jewish Émigré Directors and the Rise of Film Noir*. Rutgers University Press, 2009.

Brummer, Jamie. "Gothic Noir: Jim Thompson's *The Killer Inside Me* and the Crooked Game of Post-World War II America." *Gothic Studies*, vol. 20, nos. 1–2, November 2018, pp. 199–213.

Buchsbaum, Jonathan. "Tame Wolves and Phoney Claims: Paranoia and Film Noir." *The Book of Film Noir*, edited by Ian Cameron, Continuum, 1993, 88–97.

Butler, David. *Jazz Noir: Listening to Music from* Phantom Lady *to* The Last Seduction. Westport: Praeger, 2002.

Cain, James M. *Double Indemnity*. 1943. Vintage Crime/Black Lizard, 2011.

Carswell, Sean. "Doc, the Dude, and Marlowe: Changing Masculinities from *The Long Goodbye* to *Inherent Vice*." *Orbit*, vol. 6, no. 1, 2018, https://orbit.openlibhums.org/article /id/484/. Accessed October 12, 2023.

Chay, Crescencia. "'He Put His Disease in Me': Abjection, Depravity and Postmodern Suburbia in David Lynch's *Blue Velvet*.'" *Film International*, vol, 19, no. 1, March 2021, pp. 87–93.

Cook, Simon. "Manson Chicks and Microskirted Cuties: Pornification in Thomas Pynchon's *Inherent Vice*." *Textual Practice*, vol. 29, no. 6, 2015, pp. 1143–1164.

Coughlin, Paul. "Postmodern Parody and the Subversion of Conservative Frameworks." *Literature/Film Quarterly*, vol. 31, no. 4, 2003, pp. 304–311.

Coursen, David. "Closing Down the Open Road: *Detour*." *Movietone News* 48 (1976): 16–19.

Covey, William. "Girl Power: Female-Centered Neo-Noir." *Film Noir Reader 2*, edited by Alain Silver and James Ursini, Limelight Editions, 2004. pp. 311–328.

Cragin, Becca. "Noirish Inversions: Investigation and Victimization in *The Silence of the Lambs* and *Basic Instinct*." *Americana: The Journal of American Popular Culture (1900-Present)*, vol. 8, no. 2, Fall 2009, no pagination.

Creeber, Glen. "Killing Us Softly: Investigating the Aesthetics, Philosophy and Influence of Nordic Noir Television." *The Journal of Popular Television*, vol. 3, no. 1, April 2015, pp. 21–35.

Denzin, Norman K. *Images of Postmodern Society: Social Theory and Contemporary Cinema*. Sage, 1995.

Dickos, Andrew. *Street with No Name: A History of the Classic American Film Noir*. University Press of Kentucky, 2002.

Dobbins, Amanda. "Yes, *Gone Girl* Has a Woman Problem.'" *Vulture*, October 3, 2014, http:// www.vulture.com/2014/10/yes-gone-girl-has-a -woman-problem.html. Accessed October 6, 2023.

Durgnat, Raymond. "Paint It Black: The Family Tree of *Film Noir*." *Film Noir Reader*, edited by Alain Silver and James Ursini. Limelight Editions, 1996. 37–51.

Ebert, Roger. "*After Dark, My Sweet*." RogerEbert.com, March 13, 2005, https://www.rogerebert.com/reviews/great-movie-after-dark-my-sweet-1990. Accessed October 19, 2023.

Ebert, Roger. "*The Killer Inside Me*." RogerEbert.com, June 23, 2010, https://www.rogerebert.com/reviews/the-killer-inside-me-2010. Accessed October 21, 2023.

Ebert, Roger. "*The Last Seduction*." RogerEbert.com, November 18, 1994, https://www.rogerebert.com/reviews/the-last-seduction-1994. Accessed December 16, 2023.

Flory, Dan. "Disgust, Race and Ideology in Carl Franklin's *Devil in a Blue Dress*." *Film-Philosophy*, vol. 26, no. 2, 2022, pp. 103–129.

Flynn, Gillian. *Gone Girl*. Random House, 2012.

Forshaw, Barry. *Nordic Noir: The Pocket Essential Guide to Scandinavian Crime Fiction, Film & TV*. Oldcastle Books, 2013.

Freedman, Carl. "The End of Work: From *Double Indemnity* to *Body Heat*." *Neo-Noir*, edited by Mark Bould, Kathrina Glitre, and Greg Tuck, London: Wallflower Press, 2009, pp. 61–73.

Freer, Joanna. *Thomas Pynchon and American Counterculture.* Cambridge University Press, 2014.

Friedan, Betty. *The Feminine Mystique.* 1963. W. W. Norton, 2013.

Gjelsvik, Anne. "What Novels Can Tell that Movies Can't Show." *Adaptation Studies: New Challenges, New Directions,* edited by Jorgen Bruhn, et al., Bloomsbury Publishing, 2013, pp. 245–64.

Gold, Eleanor. "Beyond the Fog: *Inherent Vice* and Thomas Pynchon's Noir Adjustment." *New Perspectives on Detective Fiction: Mystery Magnified,* edited by Casey Cothran and Mercy Cannon, Routledge, 2016, pp. 209–224.

Gordon, Suzy. "Fatality Revisited: The Problem of 'Anxiety' in Psychoanalytic-Feminist Approaches to Film Noir." *Neo-Noir,* edited by Mark Bould, Kathrina Glitre, and Greg Tuck, Wallflower Press, 2009, pp. 203–219.

Hans, Simran. "*Under the Silver Lake* Review—Too Self-indulgent for a Parody." March 17, 2019, https://www.theguardian.com/film/2019/mar/17/under-the-silver-lake-review. Accessed December 1, 2023.

Hassan, Ihab. "POSTmodernISM." *New Literary History,* no. 3, 1971, pp. 5–30.

Haynes, Doug. "Under the Beach, the Paving-Stones!: The Fate of Fordism in Pynchon's *Inherent Vice.*" *Critique: Studies in Contemporary Fiction,* vol. 55, no. 1, 2014, pp. 1–16.

Herzogenrath, Bernd, ed. *The Films of Edgar G. Ulmer.* Scarecrow Press, 2009.

Hill, Logan. "Pynchon's Cameo, and Other Surrealities." *New York Times,* September 26, 2014, https://www.nytimes.com/2014/09/28/movies/paul-thomas-anderson-films-inherent-vice.html. Accessed October 13, 2023.

Hinson, Hal. "*After Dark, My Sweet.*" *The Washington Post,* 24 August 1990, https://www.washingtonpost.com/wp-srv/style/longterm/movies/videos/afterdarkmysweetrhinson_a0a997.htm. Accessed October 20, 1990.

Hirsch, Foster. *Detours and Lost Highways: A Map of Neo-Noir.* Limelight, 1999.

Hofstadter, Richard J. "The Paranoid Style in American Politics." *Harper's Magazine,* November 1964, pp. 77–86.

Isenberg, Noah. *Edgar G. Ulmer.* University of California Press, 2014.

Jameson, Fredric. *The Political Unconscious: Narrative as a Socially Symbolic Act.* Cornell University Press, 1981.

Jameson, Fredric. *Postmodernism, or, The Cultural Logic of Late Capitalism.* Duke University Press, 1991.

Jamieson, Gill. "Adapting *The Killer Inside Me* and the Dynamics of Deviance from Page to Screen." *Crime Uncovered: Antihero,* edited by Fiona Peters and Rebecca Stewart, Intellect Books, 2015, pp. 58–71.

Johnston, Claire. "*Double Indemnity.*" *Women in Film Noir,* edited by E. Ann Kaplan, British Film Institute, 1998, pp. 89–98.

Kaplan, E. Ann. "The Dark Continent of Film Noir: Race, Displacement and Metaphor in Tourneur's *Cat People* (1942) and Welles' *The Lady from Shanghai* (1948)." *Women in Film Noir,* edited by E. Ann Kaplan, British Film Institute, 1998, pp. 307–338.

Keiles, Jamie Lauren. "The Everyman." *The New York Times Magazine,* December 1, 2019, pp. 36–41, 56–58.

Koresky, Michael. "You Win Some, You Lose Some." *Film Comment,* vol. 55, no. 6, November–December 2019, 38–41.

Kuhn, Thomas. *The Structure of Scientific Revolutions.* 1962. 4th ed., University of Chicago Press, 2012.

Lee, Hyangjin. "The Shadow of Outlaws in Asian Noir: Hiroshima, Hong Kong and Seoul." *Neo-Noir*, edited by Mark Bould, Kathrina Glitre, Kathrina, and Greg Tuck, Wallflower Press, 2009, pp. 118–135.

Lota, Kenneth. "Cool Girls and Bad Girls: Reinventing the *Femme Fatale* in Contemporary American Fiction." *Interdisciplinary Humanities*, vol. 33, no. 1, Spring 2016, pp. 150–170.

Lott, Eric. "The Whiteness of Film Noir." *National Imaginaries, American Identities: The Cultural Work of American Iconography*, edited by Larry J. Reynolds and Gordon Hutner, Princeton University Press, 2000, pp. 159–181.

Luhr, William. *Film Noir*. Wiley-Blackwell, 2012.

Lury, Karen. *The Child in Film*. London: I. B. Tauris, 2010.

Lynch, Kevin. *The Image of the City*. MIT Press, 1960.

Lyotard, Jean-François. *The Postmodern Condition: A Report on Knowledge*, translated by Geoff Bennington and Brian Massumi. University of Minnesota Press, 1984.

Mandel, Ernest. *Delightful Murder: A Social History of the Crime Story*. University of Minnesota Press, 1984.

Mandel, Ernest. *Late Capitalism*. 2nd revised edition, Verso, 1999.

Martin, Richard. *Mean Streets and Raging Bulls: The Legacy of Film Noir in Contemporary American Cinema*. Scarecrow Press, 1997.

McCauley, Michael J. *Jim Thompson: Sleep with the Devil*. Mysterious, 1991.

Miller, John. "Present Subjunctive: Pynchon's California Novels." *Critique: Studies in Contemporary Fiction*, vol. 54, no. 3, 2013, pp. 225–237.

Moraru, Christian. *Rewriting: Postmodern Narrative and Cultural Critique in the Age of Cloning*. SUNY Press, 2001.

Mosley, Walter. "Introduction to the 30th Anniversary Edition of *Devil in a Blue Dress*." Washington Square Press, 2020, pp. vii–xi.

Murphet, Julian. "Film Noir and the Racial Unconscious." *Screen*, vol. 39, no. 1, Spring 1998, pp. 22– 35.

Murray, Terri. *Studying Feminist Film Theory*. Auteur, 2019.

Naremore, James. *More than Night: Film Noir and Its Contexts*. University of California Press, 1998.

Nestingen, Andrew. "The Nordic Noir Brand." *Journal of Scandinavian Cinema*, vol. 11, no. 1, 2021, pp. 103–112.

O'Brien, Geoffrey. *Hardboiled America: Lurid Paperbacks and the Masters of Noir*. 1981. Expanded edition, Da Capo Press, 1997.

O'Callaghan, Bren. "My Noir: John Dahl's Neo-Noir Trilogy." *Film International*, no. 65, October 2013, pp. 40–44.

O'Malley, Sheila. "*You Were Never Really Here*." RogerEbert.com, April 6, 2016, https://www .rogerebert.com/reviews/you-were-never-really-here-2018. Accessed December 7, 2023.

Palmer, R. Barton. *Hollywood's Dark Cinema: The American Film Noir*. Twayne, 1994.

Paris, James A. "'Murder Can Sometimes Smell Like Honeysuckle': Billy Wilder's *Double Indemnity* (1944)." *Film Noir Reader 4*, edited by Alain Silver and James Ursini. Limelight Editions, 2004, pp. 9–21.

Payne, Kenneth. "Billy 'The Kid' Collins: Jim Thompson's Enigmatic Savior in *After Dark, My Sweet*." *Papers on Language and Literature*, vol. 33, no. 1, Winter 1997, pp. 99–111.

Phillips, Gene D. *Creatures of Darkness: Raymond Chandler, Detective Fiction, and Film Noir*. University Press of Kentucky, 2003.

Place, Janey, and Lowell Peterson. "Some Visual Motifs of *Film Noir.*" *Film Noir Reader*, edited by Alain Silver and James Ursini. Limelight Editions, 1996, 65–76.

Polito, Robert. *Savage Art: A Biography of Jim Thompson.* Vintage-Random House, 1995.

Pynchon, Thomas. *Inherent Vice.* Penguin, 2009.

Rabinowitz, Paula. *Black & White & Noir: America's Pulp Modernism.* Columbia University Press, 2002.

Ray, Robert B. *A Certain Tendency of the Hollywood Cinema, 1930–1980.* Princeton University Press, 1985.

Rogin, Michael. "Blackface, White Noise: The Jewish Jazz Singer Finds His Voice." *New Historical Literary Study: Essays on Reproducing Texts, Representing History*, edited by Jeffrey N. Cox and Larry J. Reynolds. Princeton University Press, 1993, pp. 230–266.

Ryan, Michael, and Douglas Kellner. *Camera Politica: The Politics and Ideology of Contemporary Hollywood Film.* Indiana University Press, 1988.

Said, Edward W. *Orientalism.* New York: Vintage-Random House, 1979.

Schrader, Paul. "Notes on *Film Noir.*" *Film Noir Reader*, edited by Alain Silver and James Ursini. Limelight Editions, 1996, 53–64.

Schweiger, Daniel. "Jerry Goldsmith on Scoring *Basic Instinct.*" *Soundtrack!*, 25 June 2013, https://cnmsarchive.wordpress.com/2013/06/25/jerry-goldsmith-on-scoring-basic-instinct/comment-page-1/. Accessed December 20, 2023.

Scott, A. O. "The Pulp Inside Him as It Turns to Rot." *The New York Times*, June 17, 2010, https://www.nytimes.com/2010/06/18/movies/18 killer.html. Accessed October 21, 2023.

Shoop, Casey. "Corpse and Accomplice: Fredric Jameson, Raymond Chandler, and the Representation of History in California." *Cultural Critique*, No. 77, Winter 2011, pp. 205–238.

Silver, Alain and James Ursini. *Film Noir Fatal Women.* Silman-James, 2022.

Singer, Leigh. "Killer Joe." *Sight and Sound*, April 2018, pp. 32–36.

Spicer, Andrew. *Film Noir.* Longman, 2002.

Stables, Kate. "The Postmodern Always Rings Twice: Constructing the *Femme Fatale* in 90s Cinema." *Women in Film Noir*, edited by E. Ann Kaplan, British Film Institute, 1998, pp. 164–182.

Tallerico, Brian. "*Under the Silver Lake.*" RogerEbert.com, April 19, 2019, https://www.rogerebert.com/reviews/under-the-silver-lake-2019. Accessed December 1, 2023.

Telotte, J. P. "Voices from the Deep: Film Noir as Psychodrama." *Film Noir Reader 4: The Crucial Films and Themes*, edited by Alain Silver and James Ursini, Limelight Editions, 2004, pp. 145–160.

Thoma, Pamela. "Chick Noir: Surveilling Femininity and the Affects of Loss in *Gone Girl.*" *Noir Affect*, edited by Christopher Breu and Elizabeth A. Hatmaker, Fordham University Press, 2020, pp. 197–221.

Thomson, David. "Follow the Money." *Film Comment*, vol. 31, no. 4, July–August 1995, pp. 20–25.

Thomas, Deborah. "How Hollywood Deals with the Deviant Male." *The Book of Film Noir*, edited by Ian Cameron. Continuum, 1993, pp. 59–70.

Thornham, Sue. "Undoing Violent Masculinity: Lynne Ramsay's *You Were Never Really Here* (2018)." *Feminist Media Studies*, vol. 22, no. 1, 2022, pp. 148–165.

Turner, Kyle. "Just Like Heaven: Music in *You Were Never Really Here.*" *Paste*, April 27, 2018, https://www.pastemagazine.com/movies/you-were-never-really-here/just-like-heaven-music-in-you-were-never-really-he. Accessed December 7, 2023.

Verevis, Constantine. "Through the Past Darkly: Noir Remakes of the 1980s." *Film Noir Reader 4: The Crucial Films and Themes*, edited by Alain Silver and James Ursini. Limelight Editions, 2004. 307–322.

Walker, Michael. "Film Noir: Introduction." *The Book of Film Noir*, edited by Ian Cameron. Continuum, 1993, pp. 8–38.

Warren, Ethan. "Only I Know the Secrets: Breaking Down *Under the Silver Lake*." Bright Wall/Dark Room, July 10, 2019, https://www.brightwalldarkroom.com/2019/07/10/secrets-under-the-silver-lake/. Accessed December 1, 2023.

Williams, Linda Ruth. "A Woman Scorned: The Neo-Noir Erotic Thriller as Revenge Drama." *Neo-Noir*, edited by Mark Bould, Kathrina Glitre, and Greg Tuck, London: Wallflower Press, 2009, pp. 168–185.

Williams, Raymond. *Marxism and Literature*. Oxford University Press, 1977.

Wood, Robert E. "Somebody Has to Die: *Basic Instinct* as White Noir," *Post Script*, vol. 12, no. 3, Summer 1993, pp. 44–51.

Index

Italicized titles refer to films unless otherwise indicated.

1960s, 9, 10, 12, 135, 199n1; counterculture, 14, 15, 50, 64, 65, 67, 68, 82, 198n8

Ace in the Hole, 84, 152, 154
African Americans and noir film, 60, 96, 132, 163, 197n2. *See also Devil in a Blue Dress*
After Dark, My Sweet, 82, 101–6
Against All Odds, 82, 103
alienation, 8, 20, 25, 77, 82, 178, 81
American Dream in noir film, 1, 3, 7, 30, 58, 77, 84, 90, 91, 101, 102, 108, 119, 129, 145, 149, 151

Bacall, Lauren, 21
Basic Instinct, 141, 161, 168, 169, 171–76, 181
Batman (1989), 10
The Big Lebowski, 23, 24, 66, 198n5
The Big Sleep, 20, 21, 23, 38, 43, 65, 66, 124, 145, 175, 178, 198n8
Bigelow, Kathryn, 202n7
Blade Runner, 10, 78, 196n7
Blade Runner 2049, 11, 196n7

blaxploitation, 60
Blood Simple, 10, 23, 107
Blow Out, 23
Blue Velvet, 10, 23, 47–53
Body Heat, 9, 15, 45, 140, 159–65, 168
Bogart, Humphrey, 20, 21, 27, 38, 66, 81, 102, 124, 175, 178
Borde, Raymond, 4, 6, 13, 36

The Cabinet of Dr. Caligari, 6
Cain, James M., 101, 108, 112, 113, 137, 143–45
Cassavetes, John, 10, 60, 130
Cat People (1942), 59
Chandler, Raymond, 4, 20, 21, 23, 24, 65, 66, 78, 101, 143, 145, 149, 195nn3–4, 196n3
Chartier, Jean-Pierre, 3, 4, 19, 78
Chaumeton Etienne, 4, 6, 13, 36
Chinatown, 2, 9, 15, 22, 23, 35, 39–45, 72
Coen Brothers, 23, 66, 82, 107–13, 195n4, 196n6
Cold War, 1, 14, 21, 109, 119, 155
Communism, 1, 8, 50, 119, 155
consumerism, 15, 68, 108, 144, 146, 182–83
Citizen Kane, 13, 14, 36
Crossfire, 127

Curtiz, Michael, 7, 135

Dark City, 24
Depression (1930s), 7, 8, 44, 77, 182,
    199n3
Deep Cover, 61
De Palma, Brian, 11, 23, 140
Dead Men Don't Wear Plaid, 103
Detour, 80, 87–92, 95, 105, 111
Devil in a Blue Dress, 12, 24, 55–61
D.O.A. (1950), 80, 112, 128
D.O.A. (1988), 82
Double Indemnity, 3,33, 80, 82, 108, 135,
    140, 143–49, 151, 159–64, 166–67,
    178, 181, 199n2, 203n1, 203n4,
Dragged Across Concrete, 84
Drive, 11
Durgnat, Raymond, 143, 195n3

The Edge of the City, 60
Emily the Criminal, 142
Expressionism, 5–8, 21, 36, 109, 118,
    119, 145

Fallen Angel, 136
Fargo, 23, 24
femme fatale, 4–6, 16, 20, 23, 28, 34, 39,
    56, 64, 78–80, 90, 93, 103, 105, 108,
    112, 116, 135–41; in *Double Indemnity*,
    135, 143, 147
Fight Club, 24
The File on Thelma Jordon, 139
Flynn, Gillian, 177–78, 202n6, 205n7
Frank, Nino, 3, 4, 19, 78
Freedman, Carl, 163–64, 203n4
Fuller, Samuel, 12

Garfield, John, 102, 112, 127, 138
Gilda, 136–37
Gone Girl, 141, 177–83, 189
Good Time, 129
Gun Crazy, 135

Hammett, Dashiell, 4, 20, 27–29, 31, 32,
    101, 111, 196n6
A History of Violence, 82, 83
Hitchcock, Alfred, 112, 123, 131, 139, 175

The Hitch-Hiker, 202n7
Hollywood Production Code. *See*
    Production Code
Huston, John, 3, 19, 27, 39

In a Lonely Place, 20, 81
In the Cut, 25, 141
The Incredible Shrinking Man, 78
Inherent Vice, 24, 63–69, 198nn7–8
Invasion of the Body Snatchers, 74

Jameson, Fredric, 16, 47, 50–51, 74; on
    nostalgia films, 15, 45, 67, 163; on
    postmodernism, 13–16, 63, 182. *See also*
    postmodernism
Jews and noir film, 7, 28, 85, 127–29,
    131–33
Joker, 201n3

The Killer Inside Me (1976), 81, 115
The Killer Inside Me (2010), 10, 93, 115–20
The Killer Inside Men (Thompson novel),
    81, 93, 104, 115
The Killer, 84
Killing Them Softly, 84
Kiss Me Deadly, 21, 101, 113, 131, 200n9
Kiss of Death, 43, 102, 138

L.A. Confidential, 23
The Lady from Shanghai, 14, 59
Lang, Fritz, 6, 21, 28, 79, 127
The Last Seduction, 140, 161, 165–69, 181
Laura, 3, 19
The Long Goodbye, 9, 22, 64, 66
Lorre, Peter, 8, 28
The Lost Weekend, 3, 78, 151
Lott, Eric, 59
Luhr, William, 148
Lupino, Ida, 138, 202n7
Lynch, David, 10, 23, 24, 49, 51, 52

M, 28
The Magnificent Ambersons, 148
The Maltese Falcon, 3, 8, 13, 19–21, 27–32,
    35, 72, 131
The Man Who Wasn't There, 10, 11, 82, 84,
    107–13, 121

Manhunter, 23

Manson, Charles, 67, 198n8

Marlowe, Philip, 20–24, 30, 33–38, 43, 65–67, 72, 124, 145, 175, 198n5

Memento, 24

Metropolis, 6

Mildred Pierce, 135

Mildred Pierce (novel), 113

Mitchum, Robert, 23, 80, 93, 95, 119

modernism, 13–15, 177, 204n3

Monroe, Marilyn, 74, 75

Motherless Brooklyn, 25

Murder, My Sweet, 3, 19, 20, 22, 33–38, 66, 113, 124, 131, 145

Musuraca, Nicholas, 8, 93

The Naked Kiss, 12

Naremore, James, 3, 32, 34, 59. 92, 143, 146, 148, 149, 154

Natural Born Killers, 120

Nazism, 3, 6, 7, 28, 36, 127, 139

Night Moves, 9, 22

The Night of the Hunter, 119, 125, 190

Nightcrawler, 83

Nightmare Alley (1947), 80, 101

Nightmare Alley (2021), 83

No Country for Old Men, 25

Nosferatu, 6

Nostalgia, 48–52, 98, 118, 119, 124. *See also* postmodernism

Odds Against Tomorrow, 60

One False Move, 60, 61, 82

Orientalism, 28, 29, 35, 41, 68

Out of the Past, 80, 82, 83, 93–99, 103, 202n5

Palmer, R. Barton, 32, 37, 98, 196n3

Pitfall, 80

Point Blank, 9, 12

The Postman Always Rings Twice, 112, 137

postmodernism: and nostalgia, 15, 49–52, 67, 159, 163; and pastiche, 15, 16, 45, 163

Preminger, Otto, 3, 7, 19, 127, 136

Production Code, 9, 143, 148, 159, 160, 167–69, 171, 193, 196n4

Promising Young Woman, 141, 142, 185–91

Pynchon, Thomas, 24, 63, 64, 67, 198n8, 198n11

Reagan, Ronald, 50, 67, 164, 198n7

Rebel Without a Cause, 81

Refn, Nicolas Winding, 11

Road to Perdition, 83

Roadhouse, 138

Scarlet Street, 79

Scorsese, Martin, 10, 123, 201n3

Shadow of a Doubt, 175

Shock Corridor, 12

Showgirls, 202n4

The Silence of the Lambs, 23

Sin City, 2, 83

Siodmak, Robert, 7, 127, 139

Spade, Sam, 20, 21, 24, 27–32, 37, 43, 72

Spillane, Mickey, 21, 101, 116

Stanwyck, Barbara, 78, 135, 139, 143, 144, 148, 159

The Strange Woman, 137

The Stranger, 14, 127

Sunset Boulevard, 105, 128, 135, 149, 151–57

Tarantino, Quentin, 10, 25

Taxi Driver, 10, 123–25, 201n3

The Testament of Dr. Mabuse, 6, 7

Thomas, Deborah, 5

Thompson, Jim, 81–83, 200n1

To Have and Have Not, 21

To Live and Die in L.A., 23

Too Late for Tears, 138

Touch of Evil, 3, 12, 14, 202n5

The Treasure of the Sierra Madre, 131

Ulmer, Edgar G., 87–92, 127, 137, 199nn1–2

Uncut Gems, 10, 85, 127–33

Under the Silver Lake, 24, 71–76

Vietnam war, 41, 68

Welles, Orson, 3, 13, 14, 36, 59, 127, 148. *See also Citizen Kane; The Lady*

From Shanghai; *The Magnificent Ambersons*; *The Stranger*; *Touch of Evil While the City Sleeps*, 21
Widmark, Richard, 43, 60, 102, 138
Wilder, Billy, 3, 7, 78, 79, 83, 108, 127, 135. *See also Double Indemnity*; *Sunset Boulevard*

Winter's Bone, 25
The Woman in the Window, 79
World War II, 1, 3, 6–8, 14, 55, 77, 81, 101, 182
The Wrong Man, 112, 175

You Were Never Really Here, 84, 121–26

About the Author

M. Keith Booker is professor of English at the University of Arkansas at Fayetteville. He is the author of more than one hundred published essays and is the author or editor of more than sixty published books on literature, film, and other aspects of modern and contemporary culture.